Deep Learning for Natural Language Processing

Solve your natural language processing problems
with smart deep neural networks

Karthiek Reddy Bokka, Shubhangi Hora, Tanuj Jain
and Monicah Wambugu

Packt>

Deep Learning for Natural Language Processing

Authors: Karthiek Reddy Bokka, Shubhangi Hora, Tanuj Jain, and Monicah Wambugu

Technical Reviewer: Aashita Kesarwani

Managing Editor: Snehal Tambe

Acquisitions Editors: Kunal Sawant and Koushik Sen

Production Editor: Samita Warang

Editorial Board: David Barnes, Mayank Bhardwaj, Ewan Buckingham, Simon Cox, Mahesh Dhyani, Taabish Khan, Manasa Kumar, Alex Mazonowicz, Douglas Paterson, Dominic Pereira, Shiny Poojary, Erol Staveley, Ankita Thakur, Mohita Vyas, and Jonathan Wray

First Published: June 2019

Production Reference: 1070619

ISBN: 978-1-83855-029-5

Published by Packt Publishing Ltd.

Livery Place, 35 Livery Street

Birmingham B3 2PB, UK

Table of Contents

Preface   i

Introduction to Natural Language Processing   1

Introduction 2

The Basics of Natural Language Processing 2

    Importance of natural language processing 4

Capabilities of Natural language processing 5

Applications of Natural Language Processing 6

    Text Preprocessing 8

    Text Preprocessing Techniques 8

    Lowercasing/Uppercasing 9

    Exercise 1: Performing Lowercasing on a Sentence 10

    Noise Removal 11

    Exercise 2: Removing Noise from Words 12

    Text Normalization 13

    Stemming 14

    Exercise 3: Performing Stemming on Words 14

    Lemmatization 15

    Exercise 4: Performing Lemmatization on Words 16

    Tokenization 17

    Exercise 5: Tokenizing Words 17

    Exercise 6: Tokenizing Sentences 18

    Additional Techniques 18

    Exercise 7: Removing Stop Words 19

Word Embeddings 20

    The Generation of Word Embeddings 21

    Word2Vec 21

    Functioning of Word2Vec 22

    Exercise 8: Generating Word Embeddings Using Word2Vec 25

    GloVe 29

    Exercise 9: Generating Word Embeddings Using GloVe 30

    Activity 1: Generating Word Embeddings from a Corpus
    Using Word2Vec. 32

Summary 33

Applications of Natural Language Processing   35

Introduction 36

POS Tagging 36

    Parts of Speech 37

    POS Tagger 38

Applications of Parts of Speech Tagging 42

    Types of POS Taggers 42

    Rule-Based POS Taggers 43

    Exercise 10: Performing Rule-Based POS Tagging 44

    Stochastic POS Taggers 46

    Exercise 11: Performing Stochastic POS Tagging 48

Chunking 49

    Exercise 12: Performing Chunking with NLTK 51

    Exercise 13: Performing Chunking with spaCy 52

Chinking 53

    Exercise 14: Performing Chinking 53

    Activity 2: Building and Training Your Own POS Tagger 54

Named Entity Recognition 55

    Named Entities 56

    Named Entity Recognizers 56

    Applications of Named Entity Recognition 57

    Types of Named Entity Recognizers 58

    Rule-Based NERs 58

    Stochastic NERs 59

    Exercise 15: Perform Named Entity Recognition with NLTK 60

    Exercise 16: Performing Named Entity Recognition with spaCy 61

    Activity 3: Performing NER on a Tagged Corpus 63

Summary 65

Introduction to Neural Networks   67

Introduction 68

    Introduction to Deep Learning 68

    Comparing Machine Learning and Deep Learning 70

Neural Networks 71

    Neural Network Architecture 72

    The Layers 73

    Nodes 75

    The Edges 75

    Biases 76

    Activation Functions 76

Training a Neural Network 77

    Calculating Weights 78

    The Loss Function 80

    The Gradient Descent Algorithm 82

    Backpropagation 86

Designing a Neural Network and Its Applications 87

    Supervised neural networks 87

    Unsupervised neural networks 88

    Exercise 17: Creating a neural network 88

Fundamentals of Deploying a Model as a Service 92

    Activity 4: Sentiment Analysis of Reviews 93

Summary 94

Foundations of Convolutional Neural Network   97

Introduction 98

    Exercise 18: Finding Out How Computers See Images 99

Understanding the Architecture of a CNN 101

    Feature Extraction 101

    Convolution 102

    The ReLU Activation Function 103

    Exercise 19: Visualizing ReLU 103

    Pooling 104

    Dropout 105

    Classification in Convolutional Neural Network 105

    Exercise 20: Creating a Simple CNN Architecture 106

Training a CNN 109

    Exercise 21: Training a CNN 111

    Applying CNNs to Text 113

    Exercise 22: Application of a Simple CNN to a Reuters News
    Topic for Classification 114

Application Areas of CNNs 116

    Activity 5: Sentiment Analysis on a Real-life Dataset 120

Summary 121

Recurrent Neural Networks   123

Introduction 124

Previous Versions of Neural Networks 125

RNNs 127

    RNN Architectures 132

    BPTT 133

Updates and Gradient Flow 136

    Adjusting Weight Matrix **Wy** 136

    Adjusting Weight Matrix **Ws** 137

    For Updating **Wx** 139

Gradients 142

    Exploding Gradients 142

    Vanishing Gradients 142

    RNNs with Keras 143

    Exercise 23: Building an RNN Model to Show the Stability
    of Parameters over Time 145

    Stateful versus Stateless 148

    Exercise 24: Turning a Stateless Network into a Stateful Network
    by Only Changing Arguments 149

    Activity 6: Solving a Problem with an RNN – Author Attribution 152

Summary 153

Gated Recurrent Units (GRUs)   155

Introduction 156

The Drawback of Simple RNNs 157

    The Exploding Gradient Problem 159

Gated Recurrent Units (GRUs) 160

    Types of Gates 163

    The Update Gate 163

The Reset Gate 165

The Candidate Activation Function 168

GRU Variations 171

Sentiment Analysis with GRU 171

Exercise 25: Calculating the Model Validation Accuracy
and Loss for Sentiment Classification 172

Activity 7: Developing a Sentiment Classification Model
Using a Simple RNN 177

Text Generation with GRUs 178

Exercise 26: Generating Text Using GRUs 178

Activity 8: Train Your Own Character Generation Model
Using a Dataset of Your Choice 185

Summary 186

Long Short-Term Memory (LSTM)   189

Introduction 190

LSTM 190

The Forget Gate 192

The Input Gate and the Candidate Cell State 196

Cell State Update 199

Output Gate and Current Activation 201

Exercise 27: Building an LSTM-Based Model to Classify
an Email as Spam or Not Spam (Ham) 203

Activity 9: Building a Spam or Ham Classifier Using a Simple RNN 210

Neural Language Translation 211

Activity 10: Creating a French-to-English translation model 227

Summary 228

State-of-the-Art Natural Language Processing 231

Introduction 232

    Attention Mechanisms 232

    An Attention Mechanism Model 235

    Data Normalization Using an Attention Mechanism 236

    Encoder 237

    Decoder 237

    Attention mechanisms 237

    The Calculation of Alpha 239

    Exercise 28: Build a Date Normalization Model for
    a Database Column 241

Other Architectures and Developments 255

    Transformer 255

    BERT 256

    Open AI GPT-2 257

Activity 11: Build a Text Summarization Model 257

Summary 258

A Practical NLP Project Workflow in an Organization 261

Introduction 262

    General Workflow for the Development of a Machine Learning Product 262

    The Presentation Workflow: 262

    The Research Workflow: 263

    The Production-Oriented Workflow 264

Problem Definition 265

Data Acquisition 266

Google Colab 267

Flask 277

Deployment 280

    Making Changes to a Flask Web App 281

    Use Docker to Wrap the Flask Web Application into a Container 282

    Host the Container on an Amazon Web Services (AWS) EC2 instance 284

    Improvements 291

Summary 292

Appendix   295

Index   347

>

Preface

About

This section briefly introduces the author, the coverage of this book, the technical skills you'll need to get started, and the hardware and software requirements required to complete all of the included activities and exercises.

About the Book

Applying deep learning approaches to various NLP tasks can take your computational algorithms to a completely new level in terms of speed and accuracy. deep learning for natural language processing starts off by highlighting the basic building blocks of the natural language processing domain. The book goes on to introduce the problems that you can solve using state-of-the-art neural network models. Delving into the various neural network architectures and their specific areas of application will help you to understand how to select the best model to suit your needs. As you advance through this deep learning book, you'll study convolutional, recurrent, and recursive neural networks, in addition to covering long short-term memory networks (LSTM). In the later chapters, you will be able to develop applications using NLP techniques such as attention model and beam search.

By the end of this book, you will not only have sound knowledge of natural language processing, but you will also be able to select the best text pre-processing and neural network models to solve a number of NLP issues.

About the Authors

Karthiek Reddy Bokka is a speech and audio machine learning engineer graduate from the University of Southern California and is currently working for Bi-amp Systems in Portland. His interests include deep learning, digital signal and audio processing, natural language processing, and computer vision. He has experience in designing, building, and deploying applications with artificial intelligence to solve real-world problems with varied forms of practical data, including image, speech, music, unstructured raw data, and such.

Shubhangi Hora is a Python developer, artificial intelligence enthusiast, and a writer. With a background in computer science and psychology, she is particularly interested in mental health-related AI. She is based in Pune, India, and is passionate about furthering natural language processing through machine learning and deep learning. Apart from this, she enjoys the performing arts and is a trained musician.

Tanuj Jain is a data scientist working at a Germany-based company. He has been developing deep learning models and putting them in production for commercial use at his current job. Natural language processing is a special interest area for him, whereby he has applied his know-how to classification and sentiment rating tasks. He has a Master's degree in electrical engineering with a focus on statistical pattern recognition.

Monicah Wambugu is the lead data scientist at a financial technology company that offers micro-loans by leveraging on data, machine learning, and analytics to perform alternative credit scoring. She is a graduate student at the School of Information at UC Berkeley Masters in Information Management and Systems. Monicah is particularly interested in how data science and machine learning can be used to design products and applications that respond to the behavioral and socio-economic needs of target audiences.

Description

This book will start with the basic building blocks of natural language processing domain. It will introduce the problems that can be solved using the state-of-the-art Neural Network models. It will cover deeply the necessary pre-processing needed in the text processing tasks. The book will cover some hot topics in the NLP domain, which include Convolutional Neural Networks, Recurrent Neural Networks, and Long Short Term Memory Networks. The audience of this book will understand the importance of text pre-processing, and hyper parameter tuning as well.

Learning Objectives

- Learn the fundamentals of natural language processing.
- Understand various pre-processing techniques for deep learning problems.
- Develop Vector representation of text using word2vec & Glove.
- Understand Named Entity Recognition.
- Perform Parts of Speech Tagging using machine learning.
- Train and deploy a scalable model.
- Understand several architectures of neural networks.

Audience

Aspiring data scientists and engineers who want to be introduced to deep learning in the domain of natural language processing.

They will start with the basics of natural language processing concepts and will gradually dive deeper into the concepts of Neural Networks and their application in text processing problems. They will get to learn different Neural Network architectures along with their application areas. Strong knowledge in Python and linear algebra skills are expected.

Approach

Deep learning for natural language processing will start with the very basic concepts of natural language processing. Once the basic concepts are introduced, the audience will gradually be made aware of the applications and problems in the real world where NLP techniques are applicable. Once the user understands the problem domain, the approach for developing the solution will be introduced. As part of solution-based approach, basic building blocks of Neural Networks are discussed. Eventually, modern architectures of various Neural Networks are elaborated with their corresponding application areas with examples.

Hardware Requirements

For the optimal experience, we recommend the following hardware configuration:

- Processor: Intel Core i5 or equivalent
- Memory: 4 GB RAM
- Storage: 5 GB available space

Software Requirements

We also recommend that you have the following software installed in advance:

- OS: Windows 7 SP1 64-bit, Windows 8.1 64-bit or Windows 10 64-bit, Linux (Ubuntu, Debian, Red Hat, or Suse), or the latest version of OS X
- Python (3.6.5 or later, preferably 3.7; available through https://www.python.org/downloads/release/python-371/)
- Jupyter (go to https://jupyter.org/install and follow the instructions to install). Alternatively, you can use Anaconda to install Jupyter.
- Keras (https://keras.io/#installation)
- Google Colab: It is a free Jupyter notebook environment and runs on cloud infrastructure. It is highly recommended as it requires no setup and has pre-installed popular Python packages and libraries (https://colab.research.google.com/notebooks/welcome.ipynb)

Conventions

Code words in text, database table names, folder names, filenames, file extensions, pathnames, dummy URLs, user input, and Twitter handles are shown as follows:

A block of code is set as follows:

```
from sklearn.datasets import make_blobs
import matplotlib.pyplot as plt
import numpy as np
%matplotlib inline
```

New terms and important words are shown in bold. Words that you see on the screen, for example, in menus or dialog boxes, appear in the text like this: "Next, click **Generate file** followed by **Download now** and name the downloaded file **model.h5**."

Installation and Setup

Each great journey begins with a humble step, and our upcoming adventure in the land of data wrangling is no exception. Before we can do awesome things with data, we need to be prepared with the most productive environment. In this small note, we shall see how to do that.

Install Python on Windows

1. Find your desired version of Python on the official installation page at https://www.python.org/downloads/windows/.

2. Ensure that you install the correct "-bit' version depending on your computer system, either 32-bit or 64-bit. You can find out this information in the System Properties window of your OS.

   After you download the installer, simply double-click on the file and follow the user-friendly prompts shown on screen.

Install Python on Linux

To install Python on Linux, perform the following:

1. Open the command prompt and verify that p\Python 3 is not already installed by running `python3 --version`.

2. To install Python 3, run this:

```
sudo apt-get update
sudo apt-get install python3.6
```

3. If you encounter problems, there are numerous sources online that can help you troubleshoot the issue.

Install Python on macOS X

To install Python on macOS X, do the following:

1. Open the terminal by holding command and space (*CMD* + *Space*), typing terminal in the open search box, and hitting enter.

2. Install Xcode through the command line by running `xcode-select --install`.

3. The easiest way to install Python 3 is using homebrew, which is installed through the command line by running `ruby -e "$(curl -fsSL https://raw.githubusercon-tent.com/Homebrew/install/master/install)"`.

4. Add homebrew to your PATH environment variable. Open your profile in the command line by running `sudo nano ~/.profile` and inserting `export PATH="/usr/local/opt/python/libexec/bin:$PATH"` at the bottom.

5. The final step is to install Python. In the command line, run `brew install python`.

6. Note that if you install Anaconda, the latest version of Python will be installed automatically.

Installing Keras

To install Keras, perform the following steps:

1. Since **Keras** requires another deep learning framework to behave as the backend, you'll need to download another framework first, and **TensorFlow** is recommended.

   To install **TensorFlow** for your platform, click on https://www.tensorflow.org/install/.

2. Once the backend has been installed, you can install **Keras** using either the following command:

   ```
   sudo pip install keras
   ```

   Alternatively, you can install it from the Github source, clone **Keras** using this:

   ```
   git clone https://github.com/keras-team/keras.git
   ```

3. Install **Keras** on Python using the following commands:

   ```
   cd keras
   sudo python setup.py install
   ```

   You need to configure the backend now. Refer to the following link for more information: (https://keras.io/backend/)

Additional Resources

The code bundle for this book is also hosted on GitHub at: https://github.com/TrainingByPackt/Deep-Learning-for-Natural-Language-Processing. We also have other code bundles from our rich catalog of books and videos available at https://github.com/PacktPublishing/. Check them out!

You can download the graphic bundle for the book from here:

https://www.packtpub.com/sites/default/files/downloads/9781838558024_ColorImages.pdf

1

Introduction to Natural Language Processing

Learning Objectives

By the end of this chapter, you will be able to:

- Describe natural language processing and its applications
- Explain different text preprocessing techniques
- Perform text preprocessing on text corpora
- Explain the functioning of Word2Vec and GloVe word embeddings
- Generate word embeddings using Word2Vec and GloVe
- Use the NLTK, Gensim, and Glove-Python libraries for text preprocessing and generating word embeddings

This chapter aims to equip you with knowledge of the basics of natural language processing and experience with the various text preprocessing techniques used in Deep Learning.

Introduction

Welcome to deep learning for Natural Language Processing. This book guides you in understanding and optimizing deep learning techniques for the purpose of natural language processing, which furthers the reality of generalized artificial intelligence. You will journey through the concepts of natural language processing – its applications and implementations – and learn the ways of deep neural networks, along with utilizing them to enable machines to understand natural language.

The Basics of Natural Language Processing

To understand what natural language processing is, let's break the term into two:

- Natural language is a form of written and spoken communication that has developed organically and naturally.

- Processing means analyzing and making sense of input data with computers.

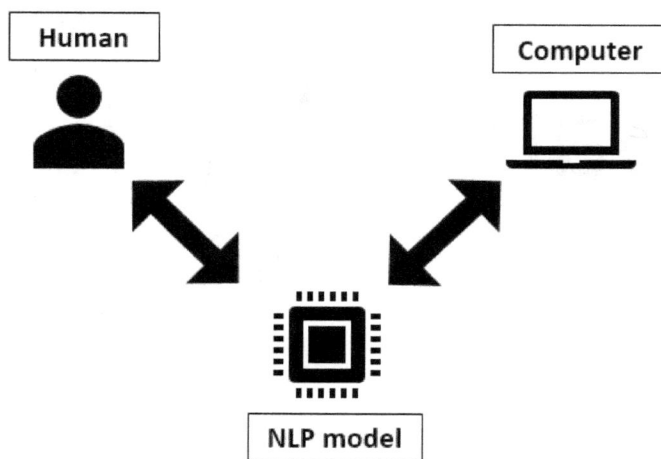

Figure 1.1: Natural language processing

Therefore, natural language processing is the machine-based processing of human communication. It aims to teach machines how to process and understand the language of humans, thereby allowing an easy channel of communication between human and machines.

For example, the personal voice assistants found in our phones and smart speakers, such as Alexa and Siri, are a result of natural language processing. They have been created in such a manner that they are able to not only understand what we say to them but also to act upon what we say and respond with feedback. Natural language processing algorithms aid these technologies in communicating with humans.

The key thing to consider in the mentioned definition of natural language processing is that the communication needs to occur in the natural language of humans. We've been communicating with machines for decades now by creating programs to perform certain tasks and executing them. However, these programs are written in languages that are not natural languages, because they are not forms of spoken communication and they haven't developed naturally or organically. These languages, such as Java, Python, C, and C++, were created with machines in mind and the consideration always being, "what will the machine be able to understand and process easily?"

While Python is a more user-friendly language and so is easier for humans to learn and be able to write code in, the basic point remains the same – to communicate with a machine, humans must learn a language that the machine is able to understand.

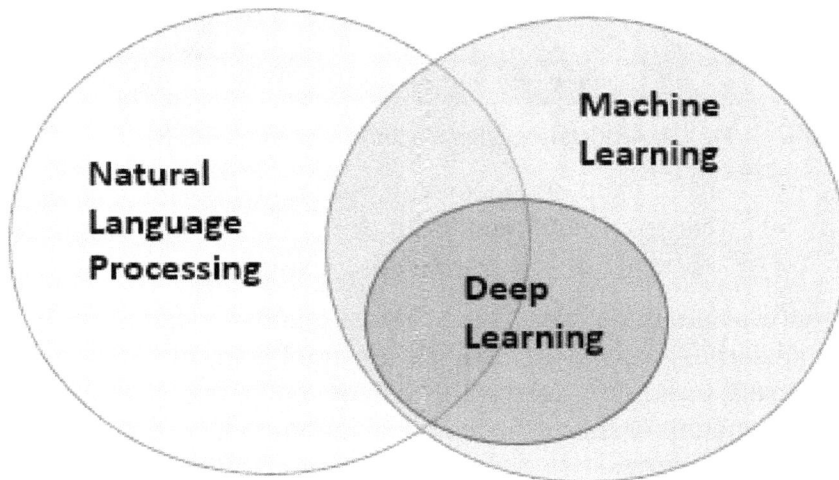

Figure 1.2: Venn diagram for natural language processing

The purpose of natural language processing is the opposite of this. Rather than having humans conform to the ways of a machine and learn how to effectively communicate with them, natural language processing enables machines to conform to humans and learn their way of communication. This makes more sense since the aim of technology is to make our lives easier.

To clarify this with an example, your first ever program was probably a piece of code that asked the machine to print 'hello world'. This was you conforming to the machine and asking it to execute a task in a language that it understood. Asking your voice assistant to say 'hello world' by voicing this command to it, and having it say 'hello world' back to you, is an example of the application of natural language processing, because you are communicating with a machine in your natural language (in this case, English). The machine is conforming to your form of communication, understanding what you're saying, processing what you're asking it to do, and then executing the task.

Importance of natural language processing

The following figure illustrates the various sections of the field of artificial intelligence:

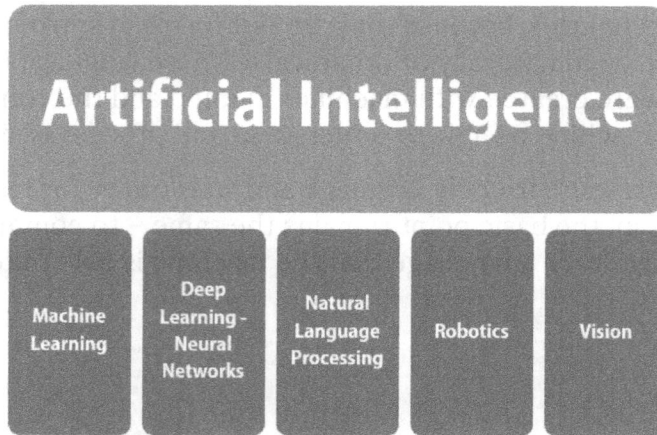

Fig 1.3: Artificial intelligence and some of its subfields

Along with machine learning and deep learning, natural language processing is a subfield of artificial intelligence, and because it deals with natural language, it's actually at the intersection of artificial intelligence and linguistics.

As mentioned, natural language processing is what enables machines to understand the language of humans, thus allowing an efficient channel of communication between the two. However, there is another reason Natural language processing is necessary, and that is because, like machines, machine learning and deep learning models work best with numerical data. Numerical data is hard for humans to naturally produce; imagine us talking in numbers rather than words. So, natural language processing works with textual data and converts it into numerical data, enabling machine learning and deep learning models to be fitted on it. Thus, it exists to bridge the communication gap between humans and machines by taking the spoken and written forms of language from humans and converting them into data that can be understood by machines. Thanks to natural language processing, the machine is able to make sense of, answer questions based on, solve problems using, and communicate in a natural language, among other things.

Capabilities of Natural language processing

Natural language processing has many real-world applications that benefit the lives of humans. These applications fall under three broad capabilities of natural language processing:

- Speech Recognition

  The machine is able to recognize a natural language in its spoken form and translate it into a textual form. An example of this is dictation on your smartphones – you can enable dictation and speak to your phone, and it will convert whatever you are saying into text.

- Natural Language Understanding

  The machine is able to understand a natural language in both its spoken and written form. If given a command, the machine is able to understand and execute it. An example of this would be saying 'Hey Siri, call home' to Siri on your iPhone for Siri to automatically call 'home' for you.

- Natural Language Generation

  The machine is able to generate natural language itself. An example of this is asking 'Siri, what time is it?' to Siri on your iPhone and Siri replying with the time – 'It's 2:08pm'.

These three capabilities are used to accomplish and automate a lot of tasks. Let's take a look at some of the things natural language processing contributes to, and how.

> **Note**
>
> Textual data is known as corpora (plural) and a corpus (singular).

Applications of Natural Language Processing

The following figure depicts the general application areas of natural language processing:

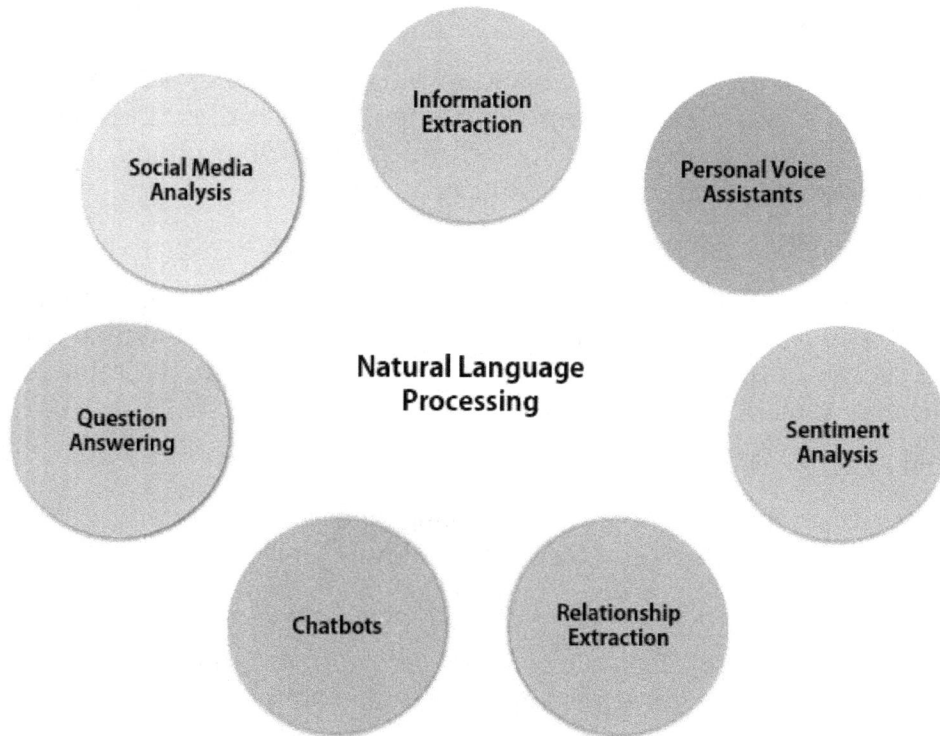

Figure 1.4: Application areas of natural language processing

- Automatic text summarization

  This involves processing corpora to provide a summary.

- Translation

  This entails translation tools that translate text to and from different languages, for example, Google Translate.

- Sentiment analysis

  This is also known as emotional artificial intelligence or opinion mining, and it is the process of identifying, extracting, and quantifying emotions and affective states from corpora, both written and spoken. Sentiment analysis tools are used to process things such as customer reviews and social media posts to understand emotional responses to and opinions regarding particular things, such as the quality of food at a new restaurant.

- Information extraction

  This is the process of identifying and extracting important terms from corpora, known as entities. Named entity recognition falls under this category and is a process that will be explained in the next chapter.

- Relationship extraction

  Relationship extraction involves extracting semantic relationships from corpora. Semantic relationships occur between two or more entities (such as people, organizations, and things) and fall into one of the many semantic categories. For example, if a relationship extraction tool was given a paragraph about Sundar Pichai and how he is the CEO of Google, the tool would be able to produce "Sundar Pichai works for Google" as output, with Sundar Pichai and Google being the two entities, and 'works for' being the semantic category that defines their relationship.

- Chatbot

  Chatbots are forms of artificial intelligence that are designed to converse with humans via speech and text. The majority of them mimic humans and make it feel as though you are speaking to another human being. Chatbots are being used in the health industry to help people who suffer from depression and anxiety.

- Social media analysis

  Social media applications such as Twitter and Facebook have hashtags and trends that are tracked and monitored using natural language processing to understand what is being talked about around the world. Additionally, natural language processing aids the process of moderation by filtering out negative, offensive, and inappropriate comments and posts.

- Personal voice assistants

  Siri, Alexa, Google Assistant, and Cortana are all personal voice assistants that leverage natural language processing techniques to understand and respond to what we say.

- Grammar checking

  Grammar-checking software automatically checks and corrects your grammar, punctuation, and typing errors.

Text Preprocessing

When answering questions on a comprehension passage, the questions are specific to different parts of the passage, and so while some words and sentences are important to you, others are irrelevant. The trick is to identify key words from the questions and match them to the passage to find the correct answer.

Text preprocessing works in a similar fashion – the machine doesn't need the irrelevant parts of the corpora; it just needs the important words and phrases required to execute the task at hand. Thus, text preprocessing techniques involve prepping the corpora for proper analysis and for the machine learning and deep learning models. Text preprocessing is basically telling the machine what it needs to take into consideration and what it can disregard.

Each corpus requires different text preprocessing techniques depending on the task that needs to be executed, and once you've learned the different preprocessing techniques, you'll understand where to use what and why. The order in which the techniques have been explained is usually the order in which they are performed.

We will be using the **NLTK** Python library in the following exercises, but feel free to use different libraries while doing the activities. **NLTK** stands for **Natural Language Toolkit** and is the simplest and one of the most popular Python libraries for natural language processing, which is why we will be using it to understand the basic concepts of natural language processing.

> **Note**
>
> For further information on NLTK, go to https://www.nltk.org/.

Text Preprocessing Techniques

The following are the most popular text preprocessing techniques in natural language processing:

- Lowercasing/uppercasing
- Noise removal
- Text normalization
- Stemming

- Lemmatization
- Tokenization
- Removing stop words

Let's look at each technique one by one.

Lowercasing/Uppercasing

This is one of the most simple and effective preprocessing techniques that people often forget to use. It either converts all the existing uppercase characters into lowercase ones so that the entire corpus is in lowercase, or it converts all the lowercase characters present in the corpus into uppercase ones so that the entire corpus is in uppercase.

This method is especially useful when the size of the corpus isn't too large and the task involves identifying terms or outputs that could be recognized differently due to the case of the characters, since a machine inherently processes uppercase and lowercase letters as separate entities – 'A' is different from 'a.' This kind of variation in the input capitalization could result in incorrect output or no output at all.

An example of this would be a corpus that contains both 'India' and 'india.' Without applying lowercasing, the machine would recognize these as two separate terms, when in reality they're both different forms of the same word and correspond to the same country. After lowercasing, there would exist only one instance of the term "India," which would be 'india,' simplifying the task of finding all the places where India has been mentioned in the corpus.

> **Note**
>
> All exercises and activities will be primarily developed on Jupyter Notebook. You will need to have Python 3.6 and NLTK installed on your system.
>
> Exercises 1 – 6 can be done within the same Jupyter notebook.

Exercise 1: Performing Lowercasing on a Sentence

In this exercise, we will take an input sentence with both uppercase and lowercase characters and convert them all into lowercase characters. The following steps will help you with the solution:

1. Open **cmd** or another terminal depending on your operating system.

2. Navigate to the desired path and use the following command to initiate a **Jupyter** notebook:

   ```
   jupyter notebook
   ```

3. Store an input sentence in an **'s'** variable, as shown:

   ```
   s = "The cities I like most in India are Mumbai, Bangalore, Dharamsala and
   Allahabad."
   ```

4. Apply the **lower()** function to convert the capital letters into lowercase characters and then print the new string, as shown:

   ```
   s = s.lower()
   print(s)
   ```

   Expected output:

   ```
   the cities i like most in india are mumbai, bangalore, dharamsala and allahabad.
   ```

   Figure 1.5: Output for lowercasing with mixed casing in a sentence

5. Create an array of words with capitalized characters, as shown:

   ```
   words = ['indiA', 'India', 'india', 'iNDia']
   ```

6. Using list comprehension, apply the **lower()** function on each element of the **words** array and then print the new array, as follows:

   ```
   words = [word.lower() for word in words]
   print(words)
   ```

   Expected output:

   ```
   ['india', 'india', 'india', 'india']
   ```

   Figure 1.6: Output for lowercasing with mixed casing of words

Noise Removal

Noise is a very general term and can mean different things with respect to different corpora and different tasks. What is considered noise for one task may be what is considered important for another, and thus this is a very domain-specific preprocessing technique. For example, when analyzing tweets, hashtags might be important to recognize trends and understand what's being spoken about around the globe, but hashtags may not be important when analyzing a news article, and so hashtags would be considered noise in the latter's case.

Noise doesn't include only words, but can also include symbols, punctuation marks, HTML markup (**<,>, *, ?,.**), numbers, whitespaces, stop words, particular terms, particular regular expressions, non-ASCII characters (**\W|\d+**), and parse terms.

Removing noise is crucial so that only the important parts of the corpora are fed into the models, ensuring accurate results. It also helps by bringing words into their root or standard form. Consider the following example:

With Noise	Without Noise
..sleepy	
sleepy!!	
#sleepy	sleepy
>>>>>sleepy>>>>	
<a>sleepy</a>	

Figure 1.7: Output for noise removal

After removing all the symbols and punctuation marks, all the instances of sleepy correspond to the one form of the word, enabling more efficient prediction and analysis of the corpus.

Exercise 2: Removing Noise from Words

In this exercise, we will take an input array containing words with noise attached (such as punctuation marks and HTML markup) and convert these words into their clean, noise-free forms. To do this, we will need to make use of Python's regular expression library. This library has several functions that allow us to filter through input data and remove the unnecessary parts, which is exactly what the process of noise removal aims to do.

> **Note**
>
> To learn more about '**re**,' click on https://docs.python.org/3/library/re.html.

1. In the same **Jupyter** notebook, import the regular expression library, as shown:

   ```
   import re
   ```

2. Create a function called '**clean_words**', which will contain methods to remove different types of noise from the words, as follows:

   ```
   def clean_words(text):

       #remove html markup
       text = re.sub("(<.*?>)","",text)

       #remove non-ascii and digits
       text=re.sub("(\W|\d+)"," ",text)

       #remove whitespace
       text=text.strip()

       return text
   ```

3. Create an array of raw words with noise, as demonstrated:

   ```
   raw = ['..sleepy', 'sleepy!!', '#sleepy', '>>>>>sleepy>>>>', '<a>sleepy</a>']
   ```

4. Apply the **clean_words()** function on the words in the raw array and then print the array of clean words, as shown:

   ```
   clean = [clean_words(r) for r in raw]
   print(clean)
   ```

Expected output:

```
['sleepy', 'sleepy', 'sleepy', 'sleepy', 'sleepy']
```

Figure 1.8: Output for noise removal

Text Normalization

This is the process of converting a raw corpus into a canonical and standard form, which is basically to ensure that the textual input is guaranteed to be consistent before it is analyzed, processed, and operated upon.

Examples of text normalization would be mapping an abbreviation to its full form, converting several spellings of the same word to one spelling of the word, and so on.

The following are examples for canonical forms of incorrect spellings and abbreviations:

Raw form	Canonical form
Spaghetti	
Spagetti	
Spageti	Spaghetti
Spaghetty	
Spagetty	

Figure 1.9: Canonical form for incorrect spellings

Raw form	Canonical form
brb	be right back

Figure 1.10: Canonical form for abbreviations

There is no standard way to go about normalization since it is very dependent on the corpus and the task at hand. The most common way to go about it is with dictionary mapping, which involves manually creating a dictionary that maps all the various forms of one word to that one word, and then replaces each of those words with one standard form of the word.

Stemming

Stemming is performed on a corpus to reduce words to their stem or root form. The reason for saying "stem or root form" is that the process of stemming doesn't always reduce the word to its root but sometimes just to its canonical form.

The words that undergo stemming are known as inflected words. These words are in a form that is different from the root form of the word, to imply an attribute such as the number or gender. For example, "journalists" is the plural form of "journalist." Thus, stemming would cut off the **'s'**, bringing "journalists" to its root form:

Before stemming	After stemming
Annoying	
Annoyed	Annoy
Annoys	

Figure 1.11: Output for stemming

Stemming is beneficial when building search applications due to the fact that when searching for something in particular, you might also want to find instances of that thing even if they're spelled differently. For example, if you're searching for exercises in this book, you might also want 'Exercise' to show up in your search.

However, stemming doesn't always provide the desired stem, since it works by chopping off the ends of the words. It's possible for the stemmer to reduce 'troubling' to 'troubl' instead of 'trouble' and this won't really help in problem solving, and so stemming isn't a method that's used too often. When it is used, Porter's stemming algorithm is the most common algorithm for stemming.

Exercise 3: Performing Stemming on Words

In this exercise, we will take an input array containing various forms of one word and convert these words into their stem forms.

1. In the same **Jupyter** notebook, import the **nltk** and **pandas** libraries as well as **Porter Stemmer**, as shown:

   ```
   import nltk
   import pandas as pd
   from nltk.stem import PorterStemmer as ps
   ```

2. Create an instance of **stemmer**, as follows:

   ```
   stemmer = ps()
   ```

3. Create an array of different forms of the same word, as shown:

```
words=['annoying', 'annoys', 'annoyed', 'annoy']
```

4. Apply the stemmer to each of the words in the **words** array and store them in a new array, as given:

```
stems =[stemmer.stem(word = word) for word in words]
```

5. Print the raw words and their stems in the form of a DataFrame, as shown:

```
sdf = pd.DataFrame({'raw word': words,'stem': stems})
sdf
```

Expected output:

Out[14]:

	raw word	stem
0	annoying	annoy
1	annoys	annoy
2	annoyed	annoy
3	annoy	annoy

Figure 1.12: Output of stemming

Lemmatization

Lemmatization is a process that is like stemming – its purpose is to reduce a word to its root form. What makes it different is that it doesn't just chop the ends of words off to obtain this root form, but instead follows a process, abides by rules, and often uses WordNet for mappings to return words to their root forms. (WordNet is an English language database that consists of words and their definitions along with synonyms and antonyms. It is considered to be an amalgamation of a dictionary and a thesaurus.) For example, lemmatization is capable of transforming the word 'better' into its root form 'good', since 'better' is just the comparative form of 'good."

While this quality of lemmatization makes it highly appealing and more efficient when compared with stemming, the drawback is that since lemmatization follows such an organized procedure, it takes a lot more time than stemming does. Hence, lemmatization is not recommended when you're working with a large corpus.

Exercise 4: Performing Lemmatization on Words

In this exercise, we will take an input array containing various forms of one word and convert these words into their root form.

1. In the same Jupyter notebook as the previous exercise, import **WordNetLemmatizer** and download **WordNet**, as shown:

    ```
    from nltk.stem import WordNetLemmatizer as wnl
    nltk.download('wordnet')
    ```

2. Create an instance of **lemmatizer**, as follows:

    ```
    lemmatizer = wnl()
    ```

3. Create an array of different forms of the same word, as demonstrated:

    ```
    words = ['troubling', 'troubled', 'troubles', 'trouble']
    ```

4. Apply **lemmatizer** to each of the words in the **words** array and store them in a new array, as follows. The **word** parameter provides the lemmatize function with the word it is supposed to lemmatize. The **pos** parameter is the part of speech you want the lemma to be. **'v'** stands for verb and thus the lemmatizer will reduce the word to its closest verb form:

    ```
    # v denotes verb in "pos"
    lemmatized = [lemmatizer.lemmatize(word = word, pos = 'v') for word in
    words]
    ```

5. Print the raw words and their root forms in the form of a DataFrame, as shown:

    ```
    ldf = pd.DataFrame({'raw word': words,'lemmatized': lemmatized})
    ldf = ldf[['raw word','lemmatized']]
    ldf
    ```

    Expected output:

	raw word	lemmatized
0	troubling	trouble
1	troubled	trouble
2	troubles	trouble
3	trouble	trouble

    Figure 1.13: Output of lemmatization

Tokenization

Tokenization is the process of breaking down a corpus into individual tokens. Tokens are the most commonly used words – thus, this process breaks down a corpus into individual words – but can also include punctuation marks and spaces, among other things.

This technique is one of the most important ones since it is a prerequisite for a lot of applications of natural language processing that we will be learning about in the next chapter, such as **Parts-of-Speech** (**PoS**) tagging. These algorithms take tokens as input and can't function with strings or paragraphs of text as input.

Tokenization can be performed to obtain individual words as well as individual sentences as tokens. Let's try both of these out in the following exercises.

Exercise 5: Tokenizing Words

In this exercise, we will take an input sentence and produce individual words as tokens from it.

1. In the same **Jupyter** notebook, import **nltk**:

   ```
   import nltk
   ```

2. From **nltk**, import **word_tokenize** and **punkt**, as shown:

   ```
   nltk.download('punkt')
   from nltk import word_tokenize
   ```

3. Store words in a variable and apply **word_tokenize()** on it, then print the results, as follows:

   ```
   s = "hi! my name is john."
   tokens = word_tokenize(s)
   tokens
   ```

   Expected output:

   ```
   ['hi', '!', 'my', 'name', 'is', 'john', '.']
   ```

   Figure 1.14: Output for the tokenization of words

As you can see, even the punctuation marks are tokenized and considered as individual tokens.

Now let's see how we can tokenize sentences.

Exercise 6: Tokenizing Sentences

In this exercise, we will take an input sentence and produce individual words as tokens from it.

1. In the same **Jupyter** notebook, import **sent_tokenize**, as shown:

    ```
    from nltk import sent_tokenize
    ```

2. Store two sentences in a variable (our sentence from the previous exercise was actually two sentences, so we can use the same one to see the difference between word and sentence tokenization) and apply **sent_tokenize()** on it, then print the results, as follows:

    ```
    s = "hi! my name is shubhangi."
    tokens = sent_tokenize(s)
    tokens
    ```

    Expected output:

    ```
    ['hi!', 'my name is john.']
    ```

    Figure 1.15: Output for tokenizing sentences

As you can see, the two sentences have formed two individual tokens.

Additional Techniques

There are several ways to perform text preprocessing, including the usage of a variety of Python libraries such as **BeautifulSoup** to strip away HTML markup. The previous exercises serve the purpose of introducing some techniques to you. Depending on the task at hand, you may need to use just one or two or all of them, including the modifications made to them. For example, at the noise removal stage, you may find it necessary to remove words such as 'the,' 'and,' 'this,' and 'it.' So, you will need to create an array containing these words and pass the corpus through a **for** loop to store only the words that are not a part of that array, removing the noisy words from the corpus. Another way of doing this is given later in this chapter and is done after tokenization has been performed.

Exercise 7: Removing Stop Words

In this exercise, we will take an input sentence and remove the stop words from it.

1. Open a **Jupyter** notebook and download '**stopwords**' using the following line of code:

    ```
    nltk.download('stopwords')
    ```

2. Store a sentence in a variable, as shown:

    ```
    s = "the weather is really hot and i want to go for a swim"
    ```

3. Import **stopwords** and create a set of the English stop words, as follows:

    ```
    from nltk.corpus import stopwords
    stop_words = set(stopwords.words('english'))
    ```

4. Tokenize the sentence using **word_tokenize**, and then store those tokens that do not occur in **stop_words** in an array. Then, print that array:

    ```
    tokens = word_tokenize(s)
    tokens = [word for word in tokens if not word in stop_words]
    print(tokens)
    ```

    Expected output:

    ```
    ['weather', 'really', 'hot', 'want', 'go', 'swim']
    ```

    Figure 1.16: Output after removing stopwords

Additionally, you may need to convert numbers into their word forms. This is also a method you can add to the noise removal function. Furthermore, you might need to make use of the contractions library, which serves the purpose of expanding the existing contractions in the text. For example, the contractions library will convert 'you're' into 'you are,' and if this is necessary for your task, then it is recommended to install this library and use it.

Text preprocessing techniques go beyond the ones that have been discussed in this chapter and can include anything and everything that is required for a task or a corpus. In some instances, some words may be important, while in others they won't be.

Word Embeddings

As mentioned in the earlier sections of this chapter, natural language processing prepares textual data for machine learning and deep learning models. The models perform most efficiently when provided with numerical data as input, and thus a key role of natural language processing is to transform preprocessed textual data into numerical data, which is a numerical representation of the textual data.

This is what word embeddings are: they are numerical representations in the form of real-value vectors for text. Words that have similar meanings map to similar vectors and thus have similar representations. This aids the machine in learning the meaning and context of different words. Since word embeddings are vectors mapping to individual words, word embeddings can only be generated once tokenization has been performed on the corpus.

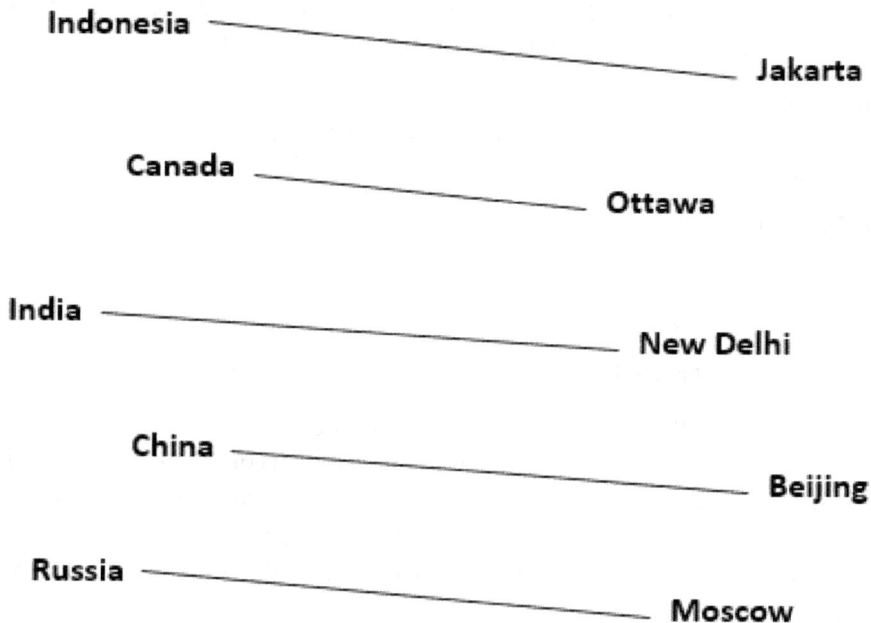

Indonesia ———————————————— Jakarta

Canada ———————————— Ottawa

India ———————————————— New Delhi

China ———————————————— Beijing

Russia ———————————————— Moscow

Figure 1.17: Example for word embeddings

Word embeddings encompass a variety of techniques used to create a learned numerical representation and are the most popular way to represent a document's vocabulary. The beneficial aspect of word embeddings is that they are able to capture contextual, semantic, and syntactic similarities, and the relations of a word with other words, to effectively train the machine to comprehend natural language. This is the main aim of word embeddings – to form clusters of similar vectors that correspond to words with similar meanings.

The reason for using word embeddings is to make machines understand synonyms the same way we do. Consider an example of online restaurant reviews – they consist of adjectives describing food, ambience, and the overall experience. They are either positive or negative, and comprehending which reviews fall into which of these two categories is important. The automatic categorization of these reviews can provide a restaurant with quick insights as to what areas they need to improve on, what people liked about their restaurant, and so on.

There exist a variety of adjectives that can be classified as positive, and the same goes with negative adjectives. Thus, not only does the machine need to be able to differentiate between negative and positive, it also needs to learn and understand that multiple words can relate to the same category because they ultimately mean the same thing. This is where word embeddings are helpful.

Consider the example of restaurant reviews received on a food service application. The following two sentences are from two separate restaurant reviews:

- Sentence A – The food here was great.

- Sentence B – The food here was good.

The machine needs to be able to comprehend that both these reviews are positive and mean a similar thing, despite the adjective in both sentences being different. This is done by creating word embeddings, because the two words 'good' and 'great' map to two separate but similar real-value vectors and, thus, can be clustered together.

The Generation of Word Embeddings

We've understood what word embeddings are and their importance; now we need to understand how they're generated. The process of transforming words into their real-value vectors is known as vectorization and is done by word embedding techniques. There are many word embedding techniques available, but in this chapter, we will be discussing the two main ones – Word2Vec and GloVe. Once word embeddings (vectors) have been created, they combine to form a vector space, which is an algebraic model consisting of vectors that follow the rules of vector addition and scalar multiplication. If you don't remember your linear algebra, this might be a good time to quickly review it.

Word2Vec

As mentioned earlier, Word2Vec is one of the word embedding techniques used to generate vectors from words – something you can probably understand from the name itself.

Word2Vec is a shallow neural network – it has only two layers – and thus does not qualify as a deep learning model. The input is a text corpus, which it uses to generate vectors as the output. These vectors are known as feature vectors for the words present in the input corpus. It transforms a corpus into numerical data that can be understood by a deep neural network.

The aim of Word2Vec is to understand the probability of two or more words occurring together and thus to group words with similar meanings together to form a cluster in a vector space. Like any other machine learning or deep learning model, Word2Vec becomes more and more efficient by learning from past data and past occurrences of words. Thus, if provided with enough data and context, it can accurately guess a word's meaning based on past occurrences and context, similar to how we understand language.

For example, we are able to create a connection between the words 'boy' and 'man', and 'girl' and 'woman,' once we have heard and read about them and understood what they mean. Likewise, Word2Vec can also form this connection and generate vectors for these words that lie close together in the same cluster so as to ensure that the machine is aware that these words mean similar things.

Once Word2Vec has been given a corpus, it produces a vocabulary wherein each word has a vector of its own attached to it, which is known as its neural word embedding, and simply put, this neural word embedding is a word written in numbers.

Functioning of Word2Vec

Word2Vec trains a word against words that neighbor the word in the input corpus, and there are two methods of doing so:

- *Continuous Bag of Words* (CBOW):

  This method predicts the current word based on the context. Thus, it takes the word's surrounding words as input to produce the word as output, and it chooses this word based on the probability that this is indeed the word that is a part of the sentence.

  For example, if the algorithm is provided with the words "the food was" and needs to predict the adjective after it, it is most likely to output the word "good" rather than output the word "delightful," since there would be more instances where the word "good" was used, and thus it has learned that "good" has a higher probability than "delightful." CBOW it said to be faster than skip-gram and has a higher accuracy with more frequent words.

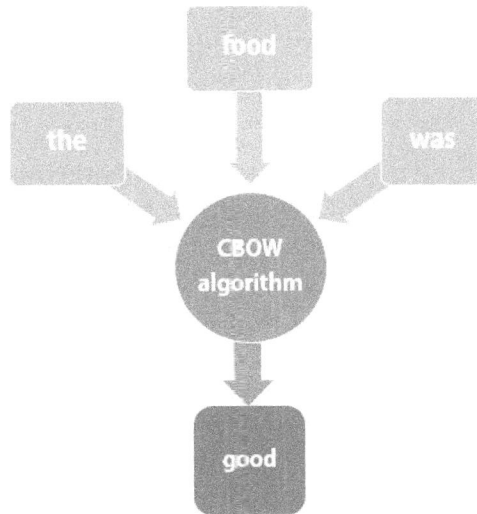

Fig 1.18: The CBOW algorithm

- *Skip-gram*

  This method predicts the words surrounding a word by taking the word as input, understanding the meaning of the word, and assigning it to a context. For example, if the algorithm was given the word "delightful," it would have to understand its meaning and learn from past context to predict that the probability that the surrounding words are "the food was" is highest. Skip-gram is said to work best with a small corpus.

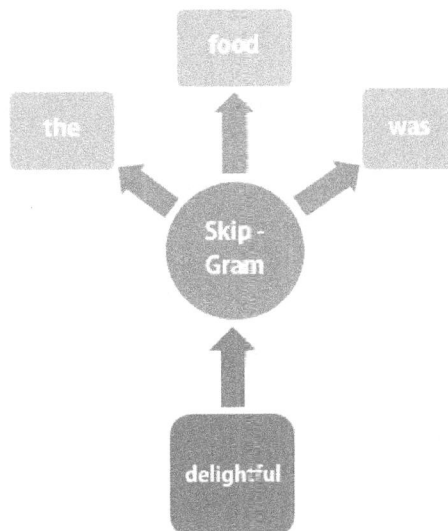

Fig 1.19: The skip-gram algorithm

While both methods seem to be working in opposite manners, they are essentially predicting words based on the context of local (nearby) words; they are using a window of context to predict what word will come next. This window is a configurable parameter.

The decision of choosing which algorithm to use depends on the corpus at hand. CBOW works on the basis of probability and thus chooses the word that has the highest probability of occurring given a specific context. This means it will usually predict only common and frequent words since those have the highest probabilities, and rare and infrequent words will never be produced by CBOW. Skip-gram, on the other hand, predicts context, and thus when given a word, it will take it as a new observation rather than comparing it to an existing word with a similar meaning. Due to this, rare words will not be avoided or looked over. However, this also means that a lot of training data will be required for skip-gram to work efficiently. Thus, depending on the training data and corpus at hand, the decision to use either algorithm should be made.

Essentially, both algorithms, and thus the model as a whole, require an intense learning phase where they are trained over thousands and millions of words to better understand context and meaning. Based on this, they are able to assign vectors to words and thus aid the machine in learning and predicting natural language. To understand Word2Vec better, let's do an exercise using Gensim's Word2Vec model.

Gensim is an open source library for unsupervised topic modeling and natural language processing using statistical machine learning. Gensim's Word2Vec algorithm takes an input of sequences of sentences in the form of individual words (tokens).

Also, we can use the **min_count** parameter. It exists to ask you how many instances of a word should be there in a corpus for it to be important to you, and then takes that into consideration when generating word embeddings. In a real-life scenario, when dealing with millions of words, a word that occurs only once or twice may not be important at all and thus can be ignored. However, right now, we are training our model only on three sentences each with only 5-6 words in every sentence. Thus, **min_count** is set to 1 since a word is important to us even if it occurs only once.

Exercise 8: Generating Word Embeddings Using Word2Vec

In this exercise, we will be using Gensim's Word2Vec algorithm to generate word embeddings post tokenization.

> **Note**
>
> You will need to have **gensim** installed on your system for the following exercise. You can use the following command to install it, if it is not already installed:
>
> ```
> pip install --upgrade gensim
> ```
>
> For further information, click on https://radimrehurek.com/gensim/models/word2vec.html.

The following steps will help you with the solution:

1. Open a new **Jupyter** notebook.

2. Import the Word2Vec model from **gensim**, and import **word_tokenize** from **nltk**, as shown:

   ```
   from gensim.models import Word2Vec as wtv
   from nltk import word_tokenize
   ```

3. Store three strings with some common words into three separate variables, and then tokenize each sentence and store all the tokens in an array, as shown:

   ```
   s1 = "Ariana Grande is a singer"
   s2 = "She has been a singer for many years"
   s3 = "Ariana is a great singer"
   sentences = [word_tokenize(s1), word_tokenize(s2), word_tokenize(s3)]
   ```

   You can print the array of sentences to view the tokens.

4. Train the model, as follows:

   ```
   model = wtv(sentences, min_count = 1)
   ```

   Word2Vec's default value for **min_count** is 5.

5. Summarize the model, as demonstrated:

```
print('this is the summary of the model: ')
print(model)
```

Your output will look something like this:

```
this is the summary of the model:
Word2Vec(vocab=12, size=100, alpha=0.025)
```

Figure 1.20: Output for model summary

Vocab = 12 signifies that there are 12 different words present in the sentences that were input to the model.

6. Let's find out what words are present in the vocabulary by summarizing it, as shown:

```
words = list(model.wv.vocab)
print('this is the vocabulary for our corpus: ')
print(words)
```

Your output will look something like this:

```
this is the vocabulary for our corpus:
['Ariana', 'Grande', 'is', 'a', 'singer', 'She', 'has', 'been', 'for', 'many', 'years', 'great']
```

Figure 1.21: Output for the vocabulary of the corpus

Let's see what the vector (word embedding) for the word 'singer' is:

```
print("the vector for the word singer: ")
print(model['singer'])
```

Expected output:

```
the vector for the word singer:
[ 3.9150659e-03  2.6659777e-03  1.0298982e-03 -2.7156321e-03
  1.9977870e-03  3.1204436e-03  1.2055682e-04  1.0450699e-03
 -6.4308796e-04  3.0822519e-03  2.1972554e-03  5.1480172e-05
 -3.7099270e-03  3.9439583e-03  6.8276987e-04  7.7137066e-04
  2.3698520e-03 -7.8547641e-04  6.0383842e-04  4.6370425e-03
 -1.6786088e-03  1.7417425e-03  2.4216413e-03  3.6545738e-03
 -1.9871239e-03  2.9489421e-03 -1.2810023e-03 -4.9174053e-04
 -3.9743204e-03 -2.7023794e-03 -3.0541950e-04 -1.5724347e-03
 -2.1029566e-03 -2.1624754e-03  2.1620055e-04 -1.4000515e-03
 -4.0824865e-03  4.6588355e-04  3.5028579e-03  4.8283348e-03
 -2.8737928e-03 -4.5569306e-03 -7.6568732e-04 -3.3311991e-03
  3.5790715e-03  4.2424244e-03  3.3478225e-03 -7.4140396e-04
  1.0030111e-03 -5.2394503e-04  5.8383477e-04 -4.8430995e-03
  2.6972082e-03 -4.8002079e-03 -2.3011414e-03  8.0388715e-04
  3.1952575e-05 -8.1621204e-04 -3.8127291e-03 -6.7428290e-04
 -1.7713077e-03 -3.0159748e-03  1.7178850e-03 -1.9258332e-03
 -2.4637436e-03  3.3779652e-03  2.7676420e-03  1.8853768e-03
 -2.4718521e-03 -1.9754141e-03  2.6104036e-03 -2.1335895e-03
  2.4405334e-03 -3.2013952e-04  3.9961869e-03  4.0419102e-03
  2.0586823e-03  4.9897884e-03  4.5599132e-03 -1.0976522e-03
  1.5563263e-03  3.9063310e-03 -2.9308300e-03 -4.8254002e-03
 -8.7642738e-06  3.9748671e-03  5.2895391e-04  6.3330121e-04
 -1.2614765e-03 -8.5018738e-04  3.7659388e-03  3.0237564e-03
  4.5014662e-03  4.3258793e-03 -4.2659100e-03  4.9081761e-03
 -3.9214552e-03 -2.4262110e-03 -8.1192164e-05 -4.1112076e-03]
```

Figure 1.22: Vector for the word 'singer'

Our Word2Vec model has been trained on these three sentences, and thus its vocabulary only includes the words present in this sentence. If we were to find words that are similar to a particular input word from our Word2Vec model, we wouldn't get words that actually make sense since the vocabulary is so small. Consider the following examples:

```
#lookup top 6 similar words to great
w1 = ["great"]
model.wv.most_similar (positive=w1, topn=6)
```

The 'positive' refers to the depiction of only positive vector values in the output.

The top six similar words to 'great' would be:

```
[('has', 0.13253481686115265),
 ('been', 0.12117968499660492),
 ('for', 0.10510198771953583),
 ('singer', 0.08586522936820984),
 ('a', 0.08413773775100708),
 ('She', 0.08044794946908951)]
```

Figure 1.23: Word vectors similar to the word 'great'

Similarly, for the word 'singer', it could be as follows:

```
#lookup top 6 similar words to singer
w1 = ["singer"]
model.wv.most_similar (positive=w1, topn=6)
```

```
[('for', 0.17918002605438232),
 ('been', 0.12124449759721756),
 ('great', 0.08586522936820984),
 ('is', 0.0768381804227829),
 ('a', 0.03302524611353874),
 ('Ariana', 0.02957470342516899)]
```

Figure 1.24: Word vector similar to word 'singer'

We know that these words are not actually similar in meaning to our input words at all, and that also shows up in the correlation value beside them. However, they show up because these are the only words that exist in our vocabulary.

Another important parameter of the **Gensim** Word2Vec model is the size parameter. Its default value is 100 and implies the size of the neural network layers that are being used to train the model. This corresponds to the amount of freedom the training algorithm has. A larger size requires more data but also leads to higher accuracy.

Note

For more information on Gensim's Word2Vec model, click on

https://rare-technologies.com/word2vec-tutorial/.

GloVe

GloVe, an abbreviation of "global vectors," is a word embedding technique that has been developed by Stanford. It is an unsupervised learning algorithm that builds on Word2Vec. While Word2Vec is quite successful in generating word embeddings, the issue with it is that is it has a small window through which it focuses on local words and local context to predict words. This means that it is unable to learn from the frequency of words present globally, that is, in the entire corpus. GloVe, as mentioned in its name, looks at all the words present in a corpus.

While Word2Vec is a predictive model as it learns vectors to improve its predictive abilities, GloVe is a count-based model. What this means is that GloVe learns its vectors by performing dimensionality reduction on a co-occurrence counts matrix. The connections that GloVe is able to make are along the lines of this:

king – man + woman = queen

This means it's able to understand that "king" and "queen" share a relationship that is similar to that between "man" and "woman".

These are complicated terms, so let's understand them one by one. All of these concepts come from statistics and linear algebra, so if you already know what's going on, you can skip to the activity!

When dealing with a corpus, there exist algorithms to construct matrices based on term frequencies. Basically, these matrices contain words that occur in a document as rows, and the columns are either paragraphs or separate documents. The elements of the matrices represent the frequency with which the words occur in the documents. Naturally, with a large corpus, this matrix will be huge. Processing such a large matrix will take a lot of time and memory, thus we perform dimensionality reduction. This is the process of reducing the size of the matrix so it is possible to perform further operations on it.

In the case of GloVe, the matrix is known as a co-occurrence counts matrix, which contains information on how many times a word has occurred in a particular context in a corpus. The rows are the words and the columns are the contexts. This matrix is then factorized in order to reduce the dimensions, and the new matrix has a vector representation for each word.

GloVe also has pretrained words with vectors attached to them that can be used if the semantics match the corpus and task at hand. The following activity guides you through the process of implementing GloVe in Python, except that the code isn't directly given to you, so you'll have to do some thinking and maybe some googling. Try it out!

Exercise 9: Generating Word Embeddings Using GloVe

In this exercise, we will be generating word embeddings using **Glove-Python**.

> **Note**
>
> To install Glove-Python on your platform, go to https://pypi.org/project/glove/#files.
>
> Download the Text8Corpus from http://mattmahoney.net/dc/text8.zip.
>
> Extract the file and store it with your Jupyter notebook.

1. Import **itertools**:

   ```
   import itertools
   ```

2. We need a corpus to generate word embeddings for, and the **gensim.models.word2vec** library, luckily, has one called **Text8Corpus**. Import this along with two modules from the **Glove-Python** library:

   ```
   from gensim.models.word2vec import Text8Corpus
   from glove import Corpus, Glove
   ```

3. Convert the corpus into sentences in the form of a list using **itertools**:

   ```
   sentences = list(itertools.islice(Text8Corpus('text8'),None))
   ```

4. Initiate the **Corpus()** model and fit it on to the sentences:

   ```
   corpus = Corpus()

   corpus.fit(sentences, window=10)
   ```

   The **window** parameter controls how many neighboring words are considered.

5. Now that we have prepared our corpus, we need to train the embeddings. Initiate the **Glove()** model:

   ```
   glove = Glove(no_components=100, learning_rate=0.05)
   ```

6. Generate a co-occurrence matrix based on the corpus and fit the **glove** model on to this matrix:

   ```
   glove.fit(corpus.matrix, epochs=30, no_threads=4, verbose=True)
   ```

The model has been trained!

7. Add the dictionary of the corpus:

```
glove.add_dictionary(corpus.dictionary)
```

8. Use the following command to see which words are similar to your choice of word based on the word embeddings generated:

```
glove.most_similar('man')
```

Expected output:

```
[('woman', 0.7866706012658177),
 ('young', 0.7787864197368234),
 ('spider', 0.7728204994207245),
 ('girl', 0.7642560909647501)]
```

Figure 1.25: Output of word embeddings for 'man'

You can try this out for several different words to see which words neighbor them and are the most similar to them:

```
glove.most_similar('queen', number = 10)
```

Expected output:

```
[('elizabeth', 0.9290495990532598),
 ('victoria', 0.8600464526851297),
 ('mary', 0.8089403382412337),
 ('anne', 0.7667713770457262),
 ('scotland', 0.6942531928211478),
 ('catherine', 0.6910265819525973),
 ('consort', 0.6906798004149294),
 ('tudor', 0.6686379422061477),
 ('isabella', 0.6666968276614551)]
```

Figure 1.26: Output of word embeddings for 'queen'

> **Note**
>
> To learn more about GloVe, go to https://nlp.stanford.edu/projects/glove/.

Activity 1: Generating Word Embeddings from a Corpus Using Word2Vec.

You have been given the task of training a Word2Vec model on a particular corpus – the Text8Corpus, in this case – to determine which words are similar to each other. The following steps will help you with the solution.

> **Note**
>
> You can find the text corpus file at http://mattmahoney.net/dc/text8.zip.

1. Upload the text corpus from the link given previously.
2. Import **word2vec** from **gensim** models.
3. Store the corpus in a variable.
4. Fit the word2vec model on the corpus.
5. Find the most similar word to 'man'.
6. *'Father'* is to *'girl'*, *'x'* is to *"boy."* Find the top 3 words for x.

> **Note**
>
> The solution for the activity can be found on page 296.

Expected Outputs:

```
[('woman', 0.6842043995857239),
 ('girl', 0.5943484306335449),
 ('creature', 0.5780946612358093),
 ('boy', 0.5204570293426514),
 ('person', 0.5135789513587952),
 ('stranger', 0.506704568862915),
 ('beast', 0.504448652267456),
 ('god', 0.50375235080871899),
 ('evil', 0.4990573525428772),
 ('thief', 0.4973783493041992)]
```

Figure 1.27: Output for similar word embeddings

Top three words for **'x'** could be:

```
[('mother', 0.7770676612854004),
 ('grandmother', 0.7024110555648804),
 ('wife', 0.6916966438293457)]
```

Figure 1.28: Output for top three words for 'x'

Summary

In this chapter, we learned about how natural language processing enables humans and machines to communicate in natural human language. There are three broad applications of natural language processing, and these are speech recognition, natural language understanding, and natural language generation.

Language is a complicated thing, and so text is required to go through several phases before it can make sense to a machine. This process of filtering is known as text preprocessing and comprises various techniques that serve different purposes. They are all task- and corpora-dependent and prepare text for operations that will enable it to be input into machine learning and deep learning models.

Since machine learning and deep learning models work best with numerical data, it is necessary to transform preprocessed corpora into numerical form. This is where word embeddings come into the picture; they are real-value vector representations of words that aid models in predicting and understanding words. The two main algorithms used to generate word embeddings are Word2Vec and GloVe.

In the next chapter, we will be building on the algorithms used for natural language processing. The processes of POS tagging and named entity recognition will be introduced and explained.

2

Applications of Natural Language Processing

Learning Objectives

By the end of this chapter, you will be able to:

- Describe POS tagging and its applications
- Differentiate between rule-based and stochastic POS taggers
- Perform POS tagging, chunking, and chinking on text data
- Perform named entity recognition for information extraction
- Develop and train your own POS tagger and named entity recognizer
- Use NLTK and spaCy to perform POS tagging, chunking, chinking, and named entity recognition

This chapter aims to introduce you to the plethora of applications of NLP and the various techniques involved within.

Introduction

This chapter begins with a quick recap of what natural language processing is and what services it can help provide. Then, it discusses two applications of natural language processing: **Parts of Speech Tagging (POS tagging)** and **Named Entity Recognition**. The functioning, necessity, and purposes of both of these algorithms are explained. Additionally, there are exercises and activities that perform POS tagging and named entity recognition and build and develop these algorithms.

Natural language processing consists of aiding machines to understand the natural language of humans in order to communicate with them effectively and automate a large number of tasks. The previous chapter discussed the applications of natural language processing along with examples of real-life use cases where these techniques could simplify the lives of humans. This chapter will specifically look into two of these algorithms and their real-life applications.

Every aspect of natural language processing can be seen to follow the same analogy of teaching a language. In the last chapter, we saw how machines need to be told what parts of a corpus to pay attention to and what parts are irrelevant and unimportant. They need to be trained to remove stop words and noisy elements and focus on key words to reduce various forms of the same word to the word's root form so that it's easier to search for and interpret. In a similar fashion, the two algorithms discussed in this chapter also teach machines particular things about languages in the way we humans have been taught.

POS Tagging

Before we dive straight into the algorithm, let's understand what parts of speech are. Parts of speech are something most of us are taught in our early years of learning the English language. They are categories assigned to words based on their syntactic or grammatical functions. These functions are the functional relationships that exist between different words.

Parts of Speech

The English language has nine main parts of speech:

- *Nouns*: Things or people
- Examples: table, dog, piano, London, towel
- *Pronouns*: Words that replace nouns
- Examples: I, you, he, she, it
- *Verbs*: Action words
- Examples: to be, to have, to study, to learn, to play
- *Adjectives*: Words that describe nouns
- Examples: intelligent, small, silly, intriguing, blue
- *Determiners*: Words that limit nouns
- Examples: a few, many, some, three

> **Note**
>
> For more examples of determiners, visit https://www.ef.com/in/english-resources/english-grammar/determiners/.

- *Adverbs*: Words that describe verbs, adjectives, or adverbs themselves
- Examples: quickly, shortly, very, really, drastically
- *Prepositions*: Words that link nouns to other words
- Examples: to, on, in, under, beside
- *Conjunctions*: Words that join two sentences or words
- Examples: and, but, yet
- *Interjections*: Words that are exclamations
- Examples: ouch! Ow! Wow!

As you can see, each word falls under a specific Parts of speech tag assigned to it that helps us understand the meaning and purpose of the word, enabling us to better understand the context in which it is being used.

POS Tagger

POS tagging is the process of assigning a tag to a word. This is done by an algorithm known as a POS tagger. The aim of the algorithm is really just as simple as this.

Most POS taggers are supervised learning algorithms. If you don't remember what supervised learning algorithms are, they are machine learning algorithms that learn to perform a task based on previously labeled data. The algorithms take rows of data as input. This data contains feature columns—data used to predict something—and usually one label column—the something that needs to be predicted. The models are trained on this input to learn and understand what features correspond to which label, thus learning how to perform the task of predicting the labels. Ultimately, they are given unlabeled data (data that just consists of feature columns), for which they must predict labels.

The following diagram is a general illustration of a supervised learning model:

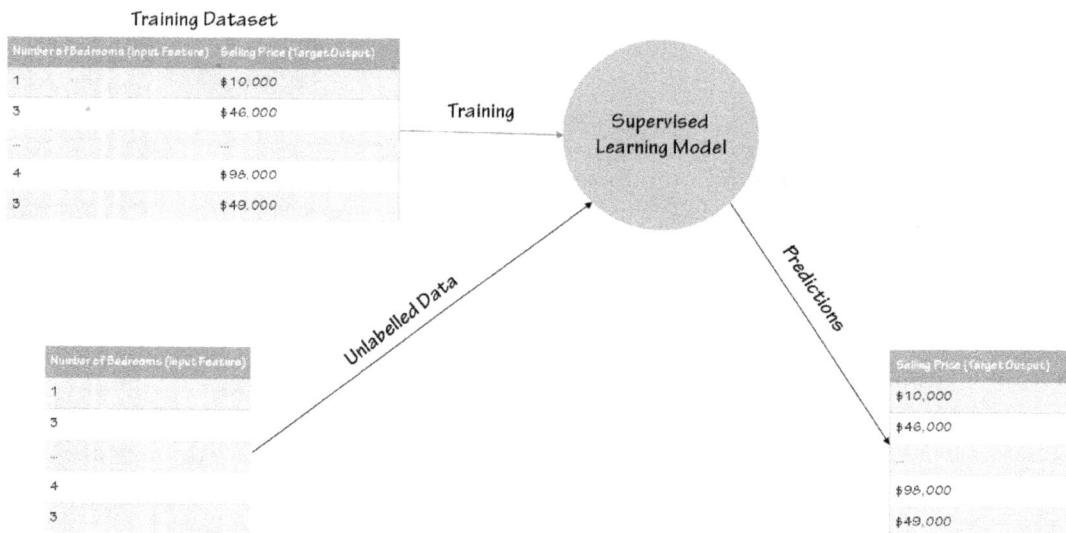

Fig 2.1: Supervised learning

Note

For more information on supervised learning, go to https://www.packtpub.com/big-data-and-business-intelligence/applied-supervised-learning-python.

Thus, POS taggers hone their predictive abilities by learning from previously labeled datasets. In this case, the datasets can consist of a variety of features, such as the word itself (obviously), the definition of the word, the relationships of the word with its preceding, proceeding, and other related word(s) that are present within the same sentence, phrase, or paragraph. These features together help the tagger predict what POS tag should be assigned to a word. The corpus used to train a supervised POS tagger is known as a pre-tagged corpus. Such corpora serve as the basis for the creation of a system for the POS tagger to tag untagged words. These systems/types of POS taggers will be discussed in the next section.

Pre-tagged corpora, however, are not always readily available, and to accurately train a tagger, the corpus must be large. Thus, recently there have been iterations of the POS tagger that can be considered as unsupervised learning algorithms. These are algorithms that take data consisting solely of features as input. These features aren't associated with labels and thus the algorithm, instead of predicting labels, forms groups or clusters of the input data.

In the case of POS tagging, the models use computational methods to automatically generate sets of POS tags. While, pre-tagged corpora are responsible for aiding the process of creating a system for the tagger in the case of supervised POS taggers, with unsupervised POS taggers, these computational methods serve as the basis for the creation of such systems. The drawback of unsupervised learning methods is that the cluster of POS tags generated automatically may not always be as accurate as those found in the pre-tagged corpora used to train supervised methods.

To summarize, the key differences between supervised and unsupervised learning methods are as follows:

- Supervised POS taggers take pre-tagged corpora as input to be trained, while unsupervised POS taggers take untagged corpora as input to create a set of POS tags.

- Supervised POS taggers create dictionaries of words with their respective POS tags based on the tagged corpora, while unsupervised POS taggers generate these dictionaries using the self-created POS tag set.

Several Python libraries (such as NLTK and spaCy) have trained POS taggers of their own. You will learn how to use one in the following sections, but let's understand the input and output of a POS tagger with an example for now. An important thing to remember is that since a POS tagger assigns a POS tag to each word in the given corpus, the input needs to be in the form of word tokens. Therefore, before performing POS tagging, tokenization needs to be carried out on the corpus. Let's say we give the trained POS tagger the following tokens as an input:

```
['I', 'enjoy', 'playing', 'the', 'piano']
```

After POS tagging, the output would look something like this:

```
['I_PRO', 'enjoy_V', 'playing_V', 'the_DT', piano_N']
```

Here, **PRO** = pronoun, **V** = verb, **DT** = determiner, and **N** = noun.

The input and output for both a trained supervised and unsupervised POS tagger are the same: tokens, and tokens with POS tags, respectively.

> **Note**
>
> This is not the exact syntax of the output; you'll see the proper output later when you perform the exercise. This is just to give you an idea of what POS taggers do.

The aforementioned parts of speech are very basic tags, and to ease the process of understanding natural language, POS algorithms create much more complicated tags that are variations of these basic ones. Here's a full list of the POS tags with their descriptions:

Number	Tag	Description
1	CC	Coordinating conjunction
2	CD	Cardinal number
3	DT	Determiner
4	EX	Existential there
5	FW	Foreign word
6	IN	Preposition or subordinating conjunction
7	JJ	Adjective
8	JJR	Adjective, comparative
9	JJS	Adjective, superlative
10	LS	List item marker
11	MD	Modal
12	NN	Noun, singular or mass
13	NNS	Noun, plural
14	NNP	Proper noun, singular
15	NNPS	Proper noun, plural
16	PDT	Predeterminer
17	POS	Possessive ending
18	PRP	Personal pronoun
19	PRP$	Possessive pronoun
20	RB	Adverb
21	RBR	Adverb, comparative
22	RBS	Adverb, superlative
23	RP	Particle
24	SYM	Symbol
25	TO	To
26	UH	Interjection
27	VB	Verb, base form
28	VBD	Verb, past tense
29	VBG	Verb, gerund or present participle
30	VBN	Verb, past participle
31	VBP	Verb, non-3rd person singular present
32	VBZ	Verb, 3rd person singular present
33	WDT	Wh-determiner
34	WP	Wh-pronoun
35	WP$	Possessive wh-pronoun
36	WRB	Wh-adverb

Figure 2.2: POS tags with descriptions

These tags are from the Penn Treebank tagset (https://www.ling.upenn.edu/courses/Fall_2003/ling001/penn_treebank_pos.html), which is one of the most popular tagsets. A majority of the pre-trained taggers for the English language are trained on this tagset, including NLTK's POS tagger.

Applications of Parts of Speech Tagging

Just like text pre-processing techniques help the machine understand natural language better by encouraging it to focus on only the important details, POS tagging helps the machine actually interpret the context of text and thus make sense of it. While text pre-processing is more of a cleaning phase, parts of speech tagging is actually the part where the machine is beginning to output valuable information about corpora on its own.

Understanding what words correspond to which parts of speech can be beneficial in processing natural language in several ways for a machine:

- POS tagging is useful in differentiating between homonyms – words that have the same spelling but mean different things. For example, the word "play" can mean the verb to play, as in engage in an activity, and also the noun, as in a dramatic work to be performed on stage. A POS tagger can help the machine understand what context the word "play" is being used in by determining its POS tag.

- POS tagging builds on the need for sentence and word segmentation – one of the basic tasks of natural language processing.

- POS tags are used in performing higher-level tasks by other algorithms, one of which we will be discussing in this chapter, named entity recognition.

- POS tags contribute to the process of sentiment analysis and question answering too. For example, in the sentence "Tim Cook is the CEO of this technology company," you want the machine to be able to replace "this technology company" with the name of the company. POS tagging can help the machine recognize that the phrase "this technology company" is a determiner ((this) + a noun phrase (technology company)). It can use this information to, for example, search articles online and check how many times "Tim Cook is the CEO of Apple" appears in them to then decide whether Apple is the correct answer.

Thus, POS tagging is an important step in the process of understanding natural language because it contributes to other tasks.

Types of POS Taggers

As we saw in the previous section, POS taggers can be both of the supervised and unsupervised learning type. This difference largely affects how a tagger is trained. There is another distinction that impacts how the tagger actually assigns a tag to an untagged word, which is the approach used to train the taggers.

The two types of POS taggers are rule-based and stochastic. Let's take a look at both of them.

Rule-Based POS Taggers

These POS taggers work pretty much exactly as their name states – by rules. The purpose for giving the taggers sets of rules is to ensure that they tag an ambiguous/unknown word accurately most of the times, thus most of the rules are applied only when the taggers come across an ambiguous/unknown word.

These rules are often known as context frame rules and provide the taggers with contextual information to understand what tag to give an ambiguous word. An example of a rule is as follows: If an ambiguous/unknown word, x, is preceded by a determiner and followed by a noun, then assign it the tag of an adjective. An example of this would be "one small girl," where "one" is a determiner and "girl" is a noun, therefore the tagger will assign adjective to the word "small."

The rules depend on your theory of grammar. Additionally, they also often include rules such as capitalization and punctuation. This can help you recognize pronouns and differentiate them from words found at the start of a sentence (following a full stop).

Most rule-based POS taggers are supervised learning algorithms, in order to be able to learn the correct rules and apply them to properly tag ambiguous words. Recently, though, there have been experiments with training these taggers the unsupervised way. Untagged text is given to the tagger to tag, and humans go through the output tags, correcting whatever tags are inaccurate. This correctly tagged text is then given to the tagger so that it can develop correction rules between the two different tagsets and learn how to accurately tag words.

An example of this correction rule-based POS tagger is Brill's tagger, which follows the process mentioned earlier. Its functioning can be compared with the art of painting – when painting a house, it is easier to first paint the background of the house (for example, a brown square) and then paint the details, such as a door and windows, on top of that background using a finer brush. Similarly, Brill's rule-based POS tagger aims to first generally tag an untagged corpus, even if some of the tags may be wrong, and then revisit those tags to understand why some are wrong and learn from them.

Note

Exercises 10-16 can be performed in the same Jupyter Notebook.

Exercise 10: Performing Rule-Based POS Tagging

NLTK has a POS tagger that is a rule-based tagger. In this exercise, we will perform POS tagging using NLTK's POS tagger. The following steps will help you with the solution:

1. Open cmd or terminal, depending on your operating system.

2. Navigate to the desired path and use the following command to initiate a **Jupyter** Notebook:

    ```
    jupyter notebook
    ```

3. Import **nltk** and **punkt**, as shown:

    ```
    import nltk
    nltk.download('punkt')
    nltk.download('averaged_perceptron_tagger')
    nltk.download('tagsets')
    ```

4. Store an input string in a variable called **s**, as follows:

    ```
    s = 'i enjoy playing the piano'
    ```

5. Tokenize the sentence, as demonstrated:

    ```
    tokens = nltk.word_tokenize(s)
    ```

6. Apply the POS tagger on the tokens and then print the tagset, as shown:

    ```
    tags = nltk.pos_tag(tokens)
    tags
    ```

    Your output will look like this:

    ```
    [('i', 'NN'),
     ('enjoy', 'VBP'),
     ('playing', 'VBG'),
     ('the', 'DT'),
     ('piano', 'NN')]
    ```

    Fig 2.3: Tagged output

7. To understand what the **"NN"** POS tag stands for, you can use the following line of code:

```
nltk.help.upenn_tagset("NN")
```

The output will be as follows:

```
NN: noun, common, singular or mass
    common-carrier cabbage knuckle-duster Casino afghan shed thermostat
    investment slide humour falloff slick wind hyena override subhumanity
    machinist ...
```

Fig 2.4: Noun details

You can do this for each POS tag by substituting "NN" with it.

Let's try this out with a sentence containing homonyms.

8. Store an input string containing homonyms in a variable called sent:

```
sent = 'and so i said im going to play the piano for the play tonight'
```

9. Tokenize this sentence and then apply the POS tagger on the tokens, as shown:

```
tagset = nltk.pos_tag(nltk.word_tokenize(sent))
tagset
```

Expected output:

```
[('and', 'CC'),
 ('so', 'RB'),
 ('i', 'JJ'),
 ('said', 'VBD'),
 ('im', 'NN'),
 ('going', 'VBG'),
 ('to', 'TO'),
 ('play', 'VB'),
 ('the', 'DT'),
 ('piano', 'NN'),
 ('for', 'IN'),
 ('the', 'DT'),
 ('play', 'NN'),
 ('tonight', 'NN')]
```

Fig 2.5: Tagged output

As you can see, the first instance of the word play has been tagged as **'VB'**, which stands for verb, base form, and the second instance of the word play has been tagged as **'NN'**, which stands for noun. Thus, POS taggers are able to differentiate between homonyms and different instances of the same word. This helps machines understand natural language better.

Stochastic POS Taggers

Stochastic POS taggers are taggers that use any method other than rule-based methods to assign tags to words. Thus, there are a large number of approaches that fall into the stochastic category. All models that incorporate statistical methods, such as probability and frequency, when determining the POS tags for words are stochastic models.

We will discuss three models:

- The Unigram or Word Frequency Approach
- The n – gram approach
- The hidden Markov Model

The Unigram or Word Frequency Approach

The simplest stochastic POS taggers assign POS tags to ambiguous words solely based on the probability that a word occurs with a tag. This basically means that whatever tag the tagger found linked with a word most often in the training set is the tag that it will assign to an ambiguous instance of the same word. For example, let's say the training set has the word "beautiful" tagged as an adjective a majority of the time. When the POS tagger encounters "beaut", it won't be able to tag this directly because it isn't a proper word. This will be an ambiguous word, and so it will calculate the probability of it being each of the POS tags, based on how many times different instances of this word have been tagged with each of those POS tags. "beaut" can be seen as an ambiguous form of "beautiful", and since "beautiful" has been tagged as an adjective a majority of the time, the POS tagger will tag "beaut" as an adjective too. This is called the word frequency approach because the tagger is checking the frequency of the POS tags assigned to words.

The n – gram Approach

This builds on the previous approach. The **n** in the name stands for how many words are considered when determining the probability of a word belonging to a particular POS tag. In the Unigram tagger, **n = 1**, and thus only the word itself is taken into consideration. Increasing the value of n results in taggers calculating the probability of a specific sequence of n POS tags occurring together and assigning a word a tag based on this probability.

When assigning a tag to a word, these POS taggers create a context of the word by factoring in the type of token it is, along with the POS tags of the n preceding words. Based on the context, the taggers select the tag that is most likely to be in sequence with the tags of the preceding words and assigns this to the word in question. The most popular n – gram tagger is known as the Viterbi algorithm.

Hidden Markov Model

The hidden Markov model combines both the word frequency approach and the n – gram approach. A Markov model is one that describes a sequence of events or states. The probability of each state occurring depends solely on the state attained by the previous event. These events are based on observations. The "hidden" aspect of the hidden Markov model is that the set of states that an event could possibly be is hidden.

In the case of POS tagging, the observations are the word tokens, and the hidden set of states are the POS tags. The way this works is that the model calculates the probability of a word having a particular tag based on what the tag of the previous word was. For example, P (V | NN) is the probability of the current word being a verb given that the previous word is a noun.

> Note
>
> This is a very basic explanation of the hidden Markov model. To learn more, go to https://medium.freecodecamp.org/an-introduction-to-part-of-speech-tagging-and-the-hidden-markov-model-953d45338f24
>
> To learn more about stochastic models, go to http://ccl.pku.edu.cn/doubtfire/NLP/Lexical_Analysis/Word_Segmentation_Tagging/POS_Tagging_Overview/POS%20Tagging%20Overview.htm.

The three approaches mentioned earlier have been explained in an order where each model builds upon and improves the accuracy of the preceding model. However, each model that builds upon a preceding model involves more calculations of probability and thus will take more time to perform computations, depending on the size of the training corpus. Therefore, the decision of which approach to use depends on the size of the corpus.

Exercise 11: Performing Stochastic POS Tagging

spaCy's POS tagger is a stochastic one. In this exercise, we will use spaCy's POS tagger on some sentences to see the difference in the results of rule-based and stochastic tagging. The following steps will help you with the solution:

> **Note**
>
> To install spaCy, click on the following link and follow the instructions: https://spacy.io/usage

1. Import **spaCy**:

   ```
   import spacy
   ```

2. Load spaCy's **'en_core_web_sm'** model:

   ```
   nlp = spacy.load('en_core_web_sm')
   ```

   spaCy has models that are specific to different languages. The 'en_core_web_sm' model is the English language model and has been trained on written web text, such as blogs and news articles, and includes vocabulary, syntax, and entities.

> **Note**
>
> To learn more about spaCy models, click on https://spacy.io/models.

3. Fit the model on the sentence you want to assign POS tags to. Let's use the sentence we gave NLTK's POS tagger:

   ```
   doc = nlp(u"and so i said i'm going to play the piano for the play tonight")
   ```

4. Now, let's tokenize this sentence, assign the POS tags, and print them:

   ```
   for token in doc:
       print(token.text, token.pos_, token.tag_)
   ```

Expected output:

```
and CCONJ CC
so ADV RB
i PRON PRP
said VERB VBD
i PRON PRP
'm VERB VBP
going VERB VBG
to PART TO
play VERB VB
the DET DT
piano NOUN NN
for ADP IN
the DET DT
play NOUN NN
tonight NOUN NN
```

Figure 2.6: Output for POS tags

To understand what a POS tag stands for, use the following line of code:

```
spacy.explain("VBZ")
```

Replace "VBZ" with the POS tag you'd like to know about. In this case, your output will be this:

```
'verb, 3rd person singular present'
```

As you can see, the results are pretty much the same as the ones obtained from the NLTK POS tagger. This is the case due to the simplicity of our input.

Chunking

POS taggers work on individual tokens of words. Tagging individual words isn't always the best way to understand corpora, though. For example, the words 'United' and 'Kingdom' don't make a lot of sense when they're separated, but 'United Kingdom' together tells the machine that this is a country, thus providing it with more context and information. This is where the process of chunking comes into the picture.

Chunking is an algorithm that takes words and their POS tags as input. It processes these individual tokens and their tags to see whether they can be combined. The combination of one or more individual tokens is known as a chunk, and the POS tag assigned to such a chunk is known as a chunk tag.

Chunk tags are combinations of basic POS tags. They are easier to define phrases by and are more efficient than simple POS tags. These phrases are chunks. There will be instances where a single word is considered a chunk and assigned a chunk tag too. There are five major chunk tags:

- *Noun Phrase* (NP): These are phrases that have nouns as the head word. They act as a subject or an object to the verb or verb phrase.

- *Verb Phrase* (VP): These are phrases that have verbs as the head word.

- *Adjective Phrase* (ADJP): These are phrases that have adjectives as the head word. Describing and qualifying nouns or pronouns is the main function of adjective phrases. They are found either directly before or after the noun or pronoun.

- *Adverb Phrase* (ADVP): These are phrases that have adverbs as the head word. They're used as modifiers for nouns and verbs by providing details that describe and qualify them.

- *Prepositional Phrase* (PP): These are phrases that have prepositions as the head word. They position an action or an entity in time or space.

For example, in the sentence 'the yellow bird is slow and is flying into the brown house', the following phrases will be assigned the following chunk tags:

'the yellow bird' – NP

'is' – VP

'slow' – ADJP

'is flying' – VP

'into' – PP

'the brown house' – NP

Thus, chunking is performed after POS tagging has been applied on a corpus. This allows the text to be broken down into its simplest form (tokens of words), have its structure analyzed, and then be grouped back together into meaningful higher-level chunks. Chunking also benefits the process of named entity recognition. We'll see how in the coming section.

The chunk parser present within the NLTK library is rule based and thus needs to be given a regular expression as a rule to output a chunk with its chunk tag. **spaCy** can perform chunking without the presence of rules. Let's take a look at both these approaches.

Exercise 12: Performing Chunking with NLTK

In this exercise, we will generate chunks and chunk tags. **nltk** has a regular expression parser. This requires an input of a regular expression of a phrase and the corresponding chunk tag. It then searches the corpus for this expression and assigns it the tag.

Since chunking works with POS tags, we can add on to our code from the POS tagging exercise. We saved the tokens with their respective POS tags in 'tagset'. Let's use this. The following steps will help you with the solution:

1. Create a regular expression that will search for a noun phrase, as shown:

   ```
   rule = r"""Noun Phrase: {<DT>?<JJ>*<NN>}"""
   ```

   This regular expression is searching for a determiner (optional), followed by one or more adjectives and then a single noun. This will form a chunk called **Noun Phrase**.

   > **Note**
   >
   > If you don't know how to write Regular Expressions, check out these quick tutorials: https://www.w3schools.com/python/python_regex.asp https://pythonprogramming.net/regular-expressions-regex-tutorial-python-3/

2. Create an instance of **RegexpParser** and feed it the rule:

   ```
   chunkParser = nltk.RegexpParser(rule)
   ```

3. Give **chunkParser** the **tagset** containing the tokens with their respective POS tags so that it can perform chunking, and then draw the chunks:

   ```
   chunked = chunkParser.parse(tagset)
   chunked.draw()
   ```

   > **Note**
   >
   > matplotlib needs to be installed on your machine for the **.draw()** function to work.

   Your output will look something like this:

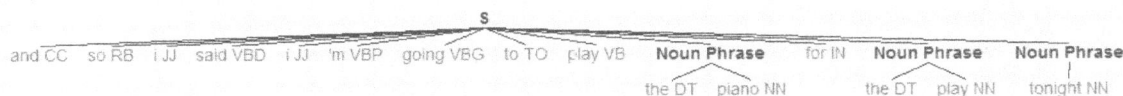

Figure 2.7: Parse tree.

This is a parse tree. As you can see, the chunking process has recognized the noun phrases and labeled them, and the remaining tokens are shown with their POS tags.

4. Let's try the same thing out with another sentence. Store an input sentence in another variable:

```
a = "the beautiful butterfly flew away into the night sky"
```

5. Tokenize the sentence and perform POS tagging using NLTK's POS tagger:

```
tagged = nltk.pos_tag(nltk.word_tokenize(a))
```

6. Repeat step 3:

```
chunked2 = chunkParser.parse(tagged)
chunked2.draw()
```

Expected output:

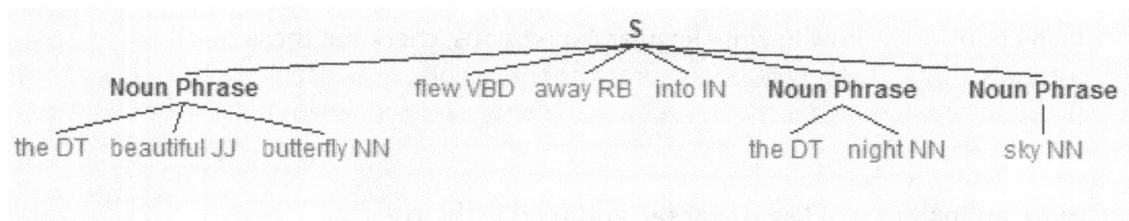

Figure 2.8: Output for chunking.

Exercise 13: Performing Chunking with spaCy

In this exercise, we will implement chunking with spaCy. **spaCy** doesn't require us to formulate rules to recognize chunks; it identifies chunks on its own and tells us what the head word is, thus telling us what the chunk tag is. Let's identify some noun chunks using the same sentence from Exercise 12. The following steps will help you with the solution:

1. Fit **spaCy**'s English model on the sentence:

```
doc = nlp(u"the beautiful butterfly flew away into the night sky")
```

2. Apply **noun_chunks** on this model, and for each chunk, print the text of the chunk, the root word of the chunk, and the dependency relation that connects the root word to its head:

```
for chunk in doc.noun_chunks:
    print(chunk.text, chunk.root.text, chunk.root.dep_)
```

Expected output:

the beautiful butterfly butterfly nsubj
the night sky sky pobj

Figure 2.9: Output for chunking with spaCy

As you can see, chunking with **spaCy** is a lot simpler than with NLTK.

Chinking

Chinking is an extension of chunking, as you've probably guessed already from its name. It's not a mandatory step in processing natural language, but it can be beneficial.

Chinking is performed after chunking. Post chunking, you have chunks with their chunk tags, along with individual words with their POS tags. Often, these extra words are unnecessary. They don't contribute to the final result or the entire process of understanding natural language and thus are a nuisance. The process of chinking helps us deal with this issue by extracting the chunks, and their chunk tags form the tagged corpus, thus getting rid of the unnecessary bits. These useful chunks are called chinks once they have been extracted from the tagged corpus.

For example, if you need only the nouns or noun phrases from a corpus to answer questions such as "what is this corpus talking about?", you would apply chinking because it would extract just what you want and present it in front of your eyes. Let's check this out with an exercise.

Exercise 14: Performing Chinking

Chinking is basically altering the things that you're looking for in a corpus. Thus, applying chinking involves altering the rule (regular expression) provided to `chinkParser`. The following steps will help you with the solution:

1. Create a rule that chunks the entire corpus and only creates chinks out of the words or phrases tagged as nouns or noun phrases:

   ```
   rule = r"""Chink: {<.*>+}
                      }<VB.?|CC|RB|JJ IN|DT|TO>+{"""
   ```

   This rule is in the form of a regular expression. Basically, this regular expression is telling the machine to ignore all words that are not nouns or noun phrases. When it comes across a noun or a noun phrase, this rule will ensure that it is extracted as a chink.

2. Create an instance of **RegexpParser** and feed it the rule:

```
chinkParser = nltk.RegexpParser(rule)
```

3. Give **chinkParser** the **tagset** containing the tokens with their respective POS tags so that it can perform chinking, and then draw the chinks:

```
chinked = chinkParser.parse(tagset)
chinked.draw()
```

Expected output:

Figure 2.10: Output for chinking

As you can see, the chinks have been highlighted and contain only nouns.

Activity 2: Building and Training Your Own POS Tagger

We've already looked at POS tagging words using the existing and pre-trained POS taggers. In this activity, we will train our own POS tagger. This is like training any other machine learning algorithm. The following steps will help you with the solution:

1. Pick a corpus to train the tagger on. You can use the nltk treebank to work on. The following code should help you import the treebank corpus:

```
nltk.download('treebank')
tagged = nltk.corpus.treebank.tagged_sents()
```

2. Determine what features the tagger will consider when assigning a tag to a word.

3. Create a function to strip the tagged words of their tags so that we can feed them into our tagger.

4. Build the dataset and split the data into training and testing sets. Assign the features to 'X' and append the POS tags to 'Y'. Apply this function on the training set.

5. Use the decision tree classifier to train the tagger.

6. Import the classifier, initialize it, fit the model on the training data, and print the accuracy score.

> **Note**
>
> The accuracy score in the output may vary, depending on the corpus used.

Expected output:

```
Training completed
Accuracy: 0.89595050061867267
```

Figure 2.11: Expected accuracy score.

> **Note**
>
> The solution for the activity can be found on page 297.

Named Entity Recognition

This is one of the first steps in the process of information extraction. Information extraction is the task of a machine extracting structured information from unstructured or semi-structured text. This furthers the comprehension of natural language by machines.

After text preprocessing and POS tagging, our corpus becomes semi-structured and machine-readable. Thus, information extraction is performed after we've readied our corpus.

The following diagram is an example of named entity recognition:

Why Is Diversity Important For Google **And India?** Sundar Pichai **Answers**

Organization   Location   Name

Figure 2.12: Example for named entity recognition

Named Entities

Named entities are real-world objects that can be classified into categories, such as people, places, and things. Basically, they are words that can be denoted by a proper name. Named entities can also include quantities, organizations, monetary values, and many more things.

Some examples of named entities and the categories they fall under are as follows:

- Donald Trump, person
- Italy, location
- Bottle, object
- 500 USD, money

Named entities can be viewed as instances of entities. In the previous examples, the categories are basically entities in their own and the named entities are instances of those. For example, London is an instance of city, which is an entity.

The most common named entity categories are as listed:

- ORGANIZATION
- PERSON
- LOCATION
- DATE
- TIME
- MONEY
- PERCENT
- FACILITY
- GPE (which stands Geo-Political Entity)

Named Entity Recognizers

Named entity recognizers are algorithms that identify and extract named entities from corpora and assign them a category. The input provided to a trained named entity recognizer consists of tokenized words with their respective POS tags. The output of named entity recognition is named entities along with their categories, among the other tokenized words and their POS tags.

The problem of named entity recognition takes place in two phases:

1. Identifying and recognizing named entities (for example, 'London')

2. Classifying these names entities (for example, 'London' is a 'location')

The first phase of identifying named entities is quite similar to the process of chunking, because the aim is to recognize things that are denoted by proper names. The named entity recognizer needs to look out for continuous sequences of tokens to be able to correctly spot named entities. For example, 'Bank of America' should be identified as a single named entity, despite the phrase containing the word 'America', which in itself is a named entity.

Much like POS taggers, most named entity recognizers are supervised learning algorithms. They are trained on input that contains named entities along with the categories that they fall under, thus enabling the algorithm to learn how to classify unknown named entities in the future.

This input containing named entities with their respective categories is often known as a knowledge base. Once a named entity recognizer has been trained and is given an unrecognized corpus, it refers to this knowledge base to search for the most accurate classification to assign to a named entity.

However, due to the fact that supervised learning requires an excessive amount of labeled data, unsupervised learning versions of named entity recognizers are also being researched. These are trained on unlabeled corpora – text that doesn't have named entities categorized. Like POS taggers, named entity recognizers categorize the named entities, and then the incorrect categories are corrected manually by humans. This corrected data is fed back to the NERs so that they can simply learn from their mistakes.

Applications of Named Entity Recognition

As mentioned earlier, named entity recognition is one of the first steps of information extraction and thus plays a major role in enabling machines to understand natural language and perform a variety of tasks based on it. Named entity recognition is and can be used in various industries and scenarios to simplify and automate processes. Let's take a look at a few use cases:

- *Online content*, including articles, reports. and blog posts, are often tagged to enable users to search for it more easily and also to get a quick overview of what exactly the content is about. Named entity recognizers can be used to scour through this content and extract named entities to automatically generate these tags. These tags help categorize articles into predefined hierarchies as well.

- *Search algorithms* also benefit from these tags. If a user were to enter a keyword into a search algorithm, instead of scouring through all the words of every article (which will take forever), the algorithm just needs to refer to the tags produced by named entity recognition to pull up articles containing or pertaining to the entered keyword. This reduces the computational time and operations by a lot.

- Another purpose for these tags is to create an *efficient recommendation system*. If you read an article that discusses the current political situation in India, and is thus maybe tagged as 'Indian Politics' (this is just an example), the news website can use this tag to suggest different articles with the same or similar tags. This also works in the case of visual entertainment such as movies and shows. Online streaming websites use tags assigned to content (for example, genres such as 'action', 'adventure', 'thriller', and so on) to understand your taste better and thus recommend similar content to you.

- *Customer feedback* is important for any service or product providing company. Running customer complaints and reviews through named entity recognizers produces tags that can help classify them based on location, type of product, and type of feedback (positive or negative). These reviews and complaints can then be sent to the people responsible for that particular product or that particular area and can be dealt with based on whether the feedback is positive or negative. The same thing can be done with tweets, Instagram captions, Facebook posts, and so on.

As you can see, there are many applications of named entity recognition. Thus, it is important to understand how it works and how to implement it.

Types of Named Entity Recognizers

As is the case with POS taggers, there are two broad methods to design a named entity recognizer: a linguistic approach by defining rules to recognize entities, or a stochastic approach using statistical models to accurately determine which category a named entity falls into best.

Rule-Based NERs

Rule-based NERs work in the same way that rule-based POS taggers do.

Stochastic NERs

These include any and all models that use statistics to name and recognize entities. There are several approaches to stochastic named entity recognition. Let's take a look at two of them:

- *Maximum Entropy Classification*

  This is a machine learning classification model. It calculates the probability of a named entity falling into a particular category solely on the basis of the information provided to it (the corpus).

  > **Note**
  >
  > For more information on Maximum Entropy Classification, go to http://blog.datumbox.com/machine-learning-tutorial-the-max-entropy-text-classifier/.

- *Hidden Markov Model*

  This method is the same as the one explained in the POS tagging section, but instead of the hidden set of states being the POS tags, they are the categories of the named entities.

  > **Note**
  >
  > For more information on stochastic named entity recognition and when to use which approach, go to http://www.datacommunitydc.org/blog/2013/04/a-survey-of-stochastic-and-gazetteer-based-approaches-for-named-entity-recognition-part-2.

Exercise 15: Perform Named Entity Recognition with NLTK

In this exercise, we'll use the **ne_chunk** algorithm of **NLTK** to perform named entity recognition on a sentence. Instead of using the sentences we used in the previous exercises, create a new sentence that contains proper names that can be classified into categories so that you can actually see the results:

1. Store an input sentence in a variable, as shown:

   ```
   ex = "Shubhangi visited the Taj Mahal after taking a SpiceJet flight from
   Pune."
   ```

2. Tokenize the sentence and assign **POS tags** to the tokens:

   ```
   tags = nltk.pos_tag(nltk.word_tokenize(ex))
   ```

3. Apply the **ne_chunk()** algorithm on the tagged words and either print or draw the results:

   ```
   ne = nltk.ne_chunk(tags, binary = True)
   ne.draw()
   ```

   Assigning the value of '**True**' to the '**binary**' parameter tells the algorithm to just recognize the named entities and not classify them. Thus, your results will look something like this:

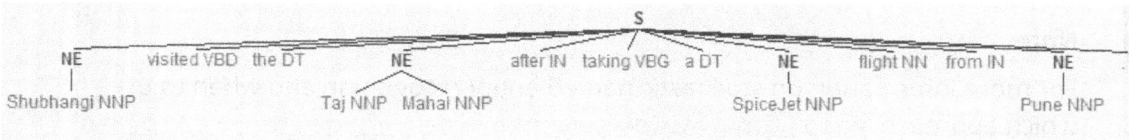

Figure 2.13: Output for named entity recognition with POS tags

As you can see, the named entities have been highlighted as '**NE**'.

4. To know which categories the algorithm has assigned to these named entities, simply assign the value of '**False**' to the '**binary**' parameter:

   ```
   ner = nltk.ne_chunk(tags, binary = False)
   ner.draw()
   ```

Expected output:

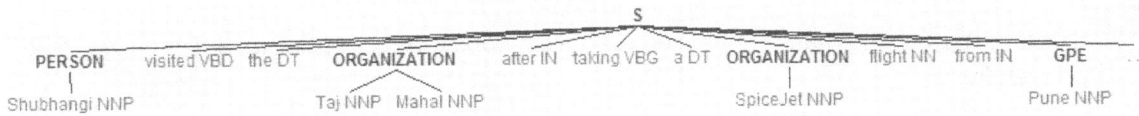

PERSON   visited VBD   the DT   ORGANIZATION   after IN   taking VBG   a DT   ORGANIZATION   flight NN   from IN   GPE
Shubhangi NNP   Taj NNP   Mahal NNP   SpiceJet NNP   Pune NNP

Figure 2.14: Output with named entities

The algorithm has accurately categorized 'Shubhangi' and 'SpiceJet'. 'Taj Mahal', however, shouldn't be an ORGANIZATION, it should be a FACILITY. Thus, NLTK's **ne_ chunk()** algorithm isn't the best one.

Exercise 16: Performing Named Entity Recognition with spaCy

In this exercise, we'll be implementing **spaCy**'s named entity recognizer on the sentence from the previous exercise and compare the results. spaCy has several NERs that have been trained on different corpora. Each model has a different set of categories; here's a list of all the categories spaCy can recognize:

PERSON	People, including fictional.
NORP	Nationalities or religious or political groups.
FAC	Buildings, airports, highways, bridges, etc.
ORG	Companies, agencies, institutions, etc.
GPE	Countries, cities, states.
LOC	Non-GPE locations, mountain ranges, bodies of water.
PRODUCT	Objects, vehicles, foods, etc. (Not services.)
EVENT	Named hurricanes, battles, wars, sports events, etc.
WORK_OF_ART	Titles of books, songs, etc.
LAW	Named documents made into laws.
LANGUAGE	Any named language.
DATE	Absolute or relative dates or periods.
TIME	Times smaller than a day.
PERCENT	Percentage, including "%".
MONEY	Monetary values, including unit.
QUANTITY	Measurements, as of weight or distance.
ORDINAL	"first", "second", etc.
CARDINAL	Numerals that do not fall under another type.

Figure 2.15: Categories of spaCy

The following steps will help you with the solution:

1. Fit **spaCy**'s English model on the sentence we used in the previous exercise:

    ```
    doc = nlp(u"Shubhangi visited the Taj Mahal after taking a SpiceJet flight
    from Pune.")
    ```

2. For each entity in this sentence, print the text of the entity and the label:

    ```
    for ent in doc.ents:
        print(ent.text, ent.label_)
    ```

    Your output will look something like this:

    ```
    SpiceJet ORG
    Pune GPE
    ```

    Figure 2.16: Output for named entity

    It's only recognizing 'SpiceJet' and 'Pune' as named entities, and not 'Shubhangi' and 'Taj Mahal'. Let's try adding a last name to 'Shubhangi' and check whether that makes a difference.

3. Fit the model on the new sentence:

    ```
    doc1 = nlp(u"Shubhangi Hora visited the Taj Mahal after taking a SpiceJet
    flight from Pune.")
    ```

4. Repeat step 2:

    ```
    for ent in doc1.ents:
        print(ent.text, ent.label_)
    ```

    Expected output:

    ```
    Shubhangi Hora PERSON
    the Taj Mahal WORK_OF_ART
    SpiceJet ORG
    Pune GPE
    ```

    Figure 2.17: Output for named entity recognition with spaCy.

So now that we've added a last name, "Shubhangi Hora" is recognized as a PERSON, and "Taj Mahal" is recognized as a **WORK_OF ART**. The latter is incorrect, since if you check the table of categories, **WORK_OF_ART** is used to describe songs and books.

Thus, the recognition and categorization of named entities strongly depends on the data that the recognizer has been trained on. This is something to keep in mind when implementing named entity recognition; it is often better to train and develop your own recognizer for specific use cases.

Activity 3: Performing NER on a Tagged Corpus

Now that we've seen how to perform named entity recognition on a sentence, in this activity, we'll perform named entity recognition on a corpus that has been through POS tagging. Imagine that you're given a corpus that you've identified the POS tags for and now your job is to extract entities from it so that you can provide an overall summary of what the corpus is discussing. The following steps will help you with the solution:

1. Import NLTK and other necessary packages.

2. Print `nltk.corpus.treebank.tagged_sents()` to see the tagged corpus that you need extract named entities from.

3. Store the first sentence of the tagged sentences in a variable.

4. Use `nltk.ne_chunk` to perform NER on the sentence. Set **binary** to **True** and print the named entities.

5. Repeat steps 3 and 4 on any number of sentences to see the different entities that exist in the corpus. Set the **binary** parameter to **False** to see what the named entities are categorized as.

Expected output:

```
(S
  (PERSON Rudolph/NNP)
  (GPE Agnew/NNP)
  ,/,
  55/CD
  years/NNS
  old/JJ
  and/CC
  former/JJ
  chairman/NN
  of/IN
  (ORGANIZATION Consolidated/NNP Gold/NNP Fields/NNP)
  PLC/NNP
  ,/,
  was/VBD
  named/VBN
  *-1/-NONE-
  a/DT
  nonexecutive/JJ
  director/NN
  of/IN
  this/DT
  (GPE British/JJ)
  industrial/JJ
  conglomerate/NN
  ./.)
```

Figure 2.18: Expected output for NER on tagged corpus

Note

The solution for the activity can be found on page 300.

Summary

Natural language processing enables a machine to understand the language of humans, and just as we learned how to comprehend and process language, machines are taught as well. Two ways of better understanding language that allow machines to contribute to the real world are POS tagging and named entity recognition.

The former is the process of assigning POS tags to individual words so that the machine can learn context, and the latter is recognizing and categorizing named entities to extract valuable information from corpora.

There are distinctions in the way these processes are performed: the algorithms can be supervised or unsupervised, and the approach can be rule-based or stochastic. Either way, the goal is the same, that is, to comprehend and communicate with humans in their natural language.

In the next chapter, we will be discussing neural networks, how they work, and how they can be used for natural language processing.

3

Introduction to Neural Networks

Learning Objectives

By the end of this chapter, you will be able to:

- Describe Deep Learning and its applications
- Differentiate between Deep Learning and machine learning
- Explore neural networks and their applications
- Understand the training and functioning of a neural network
- Use Keras to create neural networks

This chapter aims to introduce you to neural networks, their applications in Deep Learning, and their general drawbacks.

Introduction

In the previous two chapters, you learned about the basics of natural language processing, its importance, the steps required to prepare text for processing, and two algorithms that aid a machine in understanding and executing tasks based on natural language. However, to cater to higher, more complicated natural language processing problems, such as creating a personal voice assistant like *Siri* and *Alexa*, additional techniques are required. Deep learning systems, such as neural networks, are often used in natural language processing, and so we're going to cover them in this chapter. In the following chapters, you learn how to use neural networks for the purpose of natural language processing.

This chapter begins with an explanation on deep learning and how it is different from machine learning. Then, it discusses neural networks, which make up a large part of deep learning techniques, and their basic functioning along with real-world applications. Additionally, it introduces **Keras**, a Python deep learning library.

Introduction to Deep Learning

Artificial Intelligence is the idea of agents possessing the natural intelligence of humans. This natural intelligence includes the ability to plan, understand human language, learn, make decisions, solve problems, and recognize words, images and objects. When building these agents, this intelligence is known as artificial intelligence, since it is human-made. These agents do not refer to physical objects. They are, in fact, a reference to software that demonstrates artificial intelligence.

There are two types of artificial intelligence—narrow and generalized. Narrow artificial intelligence is the kind of artificial intelligence that we are currently surrounded by; it is any single agent possessing one of the several capabilities of natural intelligence. The application areas of natural language processing that you learned about in the first chapter of this book are examples of narrow Artificial Intelligence, because they are agents capable of carrying out a single task, such as, a machine being able to automatically summarize an article. There do exist Technologies do exist that are capable of more than one task, such as self-driving cars, but these are still considered a combination of several narrow AIs.

Generalized artificial intelligence is the possession of all human capabilities and more, in a single agent, rather than one or two capabilities in a single agent. AI experts claim that once AI has surpassed this goal of generalized AI and it is smarter and more adept than humans themselves in all fields, it will become super artificial intelligence.

As mentioned in the previous chapters, natural language processing is an approach to achieving artificial intelligence, by enabling machines to understand and communicate with humans in the natural language of humans. Natural language processing prepares textual data and transforms it into a form that machines are able to process—a numerical form. This is where deep learning comes in.

Like natural language processing and machine learning, deep learning is also a category of techniques and algorithms. It is a subfield of machine learning because both these approaches share the same primary principle—both machine learning and deep learning algorithms take input and use it to predict output.

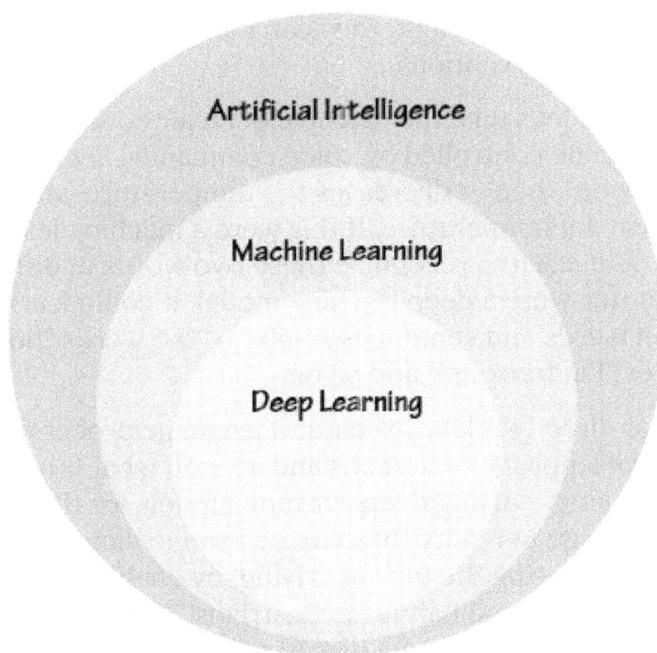

Fig 3.1: Deep learning as a subfield of machine learning

When trained on a training dataset, both types of algorithms (machine learning and deep learning) aim to minimize the difference between the actual outcomes and their predicted outcomes. This aids them in forming an association between the input and the output, thus resulting in higher accuracy.

Comparing Machine Learning and Deep Learning

While both these approaches are based on the same principle–predicting output from input–they achieve this in different ways, which is why deep learning has been categorized as a separate approach. Additionally, one of the main reasons for deep learning coming about was the increased accuracy these models provide in their prediction process.

While machine learning models are quite self-sufficient, they still need human intervention to determine that a prediction is incorrect, and thus they need to get better at performing that particular task. Deep learning models, on the other hand, are capable of determining whether a prediction is incorrect or not by themselves. Thus, deep learning models are self-sufficient; they can make decisions and improve their efficiency without human interventions.

To better understand this, let's take the example of an air conditioner whose temperature settings can be controlled by voice commands. Let's say that when the air conditioner hears the word "hot," it decreases the temperature, and when it hears the word "cold," it increases the temperature. If this were a machine learning model, then the air conditioner would learn to recognize these two words in different sentences over time. However, if this were a deep learning model, it could learn to alter the temperature based on words and sentences similar to the words "hot" and "cold," such as "It's a little warm" or "I'm freezing!" and so on.

This is an example that directly relates to natural language processing since the model understands the natural language of humans and acts on what it has understood. In this book we will be sticking to using deep learning models for the purpose of natural language processing, though in reality they can be used in almost every field. They are currently involved in automating the task of driving, by enabling a vehicle to recognize stop signs, read traffic signals, and halt for pedestrians. The medical field is also utilizing deep learning methods to detect diseases at early stages – cancer cells. But since our focus in this book is on enabling machines to understand the natural language of humans, let's get back to that.

Deep learning techniques are most often used in the supervised learning way, that is, they are provided with labelled data to learn from. However, the key difference between machine learning methods and deep learning methods is that the latter require insanely large amounts of data which didn't exist before. Thus, deep learning has only recently become advantageous. It also requires quite a bit of computing power since it needs to be trained on such large amounts of data.

The main difference, however, is in a algorithms themselves. If you've studied machine learning before, then you're aware of the variety of algorithms that exist to solve classification and regression problems, as well as unsupervised learning ones. Deep learning systems differ from these algorithms because they use Artificial Neural Networks.

Neural Networks

Often neural networks and deep learning are terms that are used interchangeably. They do not mean the same thing, however, so let's learn the difference.

As mentioned before, deep learning is an approach that follows the same principle as machine learning, but does so with more accuracy and efficiency. Deep learning systems make use of artificial neural networks, which are computing models on their own. So, basically, neural networks are a part of the deep learning approach but are not the deep learning approach on their own. They are frameworks that are incorporated by deep learning methods.

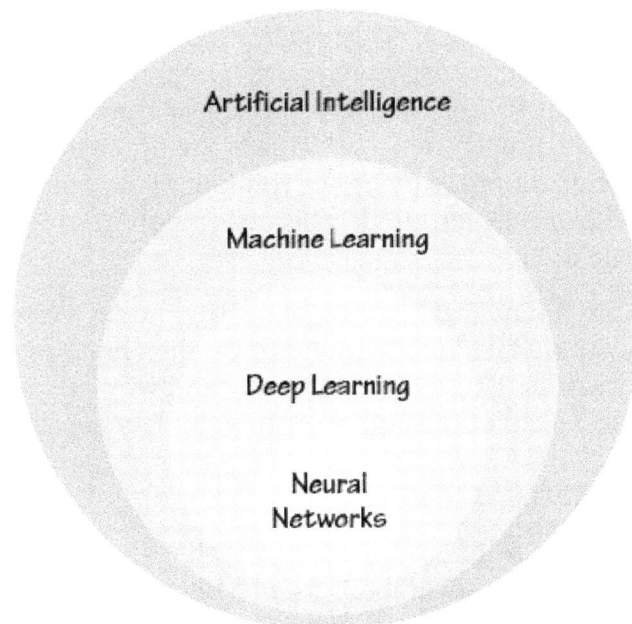

Artificial Intelligence

Machine Learning

Deep Learning

Neural
Networks

Fig 3.2: Neural Networks as a part of the deep learning Approach

Artificial neural networks are based on a framework inspired by the biological neural networks found in the human brain. These neural networks are made of nodes that enable the networks to learn from images, text, real-life objects, and other things, to be able to execute tasks and predict things accuracy.

Neural networks consist of layers, which we will take a look at in the following section. The number of layers that a network has can be anywhere from three to hundreds. Neural networks that are made of only three or four layers are called shallow neural networks, whereas networks that have many more layers than that are referred to as deep neural networks. Thus, the neural networks used by the deep learning approach are deep neural networks and they possess several layers. Due to this, deep learning models are very well suited to complex tasks such as facial recognition translating text, and so on.

These layers break down the input into several levels of abstraction. As a result, the deep learning model is better able to learn from and understand the input, be it images or text or another form of input, which aids it in making decisions and predicting things the way our human mind does.

Let's go through an example to understand these layers. Imagine that you're in your bedroom doing some work and you notice you're sweating. That's your input data–the fact that you're feeling hot and so in your head a little voice goes "I'm feeling hot!" Next, you might wonder why you're feeling so hot–"Why am I feeling so hot?" This is a thought. You'll then try to come up with a solution to this problem, maybe by taking a shower–"Let me take a quick shower." This is a decision that you've made. But then you remember that you've got to leave for work soon–"But, I need to leave the house soon." This is a memory. You might try to convince yourself by thinking "Isn't there enough time to squeeze in a quick shower, though?" This is the process of a reasoning. Lastly, you'll probably act on your thoughts by either thinking "I'm going to take a shower," or, "there's no time for a shower, never mind." This is decision making and in the event you do take a shower, it is an action.

The multiple layers in a deep neural network allow the model to go through these different levels of processing just like the mind does, thus building upon the principles of biological neural networks. These layers are how and why deep learning models are able to perform tasks and predict outputs with such high accuracy.

Neural Network Architecture

Neural network architecture refers to the elements that are the building blocks of a neural network. While there are several different types of neural networks, the basic architecture and foundation remains constant. The architecture includes:

- **Layers**
- **Nodes**

- **Edges**
- **Biases**
- **Activation functions**

The Layers

As mentioned before, neural networks are made up of layers. While the number of these layers varies from model to model and is dependent on the task at hand, there are only three types of layers. Each layer is made up of individual nodes and the number of these nodes depends on the requirement of the layer and the neural network as a whole. A node can be thought of as a neuron.

The layers present in a neural network are as follows:

- *The input layer*

  As the name suggests, this is the layer that consists of the input data entering the neural network. It is a mandatory layer as every neural network requires input data to learn from and perform operations on to be able to generate an output. This layer can only occur once in a neural network. Each input node is connected to each node present in the proceeding layer.

  The variables or characteristics of input data are known as features. The target output is dependent on these features. For example, take the iris dataset. (The Iris dataset is one of the most popular datasets for machine learning beginners. It consists of data of three different types of flowers. Each instance has four features and one target class.) The classification label of a flower is dependent on the four features—petal length and width, and sepal length and width. The features, and thus the input layer, is denoted by **X**, and each individual featured is denoted by **X1**, **X2**, ... , **Xn**.

- *The hidden layer*

  This is the layer where the actual computation is done. It comes after the input layer, since it acts on the input provided by the input layer, and before the output layer, since it generates the output that is provided by the output layer.

  A hidden layer is made up of nodes known as "activation nodes." Each node possesses an activation function, which is a mathematical function that is performed on the inputs received by an activation node to generate an output. Activation functions will be discussed later on in this chapter.

This is the only type of layer that can occur multiple times, and thus in deep neural networks, there can be up to hundreds of hidden layers present. The number of hidden layers depends on the task at hand.

The output generated by the nodes of one hidden layer are fed into the proceeding hidden layer as input. The output generated by each activation node of a hidden layer is sent to each activation node of the next layer.

- *The output layer*

This is the last layer of the neural network and it consists of nodes that provide the final outcome of all the processing and computing. This is also a mandatory layer since a neural network must produce an output based on input data.

In the case of the iris dataset, the output for a particular instance of a flower would be the category of that flower–Iris setosa, Iris virginica, or Iris versicolor.

The output, often known as the target, is denoted as **y**.

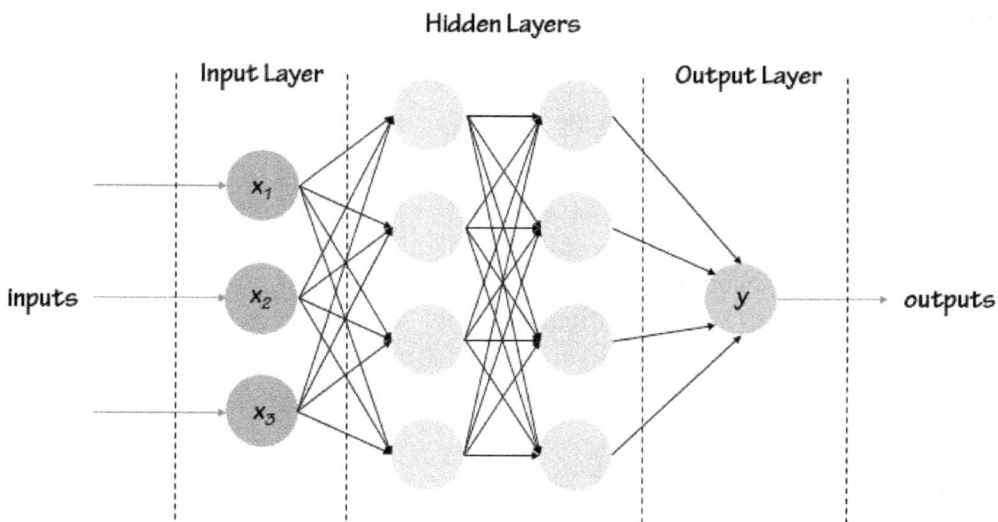

Fig 3.3: A Neural Network with 2 Hidden Layers

Nodes

Each activation node or neuron possess the following components:

- An activation

  This is the current state of the node—whether it is active or not.

- A threshold value (optional)

  If present, this determines whether a neuron is activated or not, depending on whether the weighted sum is above or below this threshold value.

- An activation function

  This is what computes a new activation for the activation node based on the inputs and the weighted sum.

- An output function

  This generates the output for the particular activation node based on the activation function.

  Input neurons have no such components as they don't perform computation, nor do they have any preceding neurons. Similarly, output neurons don't have these components, since they don't perform computation, nor do they have proceeding neurons.

The Edges

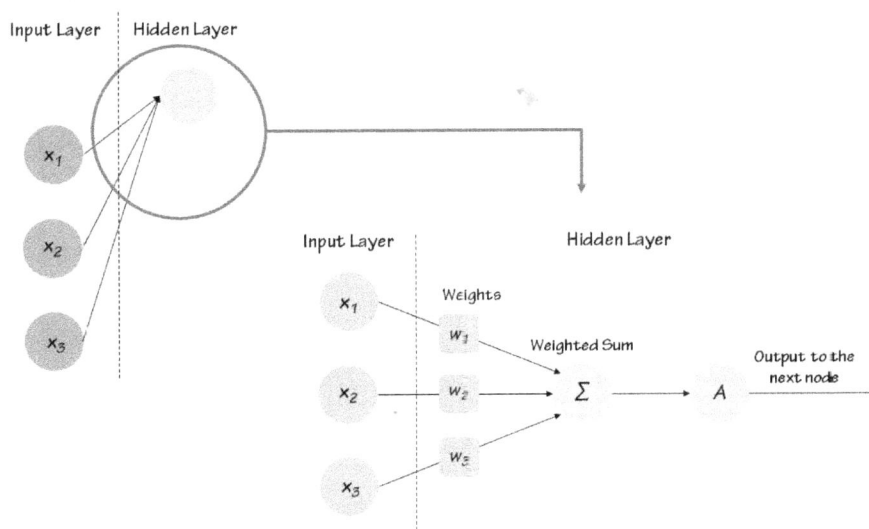

Fig 3.4: The Weighted Connect ons of a Neural Network

Each of the arrows in the preceding diagram represents a connection between two nodes from two different layers. A connection is known as an edge. Each edge that leads to an activation node has its own weight, which can be considered as a sort of impact that one node has on the other node. Weights can be either positive or negative.

Take a look at the earlier diagram. Before the values reach the activation function, their values are multiplied by the weights assigned to their respective connections. These multiplied values are then added together to obtain a weighted sum. This weighted sum is basically a measure of how much impact that node has on the output. Thus if the value is low, that means that it doesn't really affect the output that much and so it's not that important. If the value is high, then it shares a strong correlation with the target output and thus plays a role in determining what the output is.

Biases

A bias is a node, and each layer of a neural network has its own bias node, except for the output layer. Thus, each layer has its own bias node. The bias node holds a value, known as the bias. This value is incorporated in the process of calculating the weighted sum and so also plays a role in determining the output generated by a node.

Bias is an important aspect of neural networks because it allows the activation function to shift either to the right or to the left. This helps the model to better fit the data and thus produce accurate outputs.

Activation Functions

Activation functions are functions that are part of the activation nodes found in the hidden layers of neural networks. They serve the purpose of introducing non-linearity into neural networks, which is really important, as without them neural networks would just have linear functions, leaving no difference between them and linear regression models. This defeats the purpose of neural networks, because then they wouldn't be able to learn complex functional relationships that exist within data. Activation functions also need to be differentiable for backpropagation to occur. This will be discussed in future sections of this chapter.

Basically, an activation node calculates the weighted sum of the inputs it receives, adds the bias, and then applies an activation function to this value. This generates an output for that particular activation node which is then used as input by the proceeding layer. This output is known as an activation value. Therefore, the proceeding activation node in the next layer will receive multiple activation values from preceding activation nodes and calculate a new weighted sum. It will apply its activation function to this value to generate its own activation value. This is how data flows through a neural network. Thus, an activation function helps convert an input signal into an output signal.

This process of calculating the weighted sum, applying an activation function, and producing an activation value is known as feedforward.

There are several activation functions (Logistic, TanH, ReLU, and so on). The Sigmoid function is one of the most popular and simple activation functions out there. When represented mathematically, this function looks like

$$f(x) = \frac{1}{1 + e^{-x}}$$

Figure 3.5: Expression for sigmoid function

As you can see, this function is non-linear.

Training a Neural Network

So far, we know that once an input is provided to a neural network, it enters the input layer which is an interface that exists to pass on the input to the next layer. If a hidden layer is present, then the inputs are sent to the activation nodes of the hidden layer via weighted connections. The weighted sum of all the inputs received by the activations nodes is calculated by multiplying the inputs with their respective weights and adding these values up along with the bias. The activation function generates an activation value from the weighted sum and this is passed on to the nodes in the next layer. If the next layer is another hidden layer, then it uses the activation values from the previous hidden layer as inputs and repeats the activation process. However, if the proceeding layer is the output layer, then the output is provided by the neural network.

From all of this information, we can conclusively say that there are three parts of the deep learning model that have an impact on the output generated by the model—the inputs, the connection weights and biases, and the activation functions.

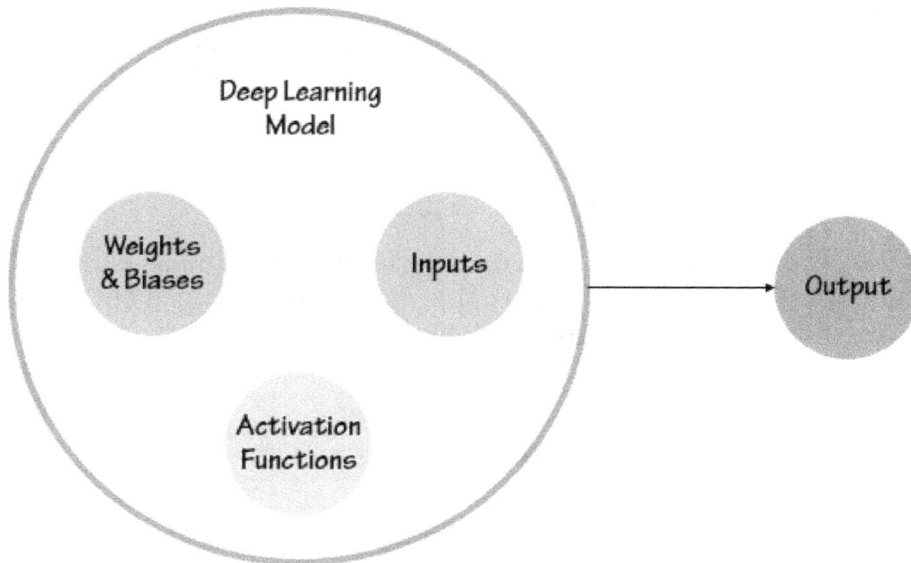

Figure 3.6: Aspects of a deep learning model that impact the output

While the inputs are taken from the dataset, the former two are not. Thus, the following two questions arise—who or what decides what the weight is for a connection? How do we know which activation functions to use? Let's tackle these questions one by one.

Calculating Weights

Weights play a very important role in multilayer neural networks, since altering the weight of a single connection can completely alter the weights assigned to further connections and thus the outputs generated by the proceeding layers. Thus, having the optimal weights is necessary to create an accurate deep learning model. This sounds like a lot of pressure, but lucky for us, deep learning models are capable of finding the optimal weights all on their own. To understand this better, let's take the example of linear regression.

Linear regression is a supervised machine learning algorithm that, as suggested by the name itself, is suitable to solve regression problems (datasets whose output is in the form of continuous numerical values, such as the selling prices of houses). This algorithm assumes there exists a linear relationship between the input (the features) and the output (the target). Basically, it believes that there exists a line of best fit that accurately describes the relationship between the input and output variables. It uses this to predict future numerical values. In a scenario where there is only one input feature, the equation for this line is:

$$y = c + mx$$

Figure 3.7: Expression for linear regression

Where,

y is the target output

c is the y-intercept

m is the model coefficient

x is the input feature

Similar to the connections in neural networks, the input features have values attached to them too–they're called model coefficients. In a way, these model coefficients determine the importance a feature has in determining the output, which is similar to what the weights in neural networks do. It is important to ensure these model coefficients are of the correct value so as to get correct predictions.

Let's say that we want to predict the selling price of a house based on how many bedrooms it has. So, the price of the house is our target output and the number of bedrooms it has is our input feature. Since this is a supervised learning method, our model will be fed a dataset that contains instances of our input feature matched with the correct target output.

Number of Bedrooms (Input Feature)	Selling Price (Target Output)
1	$10, 000
3	$46, 000
...	...
4	$98, 000
3	$49, 000

Fig 3.8: Sample Dataset for Linear Regression

Now, our linear regression model needs to find a model coefficient that describes the impact of the number of bedrooms on the selling price of the house. It does this by making use of two algorithms—the loss function and the gradient descent algorithm.

The Loss Function

The loss function is also sometimes known as the cost function.

For classification problems, the loss function calculates the difference between the predicted probability of a particular category and the category itself. For example, let's say you have a binary classification problem that needs to predict whether a house will be sold or not. There are only two outputs—"yes" and "no." A classification model when fitted on this data will predict the probability of an instance of data falling in either the "yes" category or the "no" category. Let's say the "yes" category has a value of 1, and "no" has a value of 0. Thus, if the output probability is closer to 1 it will fall in the "yes" category. The loss function for this model will measure this difference.

For regression problems, the loss function calculates the error between actual values and predicted values. The house price example from the previous section is a regression problem and so the loss function is calculating the error between the actual price of a house, and the price that our model predicted. Thus, in a way, the loss function helps the model self-evaluate its performance. Obviously, the model's aim is to predict the price that is exactly, if not closest to, the actual price. To do this, it needs to minimize the loss function as much as possible.

The only factor that is directly affecting the price predicted by the model is the model coefficient. To arrive at the model coefficient that is best suited for the problem at hand, the model needs to keep improving the values for the model coefficient. Let's call each different value an update of the model coefficient. So, with each update of the model coefficient, the model must calculate the error between the actual price and the price that the model has predicted using that update of the model coefficient.

Once the function has reached its minimum value, the model coefficient at this minimum point is chosen as the final model coefficient. This value is stored and used in the linear equation described above by the linear regression algorithm. From that point onwards, whenever the model is fed input data in the form of how many bedrooms a house has without target outputs, it uses the linear equation with the apt model coefficient to calculate and predict the price that that house will be sold at.

There are many different kinds of loss functions—such as MSE (for regression problems) and Log Loss (for classification problems). Let's take a look at how they work.

The Mean Squared Error function calculates the difference between the actual values and the predicted values, squares this difference, and then averages it out across the entire dataset. The function, when expressed mathematically, looks like this:

$$MSE = \frac{1}{n} \sum_{i}^{n} (y_i - f(x_i))^2$$

Figure 3.9: Expression for mean squared error function

Where,

n is the total number of data points

yi is the ith actual value

xi is the input

f() is the function being carried out on the input to generate the output, therefore

f(xi) is the predicted value

Log loss is used for classification models whose output is a probability value in the range of 0 and 1. The higher the difference between the predicted probability and the actual category, the higher the log loss. The mathematical representation of the log loss functions is:

$$Log\ Loss = -\frac{1}{N}\sum_{i=1}^{N} y_i\ (\log\ (p(y_i)) + (1 - y_i))(\log\ (1 - p(y_i)))$$

Figure 3.10: Expression for log loss function

Where,

N is the total number of data points

yi is the ith actual label

p is the predicted probability

The Gradient Descent Algorithm

The process of evaluating the model's performance via the loss function is one that the model carries out independently, as is the process for updating and ultimately choosing the model coefficients.

Imagine that you're on a mountain and you want to climb back down and reach the absolute bottom. It's cloudy and there are quite a few peaks so you can't exactly see where the bottom is, or which direction it is in, you just know that you need to get there. You start your journey at 5000 meters above sea level, and you decide to take large steps. You take a step and then you check your phone to see how many meters above sea level you are. Your phone says you are 5003 meters above sea level, which means you've gone in the wrong direction. Now, you take a large step in another direction and your phone says you are 4998 meters above sea level. This means you're getting closer to the bottom, but how do you know that this step was the one with the steepest descent? What if you took a step in another direction that brought you down to 4996 meters above sea level? Thus, you check your position after taking a step in each possible direction, and whichever takes you closest the bottom, is the one you choose.

You keep repeating this process, and then you reach a point where your phone says you are 100 meters above sea level. When you take another step, your phone's reading remains the same—100 meters above sea level. Finally, you have reached what seems to be the bottom since a step in any direction from this point results in you still being 100 meters above sea level.

Training Dataset

Loss
Function

Linear Regression
Model

Initial
Parameters

Final
Parameters

Gradient
Descent

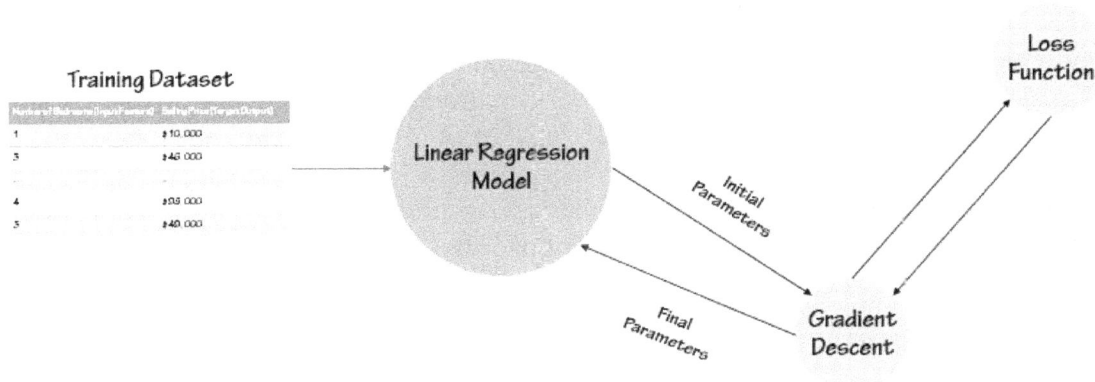

Fig 3.11: Updating Parameters

This is how the gradient descent algorithm works. The algorithm descends a plot of the loss function against possible values for the model coefficient and the y-intercept, like you descended the mountain. It starts off with an assigned value for the model coefficient—this is you standing at a point 5000 meters above sea level. It calculates the gradient of the plot at this point. This gradient tells the model which direction it should move in to update the coefficient in order to get closer to the global minimum, which is the end goal. So, it takes a step and arrives at a new point with a new model coefficient. It repeats the process of calculating the gradient, obtaining a direction to move in, updating the coefficient, and taking another step. It checks to see that this step is the one that provides it with the steepest descent. With each step that it takes, it arrives at a new model coefficient and calculates the gradient at that point. This process is repeated until the value of the gradient doesn't change for a number of trials. This means that the algorithm has reached the global minimum and has converged. The model coefficient at this point is used as the final model coefficient in the linear equations.

In neural networks, the gradient descent algorithm and loss function work together to find values to be assigned to connections as weights and to biases. These values are updated by minimizing the loss function using the gradient descent algorithm, as is the case in linear regression models. Additionally, with the case of linear regression, there is always only one minimum, due to the fact that the loss function is bowl shaped. This makes it easy for the gradient descent algorithm to find it and be sure that this is the lowest point. In the case of neural networks, however, it is not that simple. The activation functions used by neural networks serve the purpose of introducing non-linearity to the situation.

As a result, the plot of the loss function of a neural network is not a bowl-shaped curve, and this does not have just one minimum point. Instead, it has several minimums, only one of which is the global minima. The rest are known as local minima. This sounds like a major issue, but it is, in fact, alright for the gradient descent algorithm to reach a local minima and choose the weight values at that point, due to the fact that most local minima are usually quite close to the global minimum. There are modified versions of the gradient descent algorithm that are also used when designing neural networks. Stochastic and batch-sized gradient descent are two of them.

Let's say our loss function is MSE, and we need the gradient descent algorithm to update one weight (w) and one bias (b).

$$f(w, b) = \frac{1}{n} \sum_i^n (y_i - f(wx_i + b))^2$$

Figure 3.12: Expression for gradient of loss function

The gradient is the partial derivative of the loss function, with respect to the weight and the bias. The mathematical representation of this is:

$$f'(w, b) = \begin{bmatrix} \dfrac{df}{dw} \\ \dfrac{df}{db} \end{bmatrix} = \begin{bmatrix} \dfrac{1}{N} \sum -2x_i(y_i - (wx_i + b)) \\ \dfrac{1}{N} \sum -2x_i(y_i - (wx_i + b)) \end{bmatrix}$$

Figure 3.13: Expression of gradient with partial derivaive of loss function

The result of this is the gradient of the loss function at the current position. This also tells us which direction we should move in to continue updating the weight and the bias.

The size of the step taken is adjusted by a parameter called the learning rate and is a very sensitive parameter in the gradient descent algorithm. It is called alpha and is denoted by α. If the learning rate is too small, then the algorithm will take too many tiny steps and thus take too long to reach the minimum. However, if the learning rate is too large then the algorithm might miss the minimum altogether. Thus, it is important to tweak and test out the algorithm using different learning rates to ensure the right one is chosen.

The learning rate is multiplied with the gradient calculated at each step in order to modify the size of the step, thus the step size of each step is not always the same. Mathematically, this looks like:

$$w = w - \left(\frac{df/_{dw}}{N}\right) * \alpha$$

Figure 3.14: Expression for learning rate multiplied with gradient

And,

$$b = b - \left(\frac{df/_{db}}{N}\right) * \alpha$$

Figure 3.15: Expression for learning rate multiplied with gradient at each step

The values are subtracted from the previous values of the weight and bias because the partial derivatives point in the direction of the steepest ascent, but our aim is to descend.

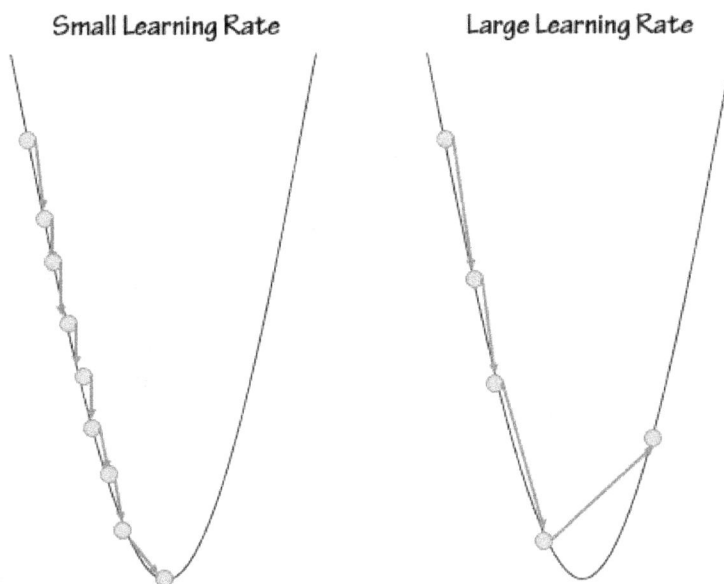

Fig 3.16: Learning Rate

Backpropagation

Linear regression is basically a neural network, but without a hidden layer and with an identity activation function (which is a linear function, therefore linearity). Hence, the learning process remains the same as the one described in the previous sections—the loss function aims to minimize the error by having the gradient descent algorithm constantly update the weights till the global minimum is reached.

However, when dealing with larger, more complicated neural networks that are not linear in nature, the loss calculated is sent back through the network to each layer, which then begins the process of weight updating again. The loss is propagated backwards, therefore this is known as backpropagation.

Backpropagation is performed using the partial derivatives of the loss function. It involves calculating the loss of every node in every layer by propagating backwards in the neural network. Knowing the loss of every node allows the network to understand which weights are having a drastic negative impact on the output and the loss. Thus, the gradient descent algorithm is able to reduce the weights of these connections that have high error rates, consequently reducing the impact that that node has on the network's output.

When dealing with many layers in a neural network, there are many activation functions working on the inputs. This can be represented as follows:

$$f(x) = X(Y(Z(x)))$$

Figure 3.17: Expression for backpropagation function

Here **X**, **Y**, and **Z** are activation functions. As we can see, **f(x)** is a composite function, thus, backpropagation can be seen as an application of the chain rule. The chain rule is the formula used to calculate the partial derivatives of a composite function, which is what we're doing through backpropagation. Therefore, by applying the chain rule to the preceding function (known as the forward propagation function since values are moving in the forward direction to generate an output) and calculating the partial derivatives with respect to each weight, we will be able to determine exactly how much of an impact each node has on the final output.

The loss of the final node present in the output layer is the total loss of the entire neural network, because it is in the output layer and so the loss of all the previous nodes gets accumulated. The input nodes present in the input layer do not have a loss because they don't have an impact on the neural network. The input layer is merely an interface that sends the input to the activation nodes present in the hidden layers.

Therefore, the process of backpropagation is the process of updating the weights using the gradient descent algorithm and the loss function.

> **Note**
>
> For more information on the math of backpropagation, click here: https://ml-cheatsheet.readthedocs.io/en/latest/backpropagation.html

Designing a Neural Network and Its Applications

Common machine learning techniques are used when training and designing a neural network. Neural networks can be classified as:

- Supervised neural networks
- Unsupervised neural networks

Supervised neural networks

These are like the example used in the previous section (predicting the price of the house based on how many rooms it has). Supervised neural networks are trained on datasets consisting of sample inputs with their corresponding outputs. These are suitable for noise classification and making predictions.

There are two types of supervised learning methods:

- Classification

  This is for problems that have discrete categories or classes as target outputs, for example the Iris dataset. The neural network learns from sample inputs and outputs how to correctly classify new data.

- Regression

  This is for problems that have a range of continuous numerical values as target outputs, like the price of a house example. The neural network describes the causal relationship between the inputs and their outputs.

Unsupervised neural networks

These neural networks are trained on data without any target output, and thus are able to recognize and draw out patterns and inferences from the data. This makes them well-suited for tasks such as identifying category relationships and discovering natural distributions in data.

- Clustering

A cluster analysis is the grouping together of similar inputs. These neural networks can be used for gene sequence analysis and object recognition, amongst other things.

Neural networks that are capable of pattern recognition can be trained both by supervised or unsupervised methods. They play a key role in text classification and speech recognition.

Exercise 17: Creating a neural network

In this exercise, we're going to implement a simple, classic neural network, by following the workflow outlined earlier, to predict whether a review is positive or negative.

This is a natural language processing problem, since the neural network is going to be fed rows of sentences that are actually reviews. Each review has a label in the training set—either 0 for negative or 1 for positive. This label is dependent on the words present in the review and so, our neural network needs to understand the meaning of the review and accordingly label it. Ultimately, our neural network needs to be able to predict whether a review is positive or negative.

> **Note**
>
> Download the dataset from the link:
>
> https://github.com/TrainingByPackt/Deep-Learning-for-Natural-Language-Processing/tree/master/Lesson%2003

The following steps will help you with the solution.

1. Open up a new Jupyter notebook by typing the following command in the directory you'd like to code in:

    ```
    jupyter notebook
    ```

2. Next, import **pandas** so that you can store the data in a dataframe:

    ```
    import pandas as pd
    df = pd.read_csv('train_comment_small_50.csv', sep=',')
    ```

3. Import the regular expressions package

    ```
    import re
    ```

4. Create a function to preprocess the reviews by removing the **HTML** tags, escaped quotes and normal quotes:

    ```
    def clean_comment(text):
        # Strip HTML tags
        text = re.sub('<[^<]+?>', ' ', text)

        # Strip escaped quotes
        text = text.replace('\\"', '')

        # Strip quotes
        text = text.replace('"', '')

        return text
    ```

5. Apply this function to the reviews currently stored in your dataframe:

    ```
    df['cleaned_comment'] = df['comment_text'].apply(clean_comment)
    ```

6. Import **train_test_split** from **scikit-learn** to divide this data into a training set and a validation set:

    ```
    from sklearn.model_selection import train_test_split

    X_train, X_test, y_train, y_test = train_test_split(df['cleaned_comment'],
    df['toxic'], test_size=0.2)
    ```

7. Import **nltk** and **stopwords** from **nltk** library:

    ```
    import nltk
    nltk.download('stopwords')
    ```

8. Now machine learning and deep learning models require numerical data as input, and currently our data is in the form of text. Thus, we're going to use an algorithm called CountVectorizer to convert the words present in the reviews into word count vectors

```
from sklearn.feature_extraction.text import CountVectorizer
from nltk.corpus import stopwords

vectorizer = CountVectorizer(binary=True, stop_words = stopwords.
words('english'), lowercase=True, min_df=3, max_df=0.9, max_features=5000)
X_train_onehot = vectorizer.fit_transform(X_train)
```

Our data is clean and prepped now!

9. We're going to create a two-layer neural network. When defining a neural network, the number of layers does not include the input layer since it's a given that an input layer exists and because the input layer isn't a part of the computation process. So, a two-layer neural network includes an input layer, one hidden layer and an output layer.

10. Import the model and the layers from Keras:

```
from keras.models import Sequential
from keras.layers import Dense
```

11. Initiate the neural network:

```
nn = Sequential()
```

12. Add the hidden layer. Specify the number of nodes the layer will have the activation function the nodes possess and what the input for the layer is:

```
nn.add(Dense(units=500, activation='relu', input_dim=len(vectorizer.get_
feature_names())))
```

13. Add the output layer. Once again, specify the number of nodes and the activation function. We're going to use the **sigmoid** function here because this is a binary classification problem (predicting whether a review is positive or negative). We're going to have only one output node since the output is just one value—either 1 or 0.

```
nn.add(Dense(units=1, activation='sigmoid'))
```

14. We're going to compile the neural network now, and decide which loss function, optimization algorithm and performance metric we want to use. Since the problem is a binary classification one, we're going to use **binary_crossentropy** as our **loss** function. The optimization algorithm is basically the gradient descent algorithm. Different versions and modifications of gradient descent exist. In this case, we're going to use the **Adam** algorithm, which is an extension of stochastic gradient descent:

```
nn.compile(loss='binary_crossentropy', optimizer='adam',
    metrics=['accuracy'])
```

15. Now, let's summarize our model and see what's going on:

```
nn.summary()
```

The output you'll get will look something like this:

```
Layer (type)                 Output Shape              Param #
=================================================================
dense_1 (Dense)              (None, 500)               28500
_____
dense_2 (Dense)              (None, 1)                 501
=================================================================
Total params: 29,001
Trainable params: 29,001
Non-trainable params: 0
_____
```

Figure 3.18: Model summary

16. Now, it's time to train the model. Fit the neural network on the **X_train** and **y_train** data we had divided earlier:

```
nn.fit(X_train_onehot[:-20], y_train[:-20],
        epochs=5, batch_size=128, verbose=1,
        validation_data=(X_train_onehot[-100:], y_train[-20:]))
```

That's it! Our neural network is now ready for testing.

17. Transform the input validation data into word count vectors and evaluate the neural network. Print the accuracy score to see how your network is doing:

```
scores = nn.evaluate(vectorizer.transform(X_test), y_test, verbose=1)
print("Accuracy:", scores[1])
```

Your score might be a little different, but it should be close to 0.875.

Which is a pretty good score. So, there you have it. You just created your first ever neural network, trained it, and validated it.

Expected output:

```
10/10 [==============================] - 0s 135us/step
Accuracy: 0.8999999761581421
```

Figure 3.19: Expected accuracy score

18. Save your model:

```
model.save('nn.hd5')
```

Fundamentals of Deploying a Model as a Service

The purpose of deploying a model as a service is for other people to view and access it with ease, and in other ways besides just looking at your code on GitHub. There are different types of model deployments, depending on why you've created the model in the first place. You could say there are three types—a streaming model (one that constantly learns as it is constantly fed data and then makes predictions), an analytics as a service model (AaaS—one that is open for anyone to interact with) and an on-line model (one which is only accessible by people working within the same company).

The most common way of showcasing your work is through a web application. There are multiple deployment platforms that aid and allow you to deploy your models through them, such as Deep Cognition, MLflow, and others.

Flask is the easiest micro web framework to use to deploy your own model without using an existing platform. It is written in Python. Using this framework, you can build a Python API for your model that will easily generate predictions and display them for you.

The flow is as follows:

1. Create a directory for the API

2. Copy your pre-trained neural network model to this directory

3. Write a program that loads this model, preprocess the input so that it matches the training input of your model, use the model to make predictions and prepare, send, display this prediction.

To test and run the API, you simply need to type the applications name along with **.run()**.

In the case of the neural network we created in, we would save that model and load it into a new Jupyter notebook. We would convert input data (the cleaned reviews) into word count vectors so that the input data for our API would be the same as the training data. Then, we would use our models to generate predictions and display them.

Activity 4: Sentiment Analysis of Reviews

In the activity, we are going to review comments from a dataset and categorize them as positive or nega**tive.** The following steps will help you with the solution.

> **Note**
>
> You will find the dataset at the following link:
>
> https://github.com/TrainingByPackt/Deep-Learning-for-Natural-Language-Processing/tree/master/Lesson%2004

1. Open a new **Jupyter** notebook. Import the dataset.

2. Import the necessary Python packages and necessary classes. Load the dataset in a dataframe.

3. Import the necessary libraries to clean and prepare the data. Create an array for your cleaned text to be stored in. Using a **for** loop, iterate through every instance (every review).

4. Import CountVectorizer and convert the words into word count vectors. Create an array to store each unique word as its own column, hence making them independent variables.

5. Import necessary label encoding entities.

6. Divide the dataset into training and testing sets.

7. Create the neural network model.

8. Train the model and validate it.

9. Evaluate the neural network and print the accuracy scores to see how it's doing.

   Expected output:

   ```
   20/20 [==============================] - 0s 160us/step
   Accuracy: 1.0
   [1.1920933321833454e-07, 1.0]
   ```

   Figure 3.20: Accuracy score

> **Note**
>
> The solution for the activity can be found on page 302.

Summary

In this chapter, we were introduced to a subset of machine learning—deep learning. You learned about the differences and similarities between the two categories of techniques and understood the requirement for deep learning and its applications.

Neural networks are artificial representations of the biological neural networks that are present in the human brain. Artificial neural networks are frameworks that are incorporated by deep learning models and have proven to be increasingly efficient and accurate. They are used in several fields, from training self-driving cars to detecting cancer cells in very early stages.

We studied the different components of a neural network and learned a network trains and corrects itself, with the help of the loss function, the gradient descent algorithm and backpropagation. You also learned how to perform sentiment analysis on text inputs! Furthermore, you learned the basics of deploying a model as a service.

In the coming chapters, you will learn more about neural networks and their different types, along with which neural network to use in what situations.

4

Foundations of Convolutional Neural Network

Learning Objectives

By the end of this chapter, you will be able to:

- Describe the inspiration for CNNs in neural sc ence
- Describe the convolution operations
- Describe a basic CNN architecture for a classi cation task
- Implement a simple CNN for image and text dassification tasks
- Implement a CNN for a sentiment analysis of text

In this chapter, we aim to cover the architecture of convolutional neural networks (CNNs) and gain an intuition of CNNs based on their applications on image data, before delving into their applications in natural language processing.

Introduction

Neural networks, as a broad field, borrow a lot from biological systems, particularly the brain. Advances in neural science have directly influenced research in to neural networks.

CNNs are inspired by the work of two neural scientists, D.H. Hubel and T.N. Wiesel. Their research focused on the mammalian visual cortex, which is the part of the brain responsible for vision. Through their research back in the sixties, they found that the visual cortex is composed of layers of neurons. Furthermore, these layers are arranged in a hierarchical structure. This hierarchy ranges from simple-to hypercomplex neurons. They also advanced the notion of a 'receptive field,' which is the space within which certain stimuli activate or fire a neuron, with a degree of spatial invariance. Spatial or shift invariance allows animals to detect objects regardless of whether they are rotated, scaled, transformed, or partially obscured.

Figure 4.1: Examples of spatial variance

Inspired by neural concepts of how animals see, computer vision scientists have modelled neural networks that adhere to the same principles of locality, hierarchy, and spatial invariance. We will dive deeper into the architecture of CNNs in the next section.

CNNs are a subset of neural networks that contain one or more 'convolution' layers. Typical neural networks are fully connected, which means every neuron is connected to every neuron in the next layer. When dealing with high-dimensional data such as images, sound, and so on, typical neural networks are slow and tend to overfit as there are too many weights being learned. Convolutional layers solve this problem by connecting a neuron to a region of the input in lower layers. We will discuss convolution layers in greater detail in the next section.

To understand the general architecture of CNNs, we will first apply them to the task of image classification and then, subsequently, to natural language processing. To begin, we'll do a small exercise to understand how computers see images.

Exercise 18: Finding Out How Computers See Images

Images and text share an important similarity. The location of a pixel in an image, or a word in text, matters. This spatial significance makes applying convolutional neural networks possible for both text and images.

In this exercise, we want to determine how computers interpret images. We will do this by using the **MNIST** dataset, which contains a repository of handwritten digits perfect for demonstrating CNNs.

> **Note**
>
> MNIST is a built-in Keras dataset.

You will need to have both Python and Keras installed. For easier visualization, you can run your code in a Jupyter notebook:

1. Start by importing the necessary classes:

   ```
   %matplotlib inline
   import keras
   import matplotlib.pyplot as plt
   ```

2. Since we'll be using this dataset throughout the chapter, we will import the training and test sets as shown here:

   ```
   (X_train, y_train), (X_test, y_test) = keras.datasets.mnist.load_data()
   ```

3. Visualize the first image in the dataset:

   ```
   sample_image = X_train[0]
   plt.imshow(sample_image)
   ```

Running the preceding code should result in an image being visualized, as shown here:

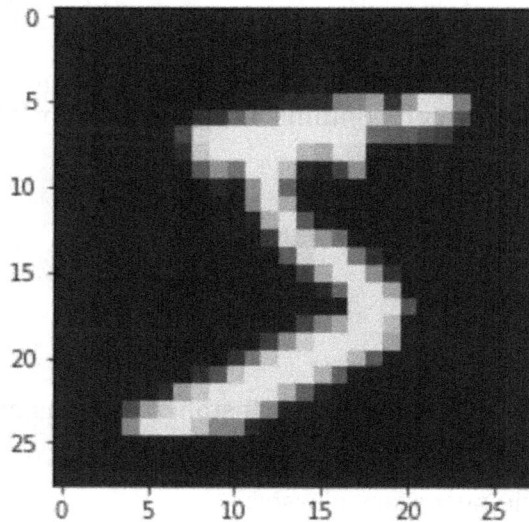

Figure 4.2: Visualization of an image

The images are 28 by 28 pixels, with each pixel being a number between 0 and 255. Try playing around with different indices to display their values as follows. You can do this by putting arbitrary numbers between **0** and **255** as **x** and **y** in:

```
print(sample_image[x][y])
```

4. When you run the print code as follows, expect to see numbers between 0 and 255:

```
print(sample_image[22][11])
print(sample_image[6][12])
print(sample_image[5][23])
print(sample_image[10][11])
```

Expected Output:

253
170
127
154

Figure 4.3: Numerical representation of an image

This exercise is meant to help you appreciate how image data is processed with each pixel as a number between **0** and **255**. This understanding is essential as we'll feed these images into a CNN as input in the next section.

Understanding the Architecture of a CNN

Let's assume we have the task of classifying each of the **MNIST** images as a number between 0 and 9. The input in the previous example is an image matrix. For a colored image, each pixel is an array with three values corresponding to the **RGB** color scheme. For grayscale images, each pixel is just one number, as we saw earlier.

To understand the architecture of a CNN, it is best to separate it into two sections as visualized in the image that follows.

A forward pass of the CNN involves a set of operations in the two sections.

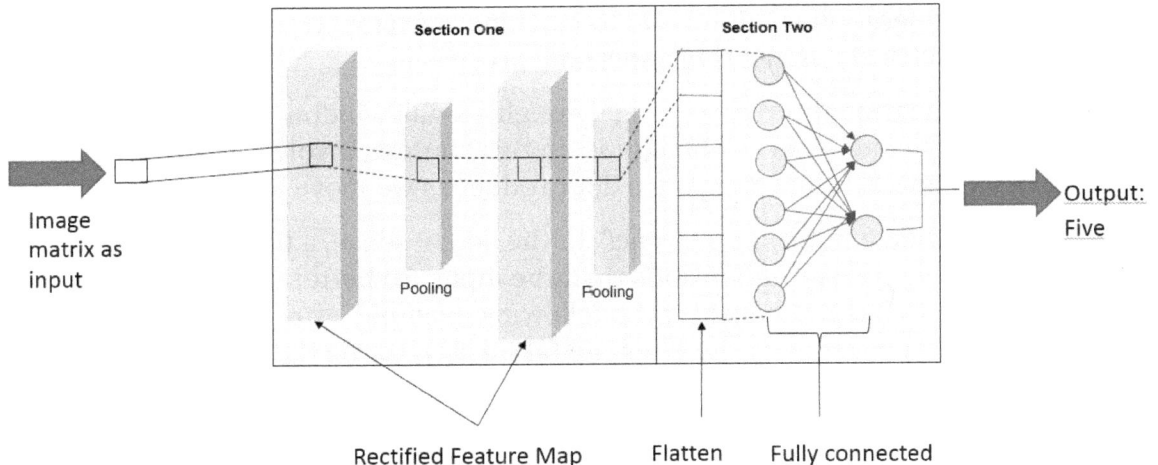

Figure 4.4: Application of convolution and ReLU operations

The figure is explained in the following sections:

- Feature extraction
- Neural network

Feature Extraction

The first section of a CNN is all about feature extraction. Conceptually, it can be interpreted as the model's attempt to learn which features distinguish one class from another. In the task of classifying images, these features might include unique shapes and colors.

CNNs learn the hierarchical structure of these features. The lower layers of a CNN abstract features such as edges, while the higher layers learn more defined features such as shapes.

Feature learning occurs through a set of three operations repeated a number of times, as follows:

1. Convolution

2. An activation function (the application of the ReLU activation function to achieve non-linearity)

3. Pooling

Convolution

Convolution is the an operation that distinguishes CNNs from other neural networks. The convolution operation is not unique to machine learning; it is applied in many other fields, such as electrical engineering and signal processing.

Convolution can be thought of as looking through a small window as we move the window to the right and down. Convolution, in this context, involves iteratively sliding a "filter" across an image, while applying a dot product as we move left and down.

This window is called a "*filter*" or a "*kernel*". In the actual sense, a filter or kernel is a matrix of preferably smaller dimensions than the input. To better understand how filters are applied to images, consider the following example. After calculating the dot product on the area covered by the filter, we take a step to the right and calculate the dot product:

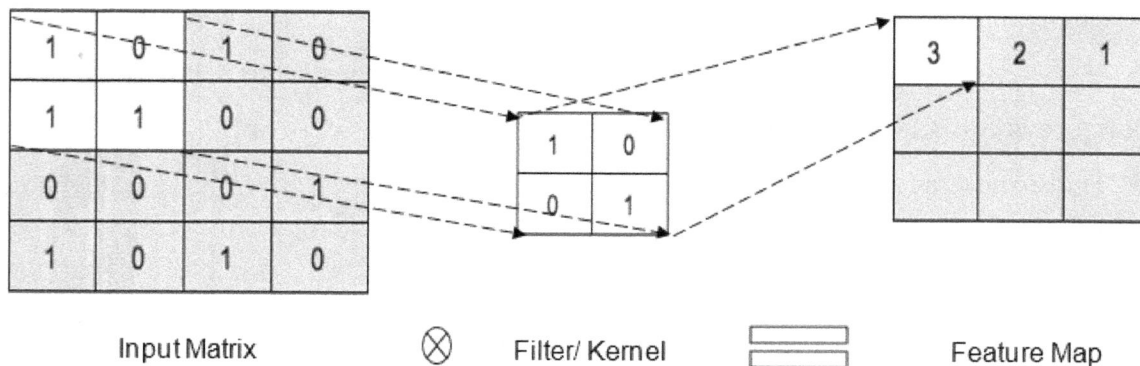

Figure 4.5: Filter application on images

The result of this convolution is known as a feature map or an activation map.

The size of the filter needs to be defined as a hyperparameter. This size can also be considered the area for which a neuron can "see" the input. This is called a neuron's *receptive field*. Additionally, we need to define the stride size, that is, the number of steps we need to take before applying the filter. Pixels at the center have the filters passing through several times compared with those at the edges. To avoid losing information at the corners, it is advisable to add an extra layer of zeros as padding.

The ReLU Activation Function

Activation functions are used all across machine learning. They are useful for introducing non-linearity and allowing the a model to learn non-linear functions. In this particular context, we apply the **Rectified Linear Unit** (**ReLU**). It basically replaces all the negative values with zero.

The following image demonstrates the change in an image after ReLU is applied.

Figure 4.6: Image after applying ReLU function

Exercise 19: Visualizing ReLU

In this exercise we will visualize the Rectified Linear Unit function. The ReLU function will be plotted on an X-Y axis, where X is numbers in the range of -15 to 15 and Y is the output after applying the ReLU function. The goal of this exercise is to visualize ReLU.

1. Import the required Python packages:

    ```
    from matplotlib import pyplot
    ```

2. Define the ReLU function:

    ```
    def relu(x):
        return max(0.0, x)
    ```

3. Specify the input and output references:

    ```
    inputs = [x for x in range(-15, 15)]
    outputs = [relu(x) for x in inputs]
    ```

4. Plot the input against the output:

```
pyplot.plot(inputs, outputs) #Plot the input against the output
pyplot.show()
```

Expected Output:

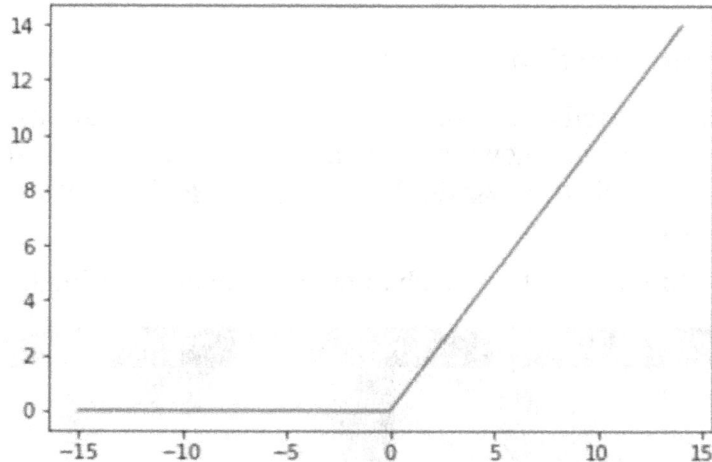

Figure 4.7: Graph plot for ReLU

Pooling

Pooling is a downsampling process that involves reducing dimensionality from a higher to a lower dimensional space. In machine learning, pooling is applied as a way to reduce the spatial complexity of the layers. This allows for fewer weights to be learned and consequently faster training times.

Historically, different techniques have been used to perform pooling, such as average pooling and L2-norm pooling. The most preferred pooling technique is max pool. Max pooling involves taking the largest element within a defined window size. The following is an example of max pooling on a matrix:

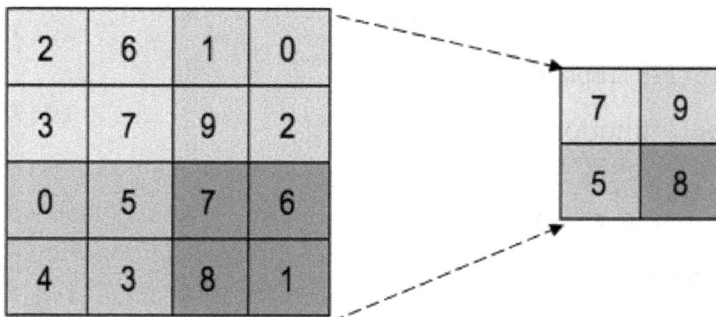

Figure 4.8: Max pool

If we apply max pooling to the preceding example, the section that has 2, 6, 3, and 7 is reduced to 7. Similarly, the section with 1, 0, 9, and 2 is reduced to 9. With max pooling, we pick the largest number in a section.

Dropout

A common problem encountered in machine learning is overfitting. Overfitting occurs when a model "memorizes" the training data and is unable to generalize when presented with different examples in testing. There are several ways to avoid overfitting, particularly through regularization:

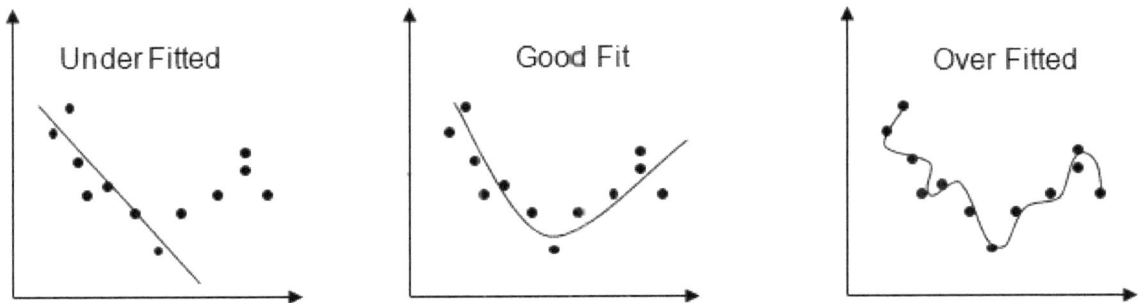

Figure 4.9: Regularization

Regulation is the process of constraining coefficients toward zero. Regularization can be summarized as techniques used to penalize learned coefficients so that they tend towards zero. Dropout is a common regularization technique that is applied by randomly "dropping" some neurons during both the forward and backward passes. To implement dropout, we specify the probability of a neuron being dropped as a parameter. By randomly dropping neurons, we ensure that the model is able to generalize better and therefore be a little more flexible.

Classification in Convolutional Neural Network

The second section of a CNN is more task-specific. For the task of classification, this section is basically a fully connected neural network. A neural network is regarded as fully connected when every neuron in one layer is connected to all the neurons in the next layer. The input to the fully connected layer is a flattened vector that is the output of section one. Flattening converts the matrix into a 1D vector.

The number of hidden layers in the fully connected layer is a hyperparameter that can be optimized and fine-tuned.

Exercise 20: Creating a Simple CNN Architecture

In this exercise, you will construct a simple CNN model using Keras. This exercise will entail creating a model with the layers discussed so far. In the first section of the model, we will have two convolutional layers with the ReLU activation function, a pooling layer, and a dropout layer. In the second section, we will have a flattened layer and a fully connected layer.

1. First, we import the necessary classes:

    ```
    from keras.models import Sequential #For stacking layers
    from keras.layers import Dense, Conv2D, Flatten, MaxPooling2D, Dropout
    from keras.utils import plot_model
    ```

2. Next, define the variables used:

    ```
    num_classes = 10
    ```

3. Let's now define the model. Keras's Sequential model allows you to stack layers as you go:

    ```
    model = Sequential()
    ```

4. We can now add section one layers. The convolution and ReLU layers are defined together. We have two convolutional layers. We define a kernel size of 3 for each. The first layer of the model receives the input. We need to define how it should expect that input to be structured. In our case, the input is in the form of 28 by 28 images. We also need to specify the number of neurons for each layer. In our case, we define 64 neurons for the first layer and 32 neurons for the second layer. Please note that these are hyperparameters that can be optimized:

    ```
    model.add(Conv2D(64, kernel_size=3, activation='relu', input_
    shape=(28,28,1)))
    model.add(Conv2D(32, kernel_size=3, activation='relu'))
    ```

5. We then add a pooling layer, followed by a dropout layer with a 25% probability of neurons being 'dropped':

    ```
    model.add(MaxPooling2D(pool_size=(2, 2)))
    model.add(Dropout(0.25))
    ```

    The section one layers are done. Please note that the number of layers is also a hyperparameter that can be optimized.

6. For section two, we first flatten the input. We then add a fully connected or dense layer. Using the softmax activation function, we can calculate the probability for each of the 10 classes:

```
model.add(Flatten())
model.add(Dense(num_classes, activation='softmax'))
```

7. To visualize the model architecture so far, we can print out the model as follows:

```
model.summary()
```

Expected Output:

```
Layer (type)                       Output Shape              Param #
=================================================================
conv2d_5 (Conv2D)                  (None, 26, 26, 64)        640

conv2d_6 (Conv2D)                  (None, 24, 24, 32)        18464

max_pooling2d_3 (MaxPooling2 (None, 12, 12, 32)              0

dropout_3 (Dropout)                (None, 12, 12, 32)        0

flatten_3 (Flatten)                (None, 4608)              0

dense_2 (Dense)                    (None, 10)                46090
=================================================================
Total params: 65,194
Trainable params: 65,194
Non-trainable params: 0
```

Figure 4.10: Model summary

8. You can also run the following code to export the image to a file:

```
plot_model(model, to_file='model.png')
```

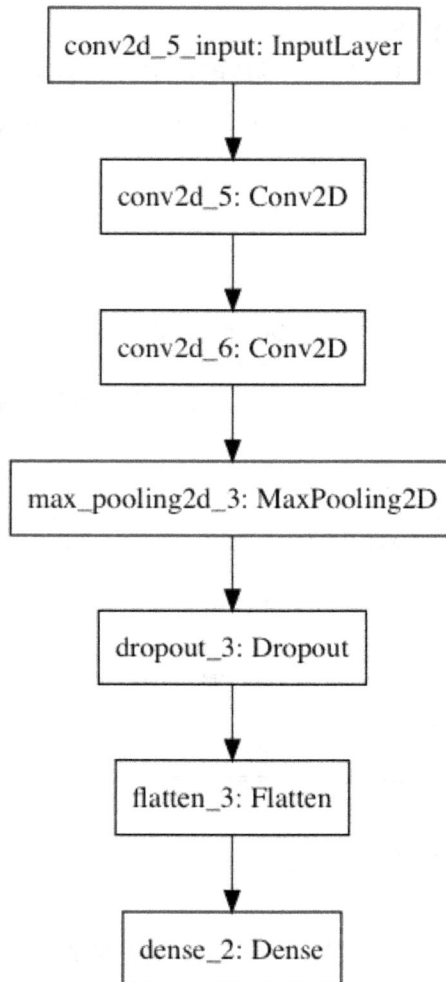

Figure 4.11: Visualized architecture of a simple CNN

In the preceding exercise, we created a simple CNN with two convolutional layers for the task of classification. In the preceding output image, you'll notice how the layers are stacked – starting from the input layer, then the two convolutional layers, the pooling, dropout, and flattening layers, and the fully connected layer at the end.

Training a CNN

During the training of a CNN, the model tries to learn the weights of the filters in feature extraction and the weights at the fully connected layers in the neural network. To understand how a model is trained, we'll discuss how the probability of each output class is calculated, how we calculate the error or the loss, and finally, how we optimize or minimize that loss while updating the weights:

1. Probabilities

   Recall that in the last layer of the neural network section, we used a softmax function to calculate the probability of each output class. This probability is calculated by dividing the exponent of that class score by the sum of the exponents of all scores:

   $$softmax = \frac{exp(y_i)}{\sum_j^c exp(y_i)} where\ i\ =\ is\ the\ class\ 0,1....9$$

   Figure 4.12: Expression to calculate probability

2. Loss

   We need to be able to quantify how well the calculated probabilities predict the actual class. This is done by calculating a loss, which in the case of classification probability is best done through the categorical cross-entropy loss function. The categorical cross-entropy loss function takes in two vectors, the predicted classes (let's call that y') and the actual classes (say y), and outputs the overall loss. Cross-entropy loss is calculated as the sum of the negative log likelihoods of the class probabilities. It can be represented as the H function here:

   $$H(y',y) = -\sum_i y' log\ (softmax(y_i))$$

   Figure 4.13: Expression to calculate loss

3. Optimization

Consider the sketch of cross-entropy loss that follows. By minimizing the loss, we can predict the correct class with a higher probability:

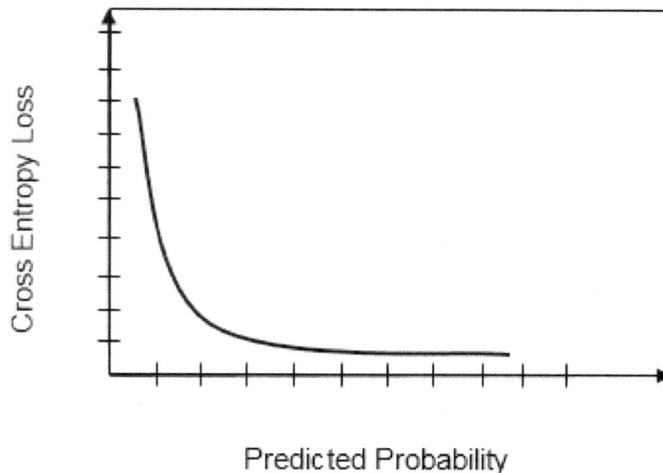

Figure 4.14: Cross-entropy loss versus predicted probability

Gradient descent is an optimization algorithm for finding the minimum of a function, such as the loss function described earlier. Although the overall error is calculated, we need to go back and calculate how much of that loss was contributed by each node. Consequently, we can update the weights, so as to minimize the overall error. Backpropagation applies the chain rule of calculus to calculate the update for each weight. This is done by taking the partial derivative of the error or loss relative to the weights.

To better visualize these steps, consider the following diagram, which summarizes the three steps. For the classification task, the first step involves the calculation of probabilities for each output class. We then apply a loss function to quantify how well the probabilities predict the actual class. In order to make a better prediction going forward, we then update our weights by performing backpropagation through gradient descent:

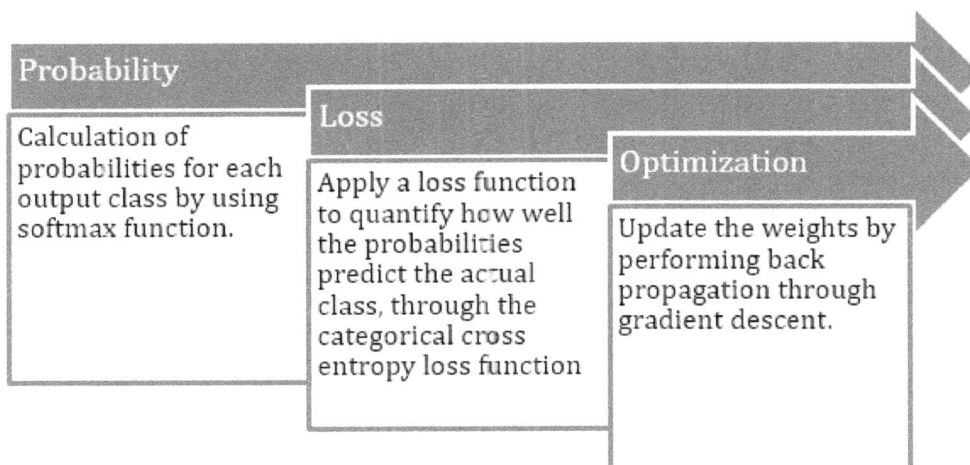

Figure 4.15: Steps for the classification task

Exercise 21: Training a CNN

In this exercise, we will train the model we created in exercise 20. The following steps will help you with the solution. Recall that this is for the overall task of classification.

1. We start by defining the number of epochs. An epoch is a common hyperparameter used in deep neural networks. One epoch is when the entire dataset is passed through a complete forward and backward pass. As training data is usually a lot, data can be divided into several batches:

    ```
    epochs=12
    ```

2. Recall that we imported the MNIST dataset by running the following command:

    ```
    (X_train, y_train), (X_test, y_test) = keras.datasets.mnist.load_data()
    ```

3. We first reshape the data to fit the model:

    ```
    X_train = X_train.reshape(60000,28,28,1) #60,000 is the number of training
    examples
    X_test = X_test.reshape(10000,28,28,1)
    ```

4. The to_categorical function changes a vector of integers to a matrix of one-hot encoded vectors. Given the following example, the function returns the array shown:

    ```
    #Demonstrating the to_categorical method
    Import numpy as np
    from keras.utils import to_categorical
    example = [1,0,3,2]
    to_categorical(example)
    ```

The array would be as follows:

```
array([[0., 1., 0., 0.],
       [1., 0., 0., 0.],
       [0., 0., 0., 1.],
       [0., 0., 1., 0.]])
```

Figure 4.16: Array output

5. We apply it to the target column as shown:

```
from keras.utils import to_categorical
y_train = to_categorical(y_train)
y_test = to_categorical(y_test)
```

6. We then define the loss function as a categorical cross-entropy loss function. Additionally, we define the optimizer and the metrics. The Adam(Adaptive Moment) optimizer is an optimization algorithm often used in place of stochastic gradient descent. It defines an adaptive learning rate for each parameter of the model:

```
model.compile(optimizer='adam', loss='categorical_crossentropy',
metrics=['accuracy'])
```

7. To train the model, run the .fit method:

```
model.fit(X_train, y_train, validation_data=(X_test, y_test),
epochs=epochs)
```

The output should be as follows:

```
Train on 60000 samples, validate on 10000 samples
Epoch 1/12
60000/60000 [==============================] - 209s 3ms/step - loss: 11.8406 - acc: 0.2646 - val_loss: 11.0491 - val_
acc: 0.3130
Epoch 2/12
60000/60000 [==============================] - 197s 3ms/step - loss: 9.8795 - acc: 0.3867 - val_loss: 9.8567 - val_ac
c: 0.3884
Epoch 3/12
60000/60000 [==============================] - 199s 3ms/step - loss: 9.8271 - acc: 0.3901 - val_loss: 9.7647 - val_ac
c: 0.3940
Epoch 4/12
60000/60000 [==============================] - 227s 4ms/step - loss: 9.6686 - acc: 0.4000 - val_loss: 9.6117 - val_ac
c: 0.4033
```

Figure 4.17: Training the model

8. To evaluate the model's performance, you can run the following:

```
score = model.evaluate(X_test, y_test, verbose=0)
print('Test loss:', score[0])
print('Test accuracy:', score[1])
```

9. For this task, we expect a fairly high accuracy after a number of epochs:

```
Test loss: 6.17029175567627
Test accuracy: 0.6169
```

Figure 4.18: Accuracy and loss output

Applying CNNs to Text

Now that we have a general intuition of how CNNs work using images, let's look at how they can be applied in natural language processing. Just like images, text has spatial qualities that make it ideal for CNN usage. However, there is one main change to the architecture that we introduce when dealing with text. Instead of having two-dimensional convolutional layers, text is one-dimensional, as shown here.

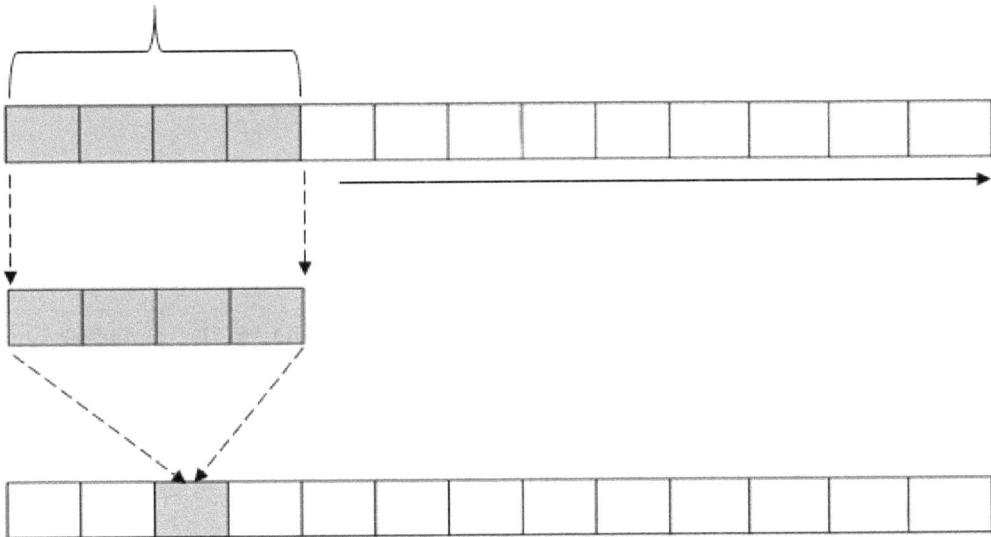

Figure 4.19: One-dimensional convolution

It is important to note that the preceding input sequence can be either the character sequence or the word sequence. The application of CNNs on text, at the character level, can be visualized as shown in the following figure. CNNs have 6 convolutional layers and 3 fully connected layers as shown here.

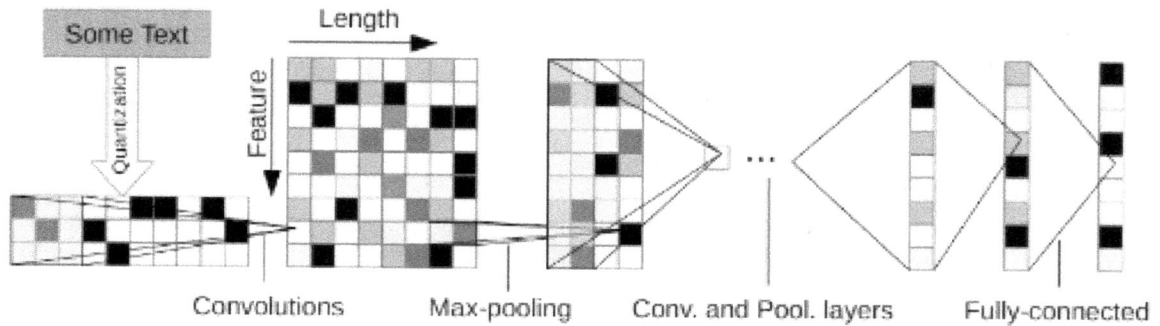

Figure 4.20: CNN with 6 convolutional and 3 fully connected layers

Character-level CNNs were shown to perform well when applied to large noisy data. They are also simpler than word-level applications because they require no preprocessing (such as stemming) and the characters are represented as one-hot encoding representations.

In the following example, we will demonstrate the application of CNNs to text at a word level. We will therefore need to perform some vectorization and padding before feeding the data into the CNN architecture.

Exercise 22: Application of a Simple CNN to a Reuters News Topic for Classification

In this exercise, we will be applying a CNN model to the built-in Keras Reuters dataset.

> **Note**
>
> If you are using Google Colab, you need to downgrade your version of **numpy** to 1.16.2 by running
>
> `!pip install numpy==1.16.1`
>
> `import numpy as np`
>
> This downgrade is necessary since this version of **numpy** has the default value of **allow_pickle** as **True**.

1. Start by importing the necessary classes:

```
import keras
from keras.datasets import reuters
from keras.preprocessing.text import Tokenizer
from keras.models import Sequential
from keras import layers
```

2. Define the variables:

```
batch_size = 32
epochs = 12
maxlen = 10000
batch_size = 32
embedding_dim = 128
num_filters = 64
kernel_size = 5
```

3. Load the Reuters dataset:

```
(x_train, y_train), (x_test, y_test) = reuters.load_data(num_words=None,
test_split=0.2)
```

4. Prepare the data:

```
word_index = reuters.get_word_index(path="reuters_word_index.json")
num_classes = max(y_train) + 1
index_to_word = {}
for key, value in word_index.items():
    index_to_word[value] = key
```

5. Tokenize the input data:

```
tokenizer = Tokenizer(num_words=maxlen)
x_train = tokenizer.sequences_to_matrix(x_train, mode='binary')
x_test = tokenizer.sequences_to_matrix(x_test, mode='binary')

y_train = keras.utils.to_categorical(y_train, num_classes)
y_test = keras.utils.to_categorical(y_test, num_classes)
```

6. Define the model:

```
model = Sequential()
model.add(layers.Embedding(512, embedding_dim, input_length=maxlen))
model.add(layers.Conv1D(num_filters, kernel_size, activation='relu'))
model.add(layers.GlobalMaxPooling1D())
model.add(layers.Dense(10, activation='relu'))
```

```
model.add(layers.Dense(num_classes, activation='softmax'))
model.compile(loss='categorical_crossentropy', optimizer='adam',
metrics=['accuracy'])
```

7. Train and evaluate the model. Print the accuracy score:

```
history = model.fit(x_train, y_train, batch_size=batch_size, epochs=epochs,
verbose=1, validation_split=0.1)
score = model.evaluate(x_test, y_test, batch_size=batch_size, verbose=1)
print('Test loss:', score[0])
print('Test accuracy:', score[1])
```

Expected output:

```
Test loss: 2.22790470276150604
Test accuracy: 0.43232413178984863
```

Figure 4.21: Accuracy score

We have thus created a model and trained it on a dataset.

Application Areas of CNNs

Now that we understand the architecture of CNNs, let's look at some applications. In general, CNNs are great for data that has a spatial structure. Examples of types of data that has a spatial structure are sound, images, video, and text.

In natural language processing, CNNs are used for various tasks such as sentence classification. One example is the task of sentiment classification, where a sentence is classified as belonging to a predetermined group of classes.

As discussed earlier, CNNs are applied at the character level to classification tasks such as sentiment classification, especially on noisy datasets such as social media posts.

CNNs are more commonly applied in computer vision. Here are some applications in this area:

- *Facial recognition*

  Most social networking sites employ CNNs to detect faces and subsequently perform tasks such as tagging.

Figure 4.22: Facial recognition

- *Object detection*

  Similarly, CNNs are able to detect objects in images. There are several CNN-based architectures that are used to detect objects, one of the most popular being R-CNN. (R-CNN stands for Region CNN.) An R-CNN works by applying a selective search to come up with regions and subsequently use using CNNs to perform classification, one region at a time.

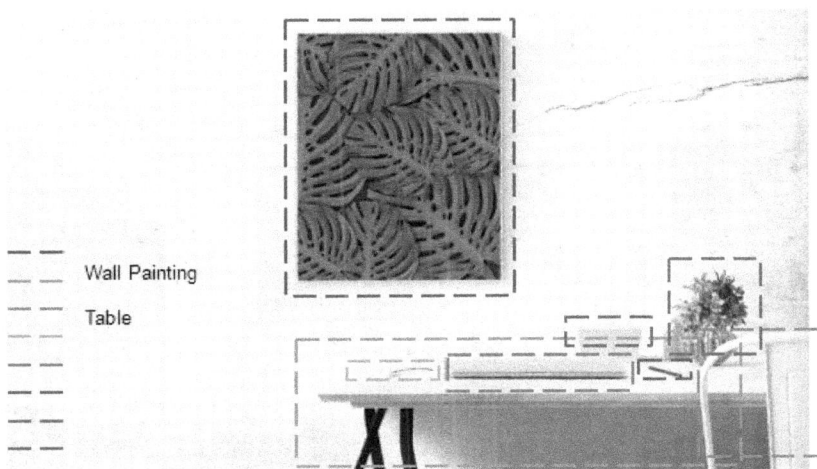

Figure 4.23: Object detection

- *Image captioning*

  This task involves creating a textual description for an image. One way to perform image captioning is to replace the fully connected layer in section two with a recurrent neural network (RNN).

  A puppy in a cup   A dog wearing   A white puppy sitting
                 sunglasses   on a sofa chair

  Figure 4.24: Image captioning

- *Semantic segmentation*

  Semantic segmentation is the task of segmenting an image into more meaningful parts. Each pixel in an image is classified as belonging to a class.

  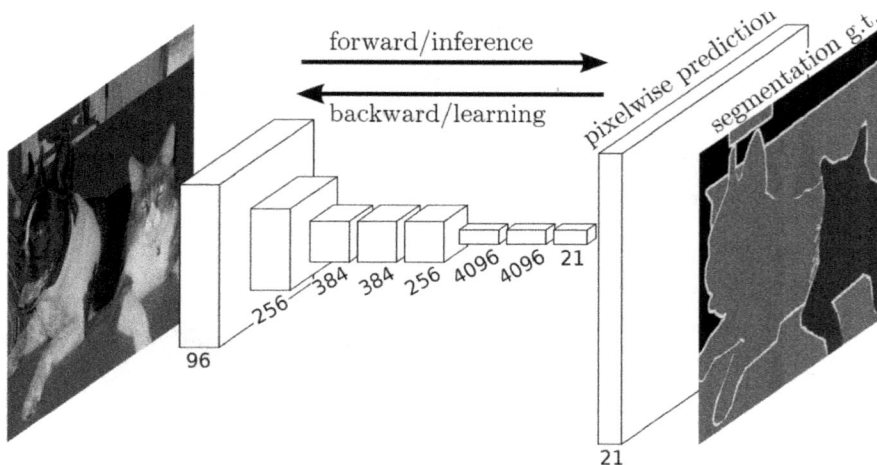

  Figure 4.25: Semantic segmentation

An architecture that can be used to perform semantic segmentation is a **Fully Convoluted Network** (**FCN**). The architecture of FCNs is slightly different from the preceding one in two ways: it has no fully connected layer and it has upsampling. Upsampling is the process of making the output image larger preferably the same size as the input image.

Here is a sample architecture:

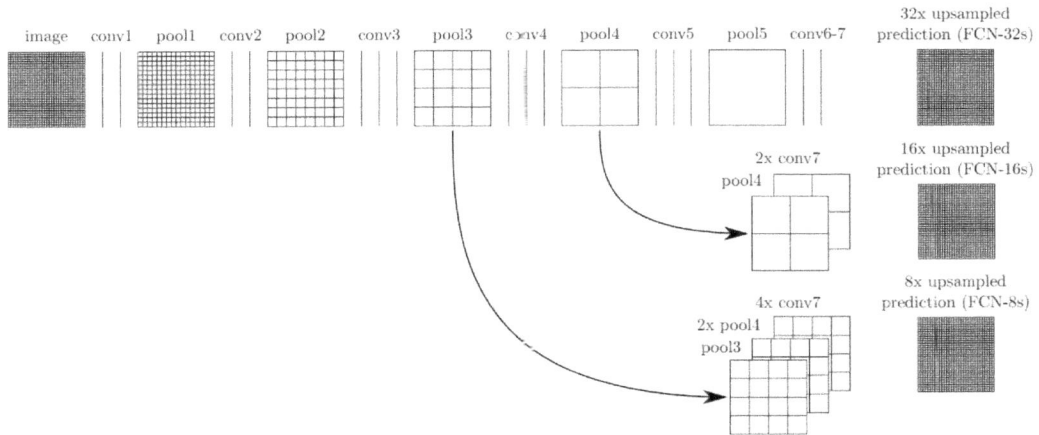

Figure 4.26: Sample architecture of semantic segmentation

Note

For more on FCNs, refer to the paper by Jonathan Long, Evan Shelhamer, and Trevor Darrell titled Fully Convolutional Networks for Semantic Segmentation.

Activity 5: Sentiment Analysis on a Real-life Dataset

Imagine that you are tasked with creating a model to classify the reviews from a dataset. In this activity, we will build a CNN that performs the binary classification task of sentiment analysis. We will be using a real-life dataset from UCI's repository.

> **Note**
>
> This dataset is downloaded from https://archive.ics.uci.edu/ml/datasets/Sentiment+Labelled+Sentences
>
> From Group to Individual Labels using Deep Features, Kotziaa et al., KDD 2015 UCI machine learning Repository [http://archive.ics.uci.edu.ml]. Irvine, CA: University of California, School of Information and Computer Science
>
> You can also download it from our GitHub repository link:
>
> https://github.com/TrainingByPackt/Deep-Learning-for-Natural-Language-Processing/tree/master/Lesson%2004

The following steps will help you with the solution.

1. Download the Sentiment Labelled Sentences dataset.

2. Create a directory labelled 'data' within your working directory and unzip the downloaded folder within the directory.

3. Create and run your working script (for example, sentiment.ipynb) on Jupyter Notebook.

4. Import your data using pandas read_csv method. Feel free to use one or all of the files in the dataset.

5. Split your data into training and test sets by using scikit learn's train_test_split.

6. Tokenize using Keras's tokenizer.

7. Convert the text into sequences using the texts_to_sequences method.

8. Ensure that all sequences have the same length by padding them. You can use Keras's pad_sequences function.

9. Define the model with a minimum of one convolutional layer and one fully connected layer. As this is a binary classification, we use a sigmoid activation function and calculate the loss through binary cross-entropy loss.

10. Train and test the model.

> **Note**
>
> The solution for the activity can be found on page 305.

Expected output:

```
Training Accuracy: 1.0000
Testing Accuracy:  0.8167
```

Figure 4.27: Accuracy scores

Summary

In this chapter, we studied the architecture and applications of convolutional neural networks (CNNs). CNNs are applied not just to text and images but also to datasets that have some form of spatial structure. In the upcoming chapters, you will explore how to apply other forms of neural networks to various natural language tasks.

5

Recurrent Neural Networks

Learning Objectives

By the end of this chapter, you will be able to:

- Describe classical feedforward networks
- Differentiate between feedforward neural networks and recurrent neural networks
- Evaluate the application of backpropagation through time for recurrent neural networks
- Describe the drawbacks of recurrent neural networks
- Use recurrent neural networks with keras to solve the author attribution problem

This chapter aims to introduce you to recurrent neural networks and their applications, as well as their drawbacks.

Introduction

We encounter different kinds of data in our day-to-day lives, and some of this data has temporal dependencies (dependencies over time) while some does not. For example, an image by itself contains the information it wants to convey. However, data forms such as audio and video have dependencies over time. They cannot convey information if a fixed point in time is taken into consideration. Based on the problem statement, the input that's needed in order to solve the problem can differ. If we have a model to detect a particular person in a frame, a single image can be used as input. However, if we need to detect their actions, we need a stream of images, contiguous in time, as the input. We can understand the person's actions by analyzing these images together, but not independently.

While watching a movie, a particular scene makes sense because its context is known, and we remember all the information gathered before in the movie to understand the current scene. This is very important, and we, as humans, can do this because our brains can store memory, analyze past data, and retrieve useful information to understand the current scene.

Networks such as multi-layered perceptron and convolutional neural networks lack this capability. Every input given to these networks is treated independently, and they don't store any information from past inputs to analyze the current inputs because they lack memory in their architecture. That being the case, maybe there is a way we can enable neural networks to have memory. We can try and make them store useful information from the past and make them retrieve information from the past that helps them to analyze the current input. This is indeed possible, and the architecture for it is called the **Recurrent Neural Network (RNN)**.

Before we delve deep into the theory of RNNs, let's take a look at their applications. Currently, RNNs are widely used. Some of the applications are as follows:

- *Speech recognition*: Whether it's Amazon's Alexa, Apple's Siri, Google's voice assistant, or Microsoft's Cortana, all their speech recognition systems use RNNs.

- *Time series predictions*: Any application with time series data, such as stock market data, website traffic, call center traffic, movie recommendations, Google Maps routes, and so on, uses RNNs to predict future data, the optimal path, optimal resource allocations, and so on.

- *Natural language processing*: Applications such as machine translation (for Google Translate, for instance), chatbots (such as those for Slack and Google), and question answering all use RNNs to model dependencies.

Previous Versions of Neural Networks

Around 40 years ago, it became clear that **Feed Forward Neural Networks (FFNNs)** could not capture time-variable dependencies, which are essential for capturing the time-variable properties of a signal. Modeling time-variable dependencies is very important in many applications involving real-world data, such as speech and video, in which data has time-variable properties. Also, human biological neural networks have a recurrent relationship, so it is the most obvious direction to take. How could this recurrent relationship be added to existing feedforward networks?

One of the first attempts to achieve this was done by adding delay elements, and the network was called the **Time-Delay Neural Network**, or **TDNN** for short.

In this network, as the following figure shows, the delay elements are added to the network and the past inputs are given to the network along with the current timestep as the input to the network. This definitely has an advantage over the traditional feed forward networks but has the disadvantage of having only so many inputs from the past as the window allows. If the window is too large, the network grows with increasing parameters and computational complexities.

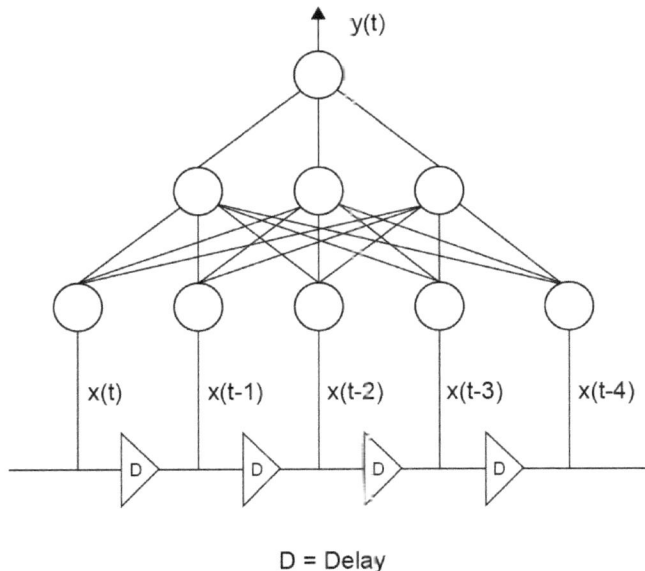

D = Delay

Figure 5.1: TDNN structure

Then came Elman networks, or simple RNNs. Elman networks are very similar to feedforward networks, except that the hidden layer of output is stored and used for the next input. This way, information from the previous timesteps can be captured in these hidden states.

One way of looking at Elman networks is that at each input, we append the previous hidden layers' outputs along with the inputs and send them all as the inputs to the network. So, if the input size is **m** and the hidden layer size is **n**, the effective input layer size becomes **m+n**.

The following figure shows a simple three-layer network, where the previous state is fed back to the network to store the context, and therefore it is called **SimpleRNN**. There are other variations to this architecture, such as Jordan networks, which we will not study in this chapter. For those are interested in the early history of RNNs, reading more on Elman networks and Jordan networks might be the best place to start.

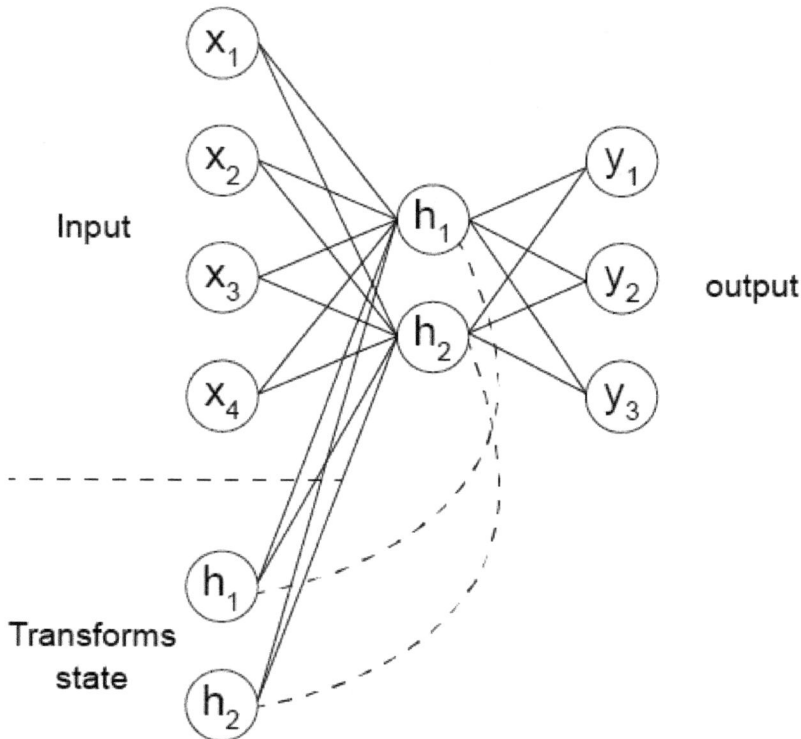

Figure 5.2: SimpleRNN structure

And then came the **RNN**, which is the topic of this chapter. We will look into RNNs in detail in the coming sections It is important to note that in recurrent networks, since there are memory units and weights associated to these units, they need to be learned during backpropagation. Since these gradients are also backpropagated through time, we call it **Back Propagation Through Time**, or **BPTT**. We will discuss BPTT in detail in the upcoming sections. However, TDNN, Elman networks, and RNNs have a major drawback due to BPTT, and it is called vanishing gradients. Vanishing gradients is a problem where gradients get smaller and smaller as they backpropagate, and in these networks, as timesteps increase, back-propagated gradients get smaller and smaller, resulting in vanishing gradients. It's almost impossible to capture time dependencies greater than 20 timesteps.

To address this issue, an architecture called the **Long Short-Term Memory** (**LSTM**) architecture was introduced. The key idea here is to hold some cell states constant and introduce them as needed in future timesteps. These decisions are made by gates, including forget gates and output gates. Another commonly used variant of the LSTM is called the **Gated Recurrent Unit**, or **GRU** for short. Don't worry much if you didn't understand this completely. There are two chapters following that are dedicated to making these concepts clear.

RNNs

Recurrent often means occurring repeatedly. The recurrent part of RNNs simply means that the same task is done over all the inputs in the input sequence (for RNNs, we give a sequence of timesteps as the input sequence). One main difference between feed forward networks and RNNs is that RNNs have memory elements called states that capture the information from the previous inputs. So, in this architecture, the current output not only depends on the current input, but also on the current state, which takes into account past inputs.

RNNs are trained by sequences of inputs rather than a single input; similarly, we can consider each input to an RNN as a sequence of timesteps. The state elements in RNNs contain information about past inputs to process the current input sequence.

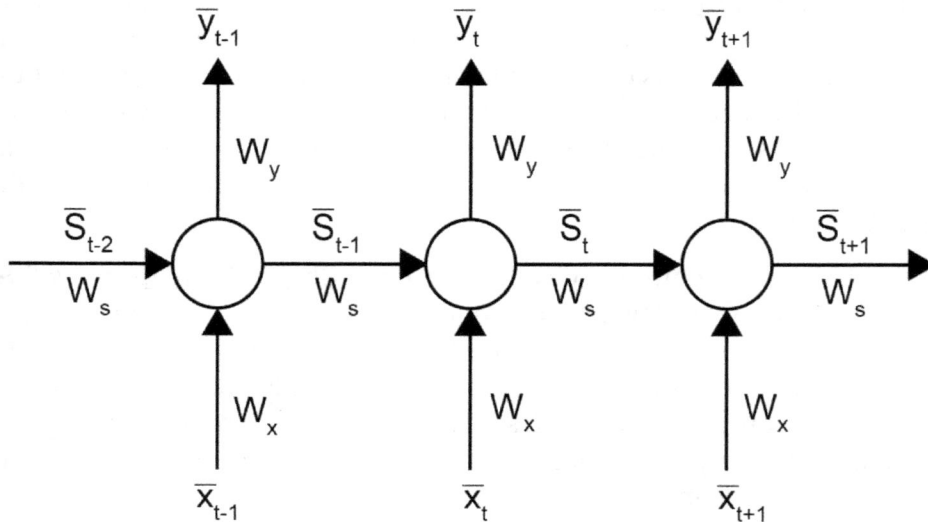

Figure 5.3: RNN structure

For each input in the input sequence, the RNN gets a state, calculates its output, and sends its state to the next input in the sequence. The same set of tasks is repeated for all the elements in the sequence.

It's easy to understand RNNs and their operations by comparing them to feedforward networks. Let's do that now.

By now, it's very clear that the inputs are independent of each other in feedforward neural networks, so we train the network by randomly drawing pairs of inputs and outputs. There is no significance to the sequence. At any given time, the output is a function of input and weights.

$$\bar{y}_t = F(\bar{x}_t, W)$$

Figure 5.4: Expression for the output of an RNN

In RNNs, our output at time **t** depends not only on the current input and the weight, but also on previous inputs. In this case, the output at time **t** will be defined as shown:

$$\bar{y}_t = F(\bar{x}_t, \bar{x}_{t-1}, \bar{x}_{t-2}, \cdots, \bar{x}_{t-t_0}, W)$$

Figure 5.5: Expression for the output of an RNN at time t

Let's look at a simple structure of an RNN that is called a folded model. In the following figure, the **S**$_t$ state vector is fed back into the network from the previous timestep. One important takeaway from this representation is that RNNs share the same weight matrices across timesteps. By increasing the timesteps, we are not learning more parameters, but we are looking at a bigger sequence.

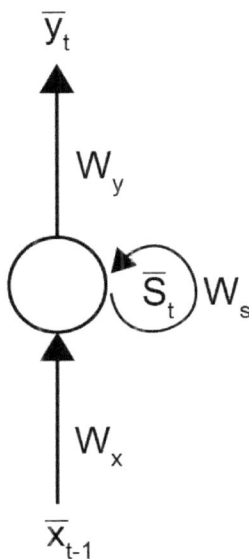

Figure 5.6: Folded model of an RNN

This is a folded model of an RNN:

Xt : Current input vector in the input sequence

Yt: Current output vector in the output sequence

St: Current state vector

Wx: Weight matrix connecting the input vector to the state vector

Wy: Weight matrix connecting the state vector to the output vector

Ws: Weight matrix connecting the state vector of previous timestep to the next one

Since the input, **x** is a sequence of timesteps and we perform the same task for elements in this sequence, we can unfold this model.

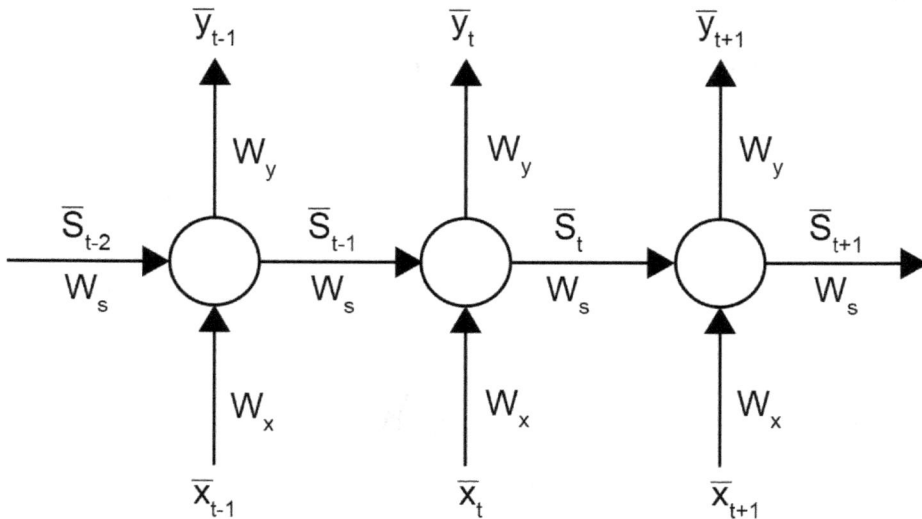

Figure 5.7: Unfolding of an RNN

For example, the output at time **t+1**,y_{t+1} depends on input at time **t+1**, weight matrices, and all the inputs before it.

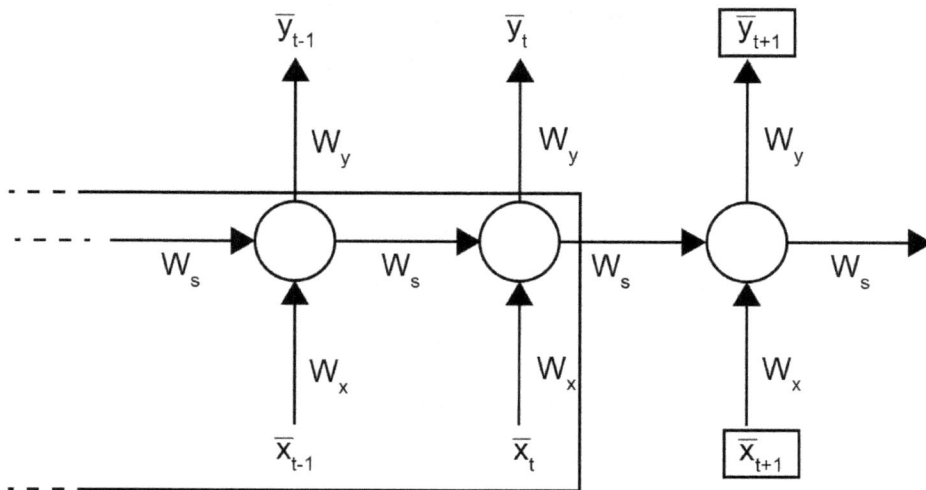

Figure 5.8: Unfolded RNN

Since RNNs are extensions of FFNNs, it's best to understand the differences between these architectures.

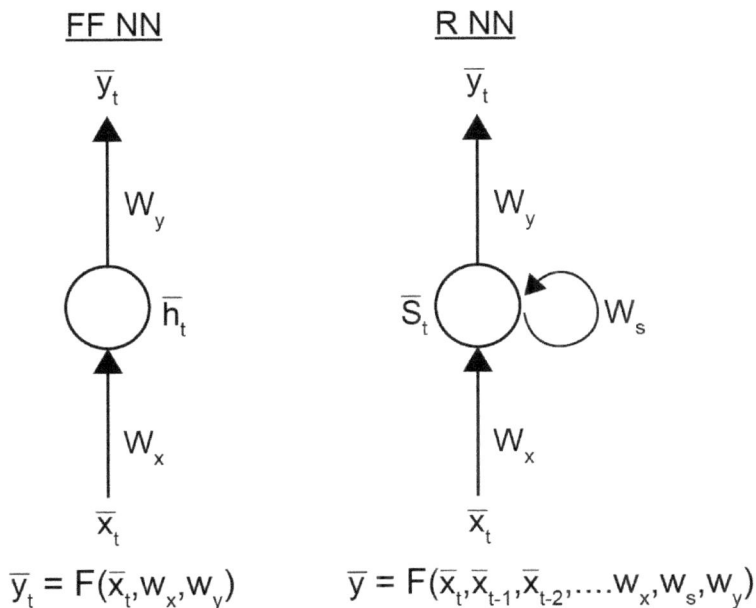

Figure 5.9: Differences between FFNNs and RNNs

The output expressions for FFNNs and RNNs are as follows:

$$\overline{h}_t = \overline{x}_t \cdot W_x \qquad \overline{S}_t = \overline{X}_t \cdot W_x + \overline{S}_{t-1} \cdot W_s$$

$$\overline{X}_t W_x + (\overline{X}_{t-1} W_x, \overline{S}_{t-2} W_s) W_s$$

$$\overline{y}_t = \overline{h}_t \cdot W_y \qquad \overline{y}_t = S_t \cdot W_y$$

Figure 5.10: Output expressions for FFNNs and RNNs

From the previous figure and equations, it is very evident that there are a lot of similarities between these two architectures. In fact, they are the same if **Ws=0**. This is obviously the case since **Ws** is the weight associated with the state that is fed back to the network. Without **Ws**, there is no feedback, which is the basis of the RNN.

In FFNNs, the output at **t** depends on the input at **t** and weight matrices. In RNNs, the output at **t** depends on input at **t**, **t-1**, **t-2**, and so on, as well as the weight matrices. This is explained with the further calculation of hidden vector **h** in the case of an FFNN and **s** in the case of an RNN. At first glance, it might look like the state at **t** depends on the input at **t**, the state at **t-1**, and the weight matrices; and the state at **t-1** depends on the input at **t-1**, the state at **t-2**, and so on; creating a chain that goes back all the way to the first timestep considered. The output calculations of both FFNNs and RNNs are same, though.

RNN Architectures

RNNs can come in many forms, and the appropriate architecture needs to be chosen depending on the problem we are solving.

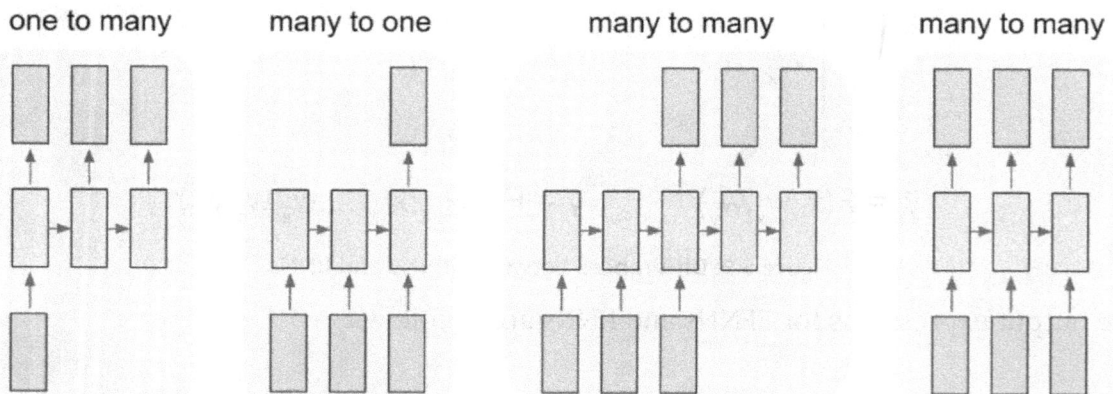

Figure 5.11 Different architectures of RNNs

One to many: In this architecture, a single input is given, and the output is a sequence. An example of this is image captioning, where the input is a single image, and the output is a sequence of words explaining the image.

Many to one: In this architecture, a sequence of inputs is given, but a single output is expected. An example is any time series prediction where the next timestep in the sequence needs to be predicted, given the previous timesteps.

Many to many: In this architecture, an input sequence is given to the network, and the network outputs a sequence. In this case, the sequence can be either synced or not synced. For example, in machine translation, the whole sentence needs to be fed in before the networks starts to translate it. Sometimes, the input and output are not in sync; for example, in the case of speech enhancement, where an audio frame is given as input and a cleaner version of the input frame is the output expected. In such cases, the input and output are in sync.

RNNs can also be stacked on top of each other. It is important to note that each RNN in the stack has its own weight matrices. So, the weight matrices are shared on the horizontal axis (the time axis) and not on the vertical axis (the number of RNNs).

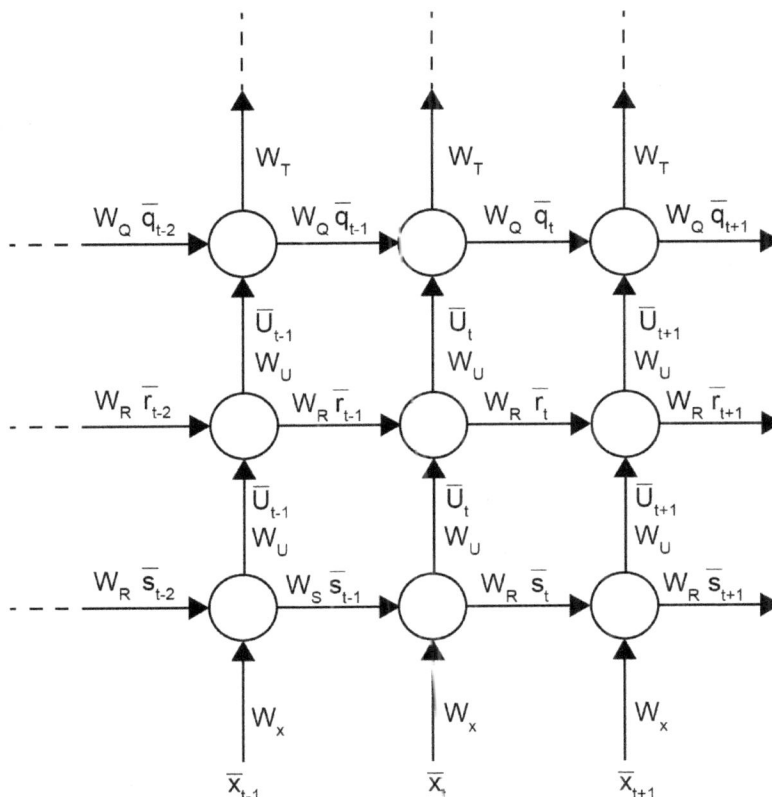

Figure 5.12: Stacked RNNs

BPTT

RNNs can deal with varying sequence lengths, can be used in different forms, and can be stacked on top of each other. Previously, you have come across the back propagation technique to backpropagate loss values to adjust weights. In the case of RNNs, something similar can be done, with a bit of a twist, which is a gate loss through time. It's called **BPTT**.

From the basic theory of back propagation, we know the following:

$$W_{new} = W_{previous} + \Delta W$$

Figure 5.13: Expression for weight update

The update value is calculated through gradient calculations using the chain rule:

$$\Delta W = -\alpha \frac{\partial E}{\partial W}$$

Figure 5.14 Partial derivative of error with regards to weight

Here, **α** is the learning rate. The partial derivative of **Error (loss)** with respect to the weight matrix is the main calculation. Once this new matrix is obtained, adjusting the weight matrices is simply adding this new matrix, scaled by a learning factor, to itself.

When calculating the update values for RNNs, we will use BPTT.

Let's look at an example to understand this better. Consider a loss function, such as the mean squared error (which is commonly used for regression problems):

$$E_t = (\bar{d}_t - \bar{y}_t)^2$$

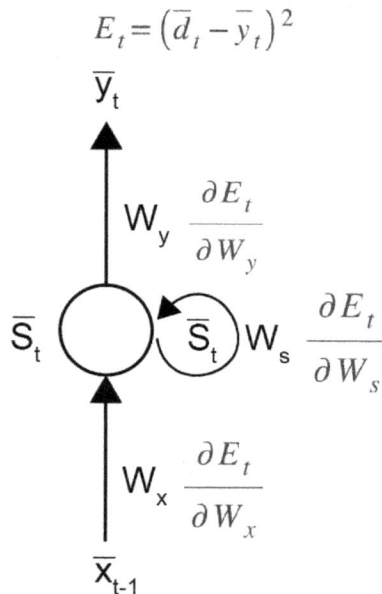

Figure 5.15: Loss function

At timestep **t = 3**, the loss calculated is as shown:

$$E_3 = (d_3 - y_3)^2$$

Figure 5.16 Loss at time t=3

This loss needs to be backpropagated, and the **Wy**, **Wx**, and **Ws** weights need to be updated.

As seen previously, we need to calculate the update value to adjust these weights, and this update value can be calculated using partial derivatives and the chain rule.

There are three parts to doing this:

- Update Weight **Wy** by calculating the partial derivative of the error with respect to **Wy**

- Update Weight **Ws** by calculating the partial derivative of the error with respect to **Ws**

- Update Weight **Wx** by calculating the partial derivative of the error with respect to **Wx**

Before we look at these updates, let's unroll the model and keep the part of the network that's actually relevant for our calculations.

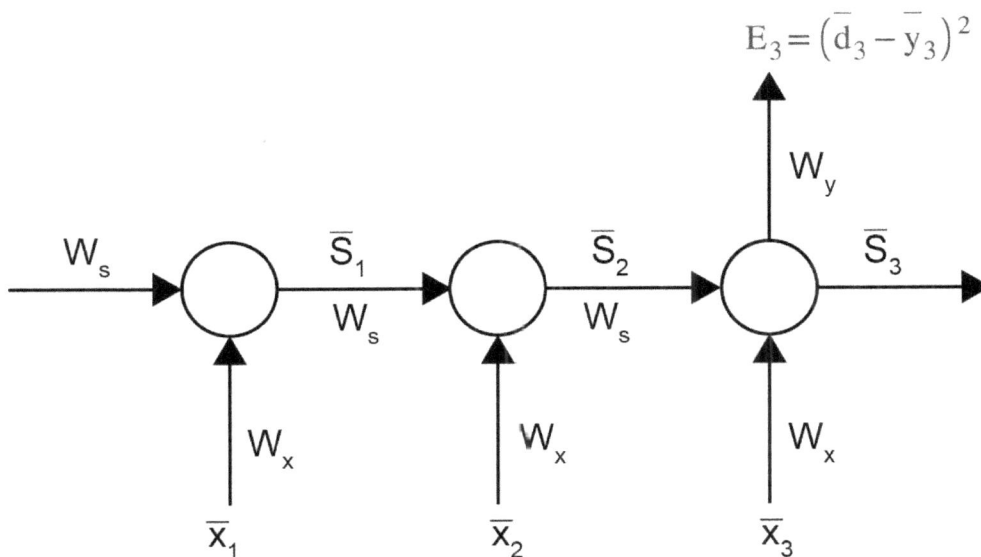

Figure 5.17 Unfolded RNN with loss at time t=3

Since we are looking at how loss at **t=3** affects the weight matrices, the loss values at and previous to **t=2** are not relevant. Now, we need to understand how to backpropagate this loss through the network.

Let's look at each of these updates and show the gradient flow for each of the updates shown in the preceding figure.

Updates and Gradient Flow

The updates can be listed as follows:

- Adjusting weight matrix **Wy**
- Adjusting weight matrix **Ws**
- For updating **Wx**

Adjusting Weight Matrix **Wy**

The model can be visualized as follows:

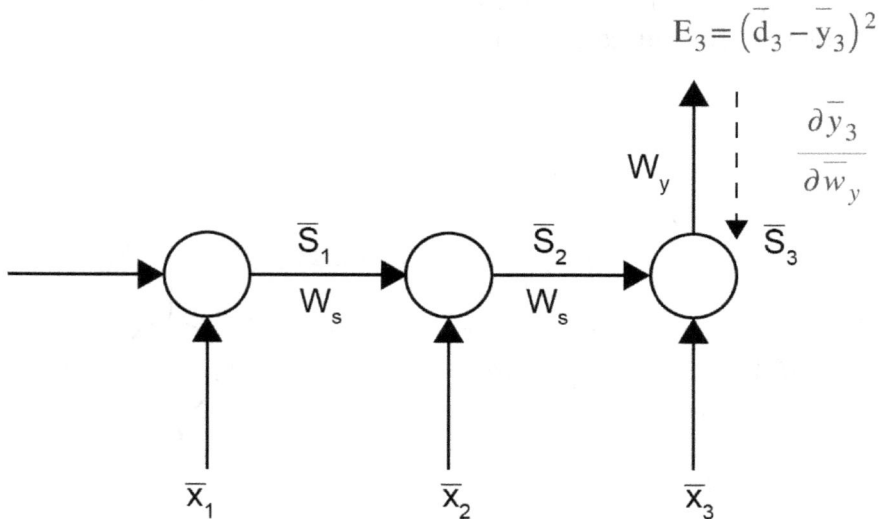

Figure 5.18: Back propagation of loss through weight matrix Wy

For Wy, the update is very simple since there are no additional paths or variables between Wy and the error. The matrix can be realized as follows:

$$\frac{\partial E_3}{\partial W_y} = \frac{\partial E_3}{\partial y_3} \frac{\partial y_3}{\partial W_y}$$

Figure 5.19: Expression for weight matrix Wy

Adjusting Weight Matrix Ws

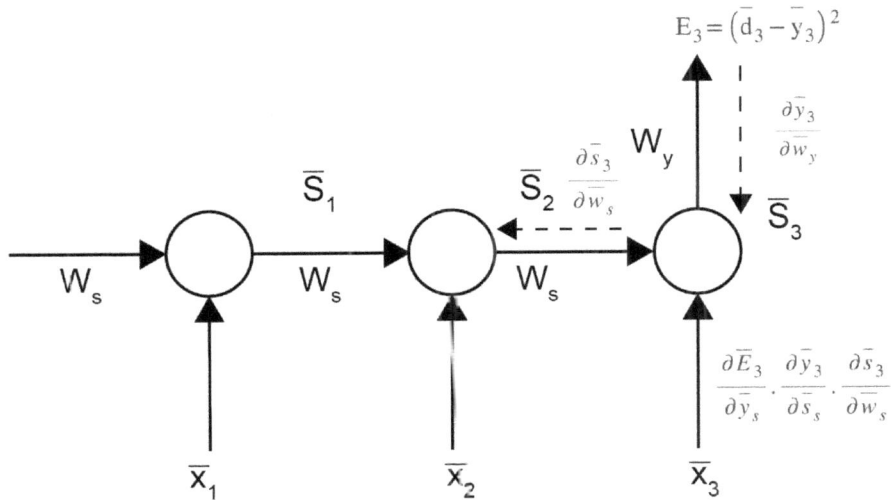

Figure 5.20: Back propagation of loss through weight matrix Ws with respect to S3

We can calculate the partial derivate of error with respect to **Ws** using the chain rule, as shown in the previous figure. It looks like that is what is needed, but it's important to remember that S_t is dependent on S_{t-1}, and therefore S_3 is dependent on S_2, so we need to consider S_2 also, as shown here:

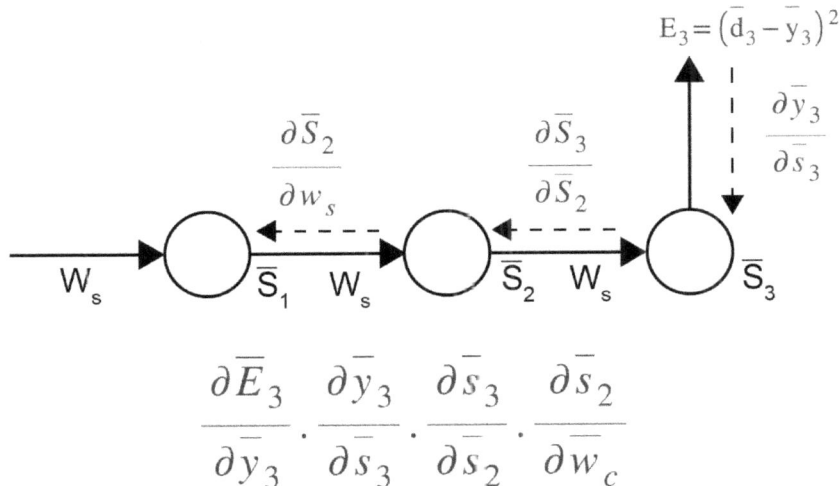

$$\frac{\partial \overline{E}_3}{\partial \overline{y}_3} \cdot \frac{\partial \overline{y}_3}{\partial \overline{s}_3} \cdot \frac{\partial \overline{s}_3}{\partial \overline{s}_2} \cdot \frac{\partial \overline{s}_2}{\partial \overline{w}_c}$$

Figure 5.21: Back propagation of loss through weight matrix Ws with respect to S_2

Again, S_2 in turn depends on S_1, and therefore S_1 needs to be considered, too, as shown here:

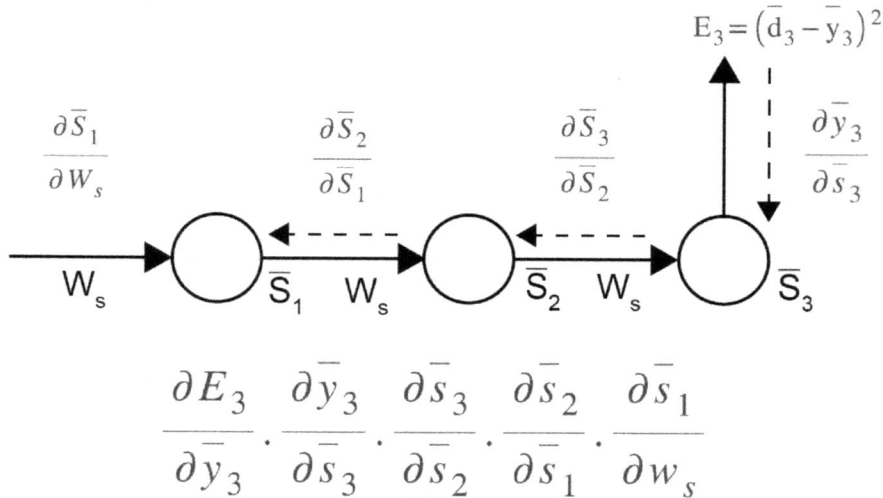

$$E_3 = (\bar{d}_3 - \bar{y}_3)^2$$

$$\frac{\partial \bar{S}_1}{\partial W_s} \qquad \frac{\partial \bar{S}_2}{\partial \bar{S}_1} \qquad \frac{\partial \bar{S}_3}{\partial \bar{S}_2} \qquad \frac{\partial \bar{y}_3}{\partial \bar{s}_3}$$

$$W_s \quad \bar{S}_1 \quad W_s \quad \bar{S}_2 \quad W_s \quad \bar{S}_3$$

$$\frac{\partial E_3}{\partial \bar{y}_3} \cdot \frac{\partial \bar{y}_3}{\partial \bar{s}_3} \cdot \frac{\partial \bar{s}_3}{\partial \bar{s}_2} \cdot \frac{\partial \bar{s}_2}{\partial \bar{s}_1} \cdot \frac{\partial \bar{s}_1}{\partial w_s}$$

Figure 5.22: Back propagation of loss through weight matrix Ws with respect to S_1

At **t=3**, we must consider the contribution of state S_3 to the error, the contribution of state S_2 to the error, and the contribution of state S_1 to the error, E_3. The final value looks like this:

$$\frac{\partial E_3}{\partial W_s} = \frac{\partial E_3}{\partial y_3} \cdot \frac{\partial \bar{y}_3}{\partial s_3} \cdot \frac{\partial s_3}{\partial s_2} \cdot \frac{\partial s_2}{\partial w_s}$$

$$+ \frac{\partial E_3}{\partial y_3} \cdot \frac{\partial \bar{y}_3}{\partial s_3} \cdot \frac{\partial s_3}{\partial s_2} \cdot \frac{\partial s_2}{\partial w_s}$$

$$+ \frac{\partial E_3}{\partial y_3} \cdot \frac{\partial y_3}{\partial s_3} \cdot \frac{\partial s_3}{\partial s_2} \cdot \frac{\partial s_2}{\partial s_1} \cdot \frac{\partial s_1}{\partial w_s}$$

Figure 5.23: Sum of all derivatives of error with respect to Ws at t=3

In general, for timestep **N**, all the contributions of the previous timesteps need to be considered. So, the general formula looks like this:

$$\frac{\partial E_N}{\partial W_s} = \sum_{i=1}^{N} \frac{\partial E_N}{\partial \overline{y}_N} \cdot \frac{\partial \overline{y}_N}{\partial \overline{S}_i} \cdot \frac{\partial \overline{S}_i}{\partial W_s}$$

Figure 5.24: General expression for the derivative of error with respect to Ws

For Updating Wx

We can calculate the partial derivate of error with respect to **Wx** using the chain rule, as shown in the next few figures. With the same reasoning that S_t is dependent on S_{t-1}, the calculation of partial derivative of error with respect to **Wx** can be divided into three stages at **t=3**.

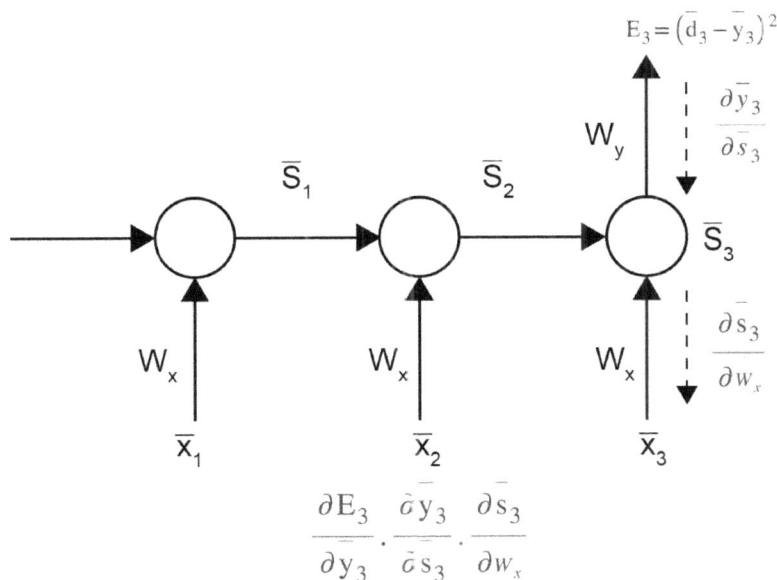

Figure 5.25: Back propagation of loss through weight matrix Wx with respect to S_2

Back propagation of loss through weight matrix Wx with respect to S_2:

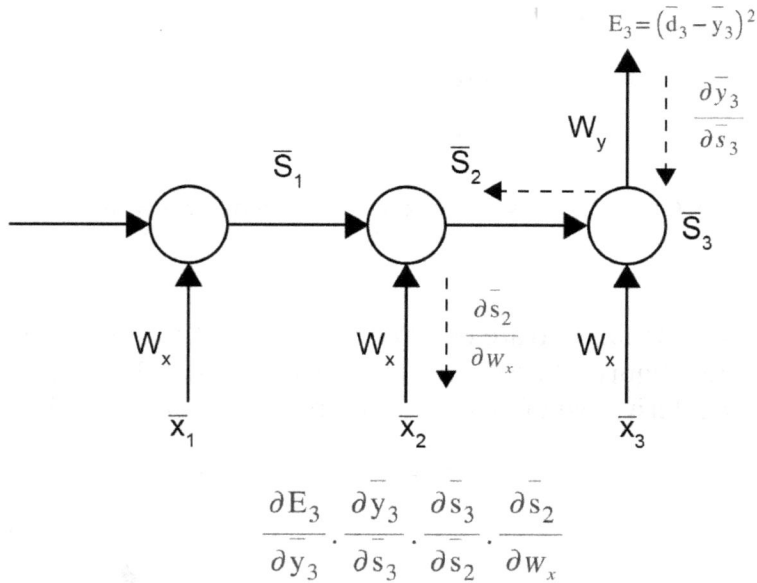

$$\frac{\partial E_3}{\partial \overline{y}_3} \cdot \frac{\partial \overline{y}_3}{\partial \overline{s}_3} \cdot \frac{\partial \overline{s}_3}{\partial \overline{s}_2} \cdot \frac{\partial \overline{s}_2}{\partial w_x}$$

Figure 5.26: Back propagation of loss through weight matrix Wx with respect to S_2

Back propagation of loss through weight matrix Wx with respect to S_1:

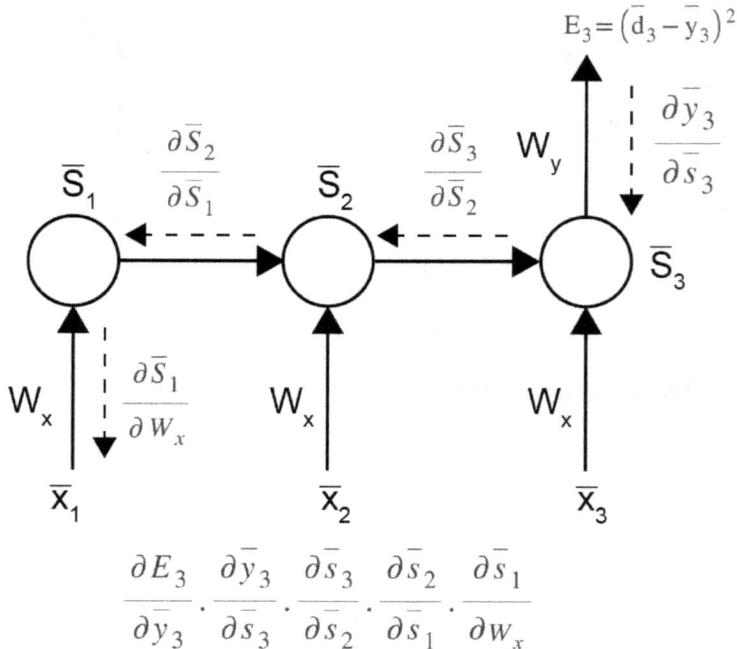

$$\frac{\partial E_3}{\partial \overline{y}_3} \cdot \frac{\partial \overline{y}_3}{\partial \overline{s}_3} \cdot \frac{\partial \overline{s}_3}{\partial \overline{s}_2} \cdot \frac{\partial \overline{s}_2}{\partial \overline{s}_1} \cdot \frac{\partial \overline{s}_1}{\partial w_x}$$

Figure 5.27: Back propagation of loss through weight matrix Wx with respect to S_1

Similar to the previous discussion, at **t=3**, we must consider the contribution of state **S₃** to the error, the contribution of state **S₂** to the error, and the contribution of state **S₁** to the error, **E₃**. The final value looks like this:

$$\frac{\partial E_3}{\partial W_x} = \begin{aligned} & \frac{\partial E_3}{\partial \bar{y}_3} \cdot \frac{\partial \bar{y}_3}{\partial \bar{s}_3} \cdot \frac{\partial \bar{s}_3}{\partial \bar{s}_2} \cdot \frac{\partial \bar{s}_2}{\partial W_x} \\[2em] + \ & \frac{\partial E_3}{\partial \bar{y}_3} \cdot \frac{\partial \bar{y}_3}{\partial \bar{s}_3} \cdot \frac{\partial \bar{s}_3}{\partial \bar{s}_2} \cdot \frac{\partial \bar{s}_2}{\partial W_x} \\[2em] + \ & \frac{\partial E_3}{\partial \bar{y}_3} \cdot \frac{\partial \bar{y}_3}{\partial \bar{s}_3} \cdot \frac{\partial \bar{s}_3}{\partial \bar{s}_2} \cdot \frac{\partial \bar{s}_2}{\partial \bar{s}_1} \cdot \frac{\partial \bar{s}_1}{\partial W_x} \end{aligned}$$

Figure 5.28: Sum of all derivatives of error with respect to Wx at t=3

In general, for timestep N, all the contributions of the previous timesteps need to be considered. So, the general formula looks as follows:

$$\frac{\partial E_N}{\partial W_X} = \sum_{i=1}^{N} \frac{\partial E_N}{\partial \bar{y}_N} \cdot \frac{\partial \bar{y}_N}{\partial \bar{S}_i} \cdot \frac{\partial \bar{S}_i}{\partial W_X}$$

Figure 5.29: General expression of derivative of error with respect to Wx

Since the chain of derivatives already has 5 multiplicative terms at **t=3**, this number grows to 22 multiplicative terms for timestep 20. It's possible that each of these derivatives could be either greater than 0 or less than 0. Due to consecutive multiplications with longer timesteps, the total derivative gets smaller or larger. This problem is either vanishing gradients or exploding gradients.

Gradients

The two types of gradients that have been identified are:

- Exploding gradients
- Vanishing gradients

Exploding Gradients

As the name indicates, this happens when gradients explode to much bigger values. This could be one of the problems that RNN architectures could encounter with larger timesteps. This could happen when each of the partial derivatives is larger than **1**, and multiplication of these partial derivatives leads to an even larger value. These larger gradient values cause a dramatic shift in the weight values each time they are adjusted using back propagation, leading to a network that doesn't learn well.

There are some techniques used to mitigate this issue, such as gradient clipping, wherein the gradient is normalized once it exceeds a set threshold.

Vanishing Gradients

Whether it is RNNs or CNNs, vanishing gradients could be a problem if calculated loss has to travel back a lot. In CNNs, this problem could occur when there are a lot of layers with activations such as sigmoid or tanh. The loss has to travel all the way back to the initial layers, and these activations generally dilute them by the time they reach the initial layers, which means there are almost no weight updates for the initial layers, resulting in underfitting. This is even common in RNNs, since even if a network has one RNN layer but a large number of timesteps, the loss has to travel all the way through the timesteps due to backpropagation through time. Since the gradients are multiplicative, as seen in the generalized derivative expressions earlier, these values tend to become low, and weights are not updated after a certain timestep. This means that even if more timesteps are shown to a network, the network can't benefit because the gradients cannot travel all the way back. This limitation in RNNs is due to vanishing gradients.

As the name indicates, this happens when the gradients become too small. This could happen when each of partial derivatives is smaller than 1 and multiplication of these partial derivatives leads to a much smaller value. With this geometric decay of information, the network cannot learn properly. There are almost no changes in the weight values, which leads to underfitting.

There must be a better mechanism to use to know what parts of the previous timesteps to remember, what to forget, and so on. To address this issue, architectures such as LSTM networks and GRUs were created.

RNNs with Keras

So far, we have discussed the theory behind RNNs, but there are a lot of frameworks available that can abstract away the implementation details. As long as we know how to use these frameworks, we can successfully get our projects working. **TensorFlow**, **Theano**, **Keras**, **PyTorch**, and **CNTK** are some of these frameworks. In this chapter, let's take a closer look at the most commonly used framework, called **Keras**. It uses either Tensorflow or Theano as the backend, indicating that it creates an even higher level of abstraction than other frameworks. It is a tool best suited for beginners. Once comfortable with Keras, tools such as TensorFlow give much more power in implementing custom functions.

There are many variants of RNNs that you will study in the next few chapters, but all of them use the same base class, called RNN:

```
keras.layers.RNN(cell, return_sequences=False, return_state=False, go_
backwards=False, stateful=False, unroll=False)
```

In this chapter, we have discussed the simple form of the RNN, which is called **SimpleRNN** in Keras:

```
keras.layers.SimpleRNN(units, activation='tanh', use_bias=True, kernel_
initializer='glorot_uniform', recurrent_initializer='orthogonal', bias_
initializer='zeros', kernel_regularizer=None, recurrent_regularizer=None,
bias_regularizer=None, activity_regularizer=None, kernel_constraint=None,
recurrent_constraint=None, bias_constraint=None, dropout=0.0, recurrent_
dropout=0.0, return_sequences=False, return_state=False, go_backwards=False,
stateful=False, unroll=False)
```

As you can see from the arguments here, there are two kinds: one for regular kernels, used to compute the outputs of a layer, and the other for recurrent kernels used to compute states. Don't worry too much about constraints, regularizers, initializers, and dropout. You can find more about them at https://keras.io/layers/recurrent/. They are mostly used to avoid overfitting. The role of activation here is the same as the role of activation with any other layer.

The units are the number of recurrent units in a particular layer. The greater the number of units, the more parameters there are that need to be learned.

return_sequences is the argument that specifies whether the RNN layer should return the whole sequence or just the last timestep. If **return_sequences** is false, the output of the RNN layer is just the last timestep, so we cannot stack this with another RNN layer. In other words, if an RNN layer needs to be stacked by another RNN layer, **return_sequences** need to be true. If an RNN layer is connected to the Dense layer, this can argument can be either true or false, depending on the application.

The **return_state** argument specifies whether the last state of the RNN needs to be returned along with the output. This can be set to either True or False, depending on the application.

go_backwards can be used if, for any reason, the input sequence needs to be processed backward. Keep a note that if this is set to True, even the returned sequence is reversed.

stateful is an argument that can be set to true if a state needs to be passed between batches. If this argument is set to true, the data needs to be handled carefully; we have a topic covering this in detail.

unroll is an argument that leads to the network being unrolled if set to true, which can speed up operations but can be very memory extensive depending on the timesteps. Generally, this argument is set to true for short sequences.

The number of timesteps is not an argument for a particular layer since it stays the same for the whole network, which is represented in the input shape. This brings us to the important point of the shape of the network when using RNNs:

Input_shape

3D tensor with shape (batch_size, timesteps, input_dim)

Output_shape

If return_sequences is true, 3D tensor with shape (batch_size, timesteps, units)

If return_sequences is false, 2D tensor with shape (batch_size, units)

If return_state is True, a list of 2 tensors, 1 is output tensor same as above depending on return_sequences, the other is state tensor of shape (batch_size, units)

> **Note**
>
> If you start building a network with an RNN layer, **input_shape** must be specified.

After a model is built, `model.summary()` can be used to see the shapes of each layer and the total number of parameters.

Exercise 23: Building an RNN Model to Show the Stability of Parameters over Time

Let's build a simple RNN model to show that the parameters do not change with timesteps. Note that while mentioning the **input_shape** argument, **batch_size** need not be mentioned unless needed. It is needed for a stateful network, which we will discuss next. **batch_size** is mentioned while training the model with the fit() or **fit_generator()** functions.

The following steps will help you with the solution:

1. Import the necessary Python packages. We will be using Sequential, SimpleRNN, and Dense.

    ```
    from keras.models import Sequential
    from keras.layers import SimpleRNN, Dense
    ```

2. Next, we define the model and its layers:

```
model = Sequential()
# Recurrent layer
model.add(SimpleRNN(64, input_shape=(10,100), return_sequences=False))
# Fully connected layer
model.add(Dense(64, activation='relu'))
# Output layer
model.add(Dense(100, activation='softmax'))
```

3. You can check the summary of the model:

```
model.summary()
```

model.summary() gives the following output:

```
Layer (type)                  Output Shape             Param #
=================================================================
simple_rnn_1 (SimpleRNN)      (None, 64)               10560
_____
dense_1 (Dense)               (None, 64)               4160
_____
dense_2 (Dense)               (None, 100)              6500
=================================================================
Total params: 21,220
Trainable params: 21,220
Non-trainable params: 0
_____
```

Figure 5.30: Model summary for model layers

In this case, **None** is the **batch_size** parameter, which will be provided by the **fit()** function. The output of the RNN layer is **(None, 64)** since it is not returning the sequence.

4. Let's look at the model that returns sequence:

```
model = Sequential()
# Recurrent layer
model.add(SimpleRNN(64, input_shape=(10,100), return_sequences=True))
# Fully connected layer
model.add(Dense(64, activation='relu'))
```

```
# Output layer
model.add(Dense(100, activation='softmax'))

model.summary()
```

The summary of the model that returns sequence looks like this:

```
Layer (type)                    Output Shape              Param #
=================================================================
simple_rnn_3 (SimpleRNN)        (None, 10, 64)            10560

dense_5 (Dense)                 (None, 10, 64)            4160

dense_6 (Dense)                 (None, 10, 100)           6500
=================================================================
Total params: 21,220
Trainable params: 21,220
Non-trainable params: 0
```

Figure 5.31: Model summary of sequence-returning model

Now the RNN layer is returning a sequence, and therefore its output shape is 3D instead of 2D, as seen earlier. Also, note that the **Dense** layer is automatically adjusted to this change in its input. The **Dense** layer with the current Keras version has the capability of adjusting to time_steps from a previous RNN layer. In the previous versions of Keras, **TimeDistributed(Dense)** was used to achieve this.

5. We have previously discussed how the RNN shares its parameters over timesteps. Let's see that in action and change the timesteps of the previous model from 10 to 1,000:

```
model = Sequential()
# Recurrent layer
model.add(SimpleRNN(64, input_shape=(1000,100), return_sequences=True))
```

```
# Fully connected layer
model.add(Dense(64, activation='relu'))
# Output layer
model.add(Dense(100, activation='softmax'))

model.summary()
```

Layer (type)	Output Shape	Param #
simple_rnn_5 (SimpleRNN)	(None, 1000, 64)	10560
dense_9 (Dense)	(None, 1000, 64)	4160
dense_10 (Dense)	(None, 1000, 100)	6500

```
Total params: 21,220
Trainable params: 21,220
Non-trainable params: 0
```

Figure 5.32: Model summary for timesteps

Clearly, the output shapes of the network changed to this new time_steps. However, there is no change in the parameters between the two models.

This indicates that the parameters are shared over time and are not impacted by changing the number of timesteps. Note that the same is applicable to the **Dense** layer when operating on more than one timestep.

Stateful versus Stateless

There are two modes of operation available with RNNs considering the states: the stateless and stateful modes. If the **argument stateful=True**, you are working with stateful mode, and **False** signifies stateless mode.

Stateless mode is basically saying that one example in a batch is not related to any example in the next batch; that is, every example is independent in the given case. The state is reset after every example. Each example has a certain number of timesteps depending on the model architecture. For example, the last model we saw had 1,000 timesteps, and between these 1000 timesteps, the state vector was calculated and passed from one timestep to the next. However, at the end of the example or the beginning of the next example, there was no state passed. Each example was independent and therefore there was no consideration needed regarding the way the data was shuffled.

In stateful mode, the state from example **i** of **batch 1** is passed to the **i+1** example of **batch 2**. This means that the state is passed from one example to the next among batches. For this reason, the examples must be contiguous across batches and cannot be random. The following figure explains this situation. The examples **i**, **i+1**, **i+2**, and so on are contiguous, and so are **j**, **j+1**, **j+2**, and so on, and **k**, **k+1**, **k+2**, and so on.

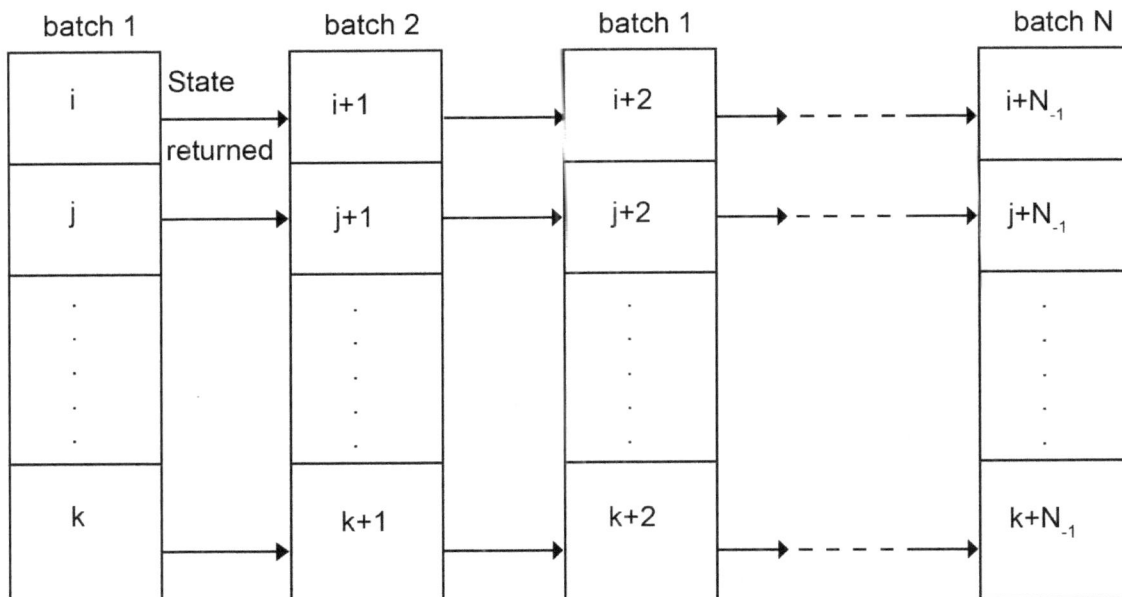

Figure 5.33 Batch formations for stateful RNN

Exercise 24: Turning a Stateless Network into a Stateful Network by Only Changing Arguments

In order to turn a network from stateless to stateful by changing the arguments, the following steps should be taken.

1. First, we would need to import the required Python packages:

```
from keras.models import Sequential
from keras.layers import SimpleRNN, Dense
```

2. Next, build the model using **Sequential** and define the layers:

```
model = Sequential()
# Recurrent layer
model.add(SimpleRNN(64, input_shape=(1000,100), return_sequences=True,
stateful=False))
# Fully connected layer
```

```
model.add(Dense(64, activation='relu'))
# Output layer
model.add(Dense(100, activation='softmax'))

model.summary()
```

3. Set the optimizer to **Adam**, set **categorical crosstropy** as the loss parameter, and set the metrics to fit the model. Compile the model and fit the model over 100 epochs:

```
model.compile(optimizer='adam', loss='categorical_crossentropy',
metrics=['accuracy'])
model.fit(X, Y, batch_size=32, epochs=100, shuffle=True)
```

4. Assume that **X** and **Y** are training data as contiguous examples. Turn this model into a stateful one:

```
model = Sequential()
# Recurrent layer
model.add(SimpleRNN(64, input_shape=(1000,100), return_sequences=True,
stateful=True))
# Fully connected layer
model.add(Dense(64, activation='relu'))
# Output layer
model.add(Dense(100, activation='softmax'))
```

5. Set the optimizer to **Adam**, set **categorical crossentropy** as the loss parameter, and set the metrics to fit the model. Compile the model and fit the model over 100 epochs:

```
model.compile(optimizer='adam', loss='categorical_crossentropy',
metrics=['accuracy'])
model.fit(X, Y, batch_size=1, epochs=100, shuffle=False)
```

6. You can use a box and whisker plot to visualize the output.

```
results.boxplot()
pyplot.show()
```

Expected output:

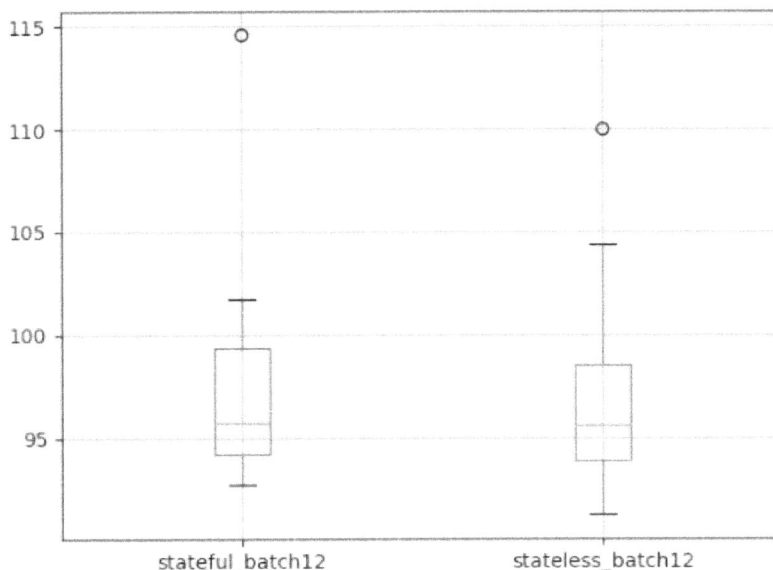

Figure 5.34: Box and whisker plot for stateful vs stateless

> **Note**
>
> The output may vary depending on the data used.

From the concept of stateful models, we understand that the data fed in batches need to be contiguous, so turn randomization **OFF**. However, even with **batch_size >1**, the data across batches will not be contiguous, so make **batch_size=1**. By turning the network to **stateful=True** and fitting it with the mentioned parameters, we are essentially training the model correctly in a stateful manner.

However, we are not using the concept of mini batch gradient descent, and nor are we shuffling the data. So, a generator needs to be implemented that can carefully train a stateful network, which is outside the scope of this chapter.

`model.compile` is a function where an optimizer and a loss function are assigned to the network, along with the metrics that we care about.

`model.fit()` is a function that is used to train a model by specifying its training data, validation data, the number of epochs, the batch size, the mode of shuffling, and more.

Activity 6: Solving a Problem with an RNN – Author Attribution

Author attribution is a classic text classification problem that comes under the umbrella of natural language processing (NLP). Authorship attribution is a well-studied problem that led to the field of **stylometry**.

In this problem, we are given a set of documents from certain authors. We need to train a model to understand the authors' styles and use the model to identify the authors of the unknown documents. As with many other NLP problems, it has benefited greatly from the increase in available computer power, data, and advanced machine learning techniques. This makes authorship attribution a natural candidate for the use of **deep learning (DL)**. In particular, we can benefit from DL's ability to automatically extract the relevant features for a specific problem.

In this activity, we will focus on the following:

1. Extracting character-level features from the text of each author (to get each author's style)

2. Using those features to build a classification model for authorship attribution

3. Applying the model for identifying the author of a set of unknown documents

> **Note**
>
> You can find the required data for the activity at https://github.com/ TrainingByPackt/Deep-Learning-for-Natural-Language-Processing/tree/master/ Lesson%2005.

The following steps will help you with the solution.

1. Import the necessary Python packages.

2. Upload the text document to be used. Then, pre-process the text file by converting all text into lowercase, converting all newlines and multiple whitespaces into single whitespaces, and removing any mention of the authors' names, otherwise we risk data leakage.

3. To break the long texts into smaller sequences, we use the **Tokenizer** class from the Keras framework.

4. Proceed to create the training and validation sets.

5. We construct the model graph and perform the training procedure.

6. Apply the model to the unknown papers. Do this for all the papers in the **Unknown** folder.

   Expected output:

```
Paper 5 is predicted to have been written by Author A, 6142 to 5612
Paper 4 is predicted to have been written by Author B, 5215 to 4558
Paper 1 is predicted to have been written by Author B, 13924 to 6850
Paper 3 is predicted to have been written by Author B, 7620 to 5764
Paper 2 is predicted to have been written by Author B, 12840 to 6806
```

Figure 5.35: Output for author attribution

> **Note**
>
> The solution for the activity can be found on page 309.

Summary

In this chapter, we were introduced to RNNs and covered the major differences between the architectures of RNNs and FFNNs. We looked at BPTT and how weight matrices are updated. We learned how to use RNNs using Keras and solved a problem of author attribution using RNNs in Keras. We looked at the shortcomings of RNNs by looking at vanishing gradients and exploding gradients. In the next chapters, we will look into architectures that will address these issues.

6

Gated Recurrent Units (GRUs)

Learning Objectives

By the end of this chapter, you will be able to:

- Assess the drawback of simple Recurrent Neural Networks (RNNs)
- Describe the architecture of Gated Recurrent Units (GRUs)
- Perform sentiment analysis using GRUs
- Apply GRUs for text generation

The chapter aims to provide a solution to the existing drawbacks of the current architecture of RNNs.

Introduction

In previous chapters, we studied text processing techniques such as word embedding, tokenization, and Term Frequency Inverse Document Frequency (TFIDF). We also learned about a specific network architecture called a Recurrent Neural Network (RNN) that has the drawback of vanishing gradients.

In this chapter, we are going to study a mechanism that deals with vanishing gradients by using a methodical approach of adding memory to the network. Essentially, the gates that are used in GRUs are vectors that decide what information should be passed onto the next stage of the network. This, in turn, helps the network to generate output accordingly.

A basic RNN generally consists of an input layer, output layer, and several interconnected hidden layers. The following diagram displays the basic architecture of an RNN:

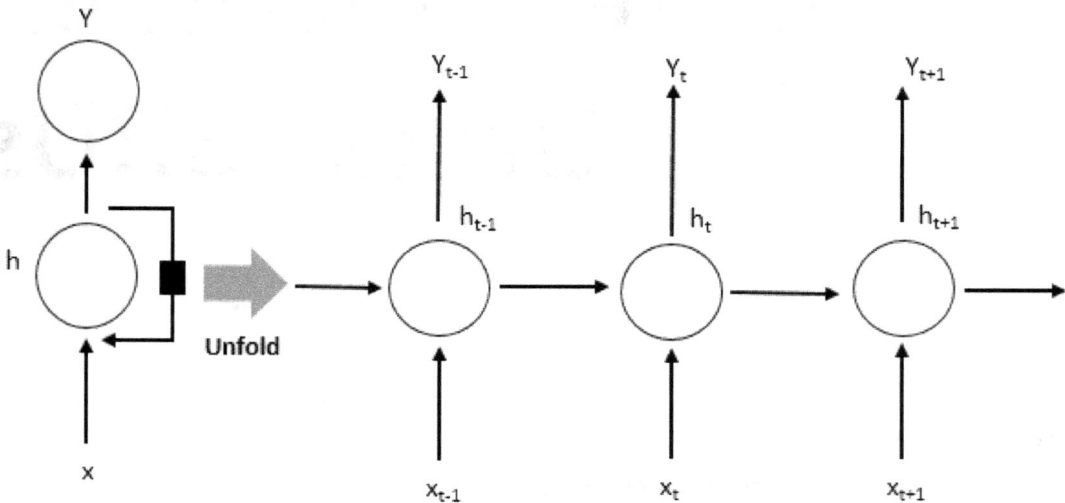

Figure 6.1: A basic RNN

RNNs, in their simplest form, suffer from a drawback, that is, their inability to retain long-term relationships in the sequence. To rectify this flaw, a special layer called Gated Recurrent Unit (GRU) needs to be added to the simple RNN network.

In this chapter, we will first explore the reason behind the inability of Simple RNNs to retain long term dependencies, followed by the introduction of the GRU layer and how it attempts to solve this specific issue. We will then go on to build a network with the GRU layer included.

The Drawback of Simple RNNs

Let's take a look at a simple example in order to revisit the concept of vanishing gradients.

Essentially, you wish to generate an English poem using an RNN. Here, you set up a simple RNN to do your bidding and it ends up producing the following sentence:

"The flowers, despite it being autumn, blooms like a star".

One can easily spot the grammatical error here. The word 'blooms' should be 'bloom' since at the beginning of the sentence, the word 'flowers' indicates that you should be using the plural form of the word 'bloom' to bring about the subject-verb agreement in the sentence. A simple RNN fails at this job because it is incapable of retaining any information about a dependency between the word 'flowers' that occurs early in the sentence and the word 'blooms', which occurs much later (theoretically, it should be able to!).

A **GRU** helps to solve this issue by eliminating the 'vanishing gradient' problem that hinders the learning ability of the network where long-term relationships within the text are not preserved by the network. In the following sections, we'll focus our attention on understanding the vanishing gradient problem and discuss how a GRU resolves the issue in more detail

Let's now recall how a neural network learns. In the training phase, the inputs get propagated, layer by layer, up to the output layer. Since we know the exact value that the output should be producing for a given input during training, we calculate the error between the expected output and the output obtained. This error is then fed into a cost function (which varies depending on the problem and the creativity of the network developer). Now, the next step is to calculate the gradient of this cost function with respect to every parameter of the network, starting from the layer nearest to the output layer right down to the bottom layer where the input layer is present:

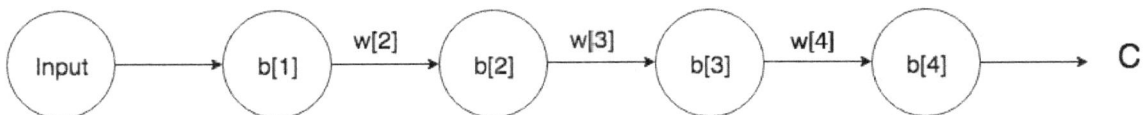

Figure 6.2: A simple neural network

Consider a very simple neural network with only four layers and only one connection between each layer and one single output, as shown in the preceding diagram. Note that you will never use such a network in practice; it is presented here only for demonstrating the concept of vanishing gradients.

Now, to calculate the gradient of the cost function with respect to the bias term of the first hidden layer (b[1]), the following calculation needs to be carried out:

$$\text{grad}(C, b[1]) = d(z[1]) * w[2] * d(z[2]) * w[3] * d(z[3]) * w[4] * d(z[4]) * \text{grad}(C, a[4])$$

Figure 6.3: Gradient calculation using chain rule

Here, each element can be explained as follows:

grad(x, y) = the gradient of x with respect to y

d(var) = the derivative of 'sigmoid' of the 'var' variable

w[i] = the weight of the 'i' layer

b[i] = the bias term in the 'i' layer

a[i] = the activation function of the 'i' layer

z[j] = w[j]*a[j-1] + b[j]

The preceding expression can be attributed to the chain rule of differentiation.

The preceding equation involves the multiplication of several terms. If the values of most of these terms are a fraction between -1 and 1, the multiplication of such fractions will yield a term with a very small value at the end. In the preceding example, the value of grad(C,b[1]) will a very small fraction. The problem here is, this gradient is the term that will be used to update the value of b[1] for the next iteration:

$$b[1] = b[1] + \text{lambda}*\text{grad}(C, b[1])$$

Figure 6.4: Updating value of b[1] using the gradient

Note

There could be several ways of performing an update using different optimizers, but the concept remains essentially the same.

The consequence of this action is that the value of b[1] hardly changes from the last iteration, which leads to a very slow learning progress. In a real-world network, which might be several layers deep, this update will be still smaller. Hence, the deeper the network, the more severe the problem with gradients. Another observation made here is that the layers that are closer to the output layer learn quicker than those that are closer to the input layer since there are fewer multiplication terms. This also leads to an asymmetry in learning, leading to the instability of the gradients.

So, what bearing does this issue have on simple RNNs? Recall the structure of RNNs;. it is essentially an unfolding of layers in time with as many layers as there are words (for a modelling problem). The learning proceeds through Backpropagation Through Time (BPTT), which is exactly the same as the regime that was described previously. The only difference is that the same parameters are updated in every layer. The later layers correspond to the words that appear later in the sentence, while the earlier layers are those that correspond to the words appearing earlier in the sentence. With vanishing gradients, the earlier layers do not change much from their initial values and, hence, they fail to have much effect on the later layers. The more far-back-in-time a layer is from a given layer at time, 't', the less influential it is for determining the output of the layer at 't'. Hence, in our example sentence, the network struggles to learn that the word 'flowers' is plural, which results in the wrong form of the word 'bloom' being used.

The Exploding Gradient Problem

As it turns out, gradients not only vanish but they can explode as well – that is, early layers can learn too quickly with a large deviation in values from one training iteration to the next, while the gradients of the later layers don't change very quickly. How can this happen? Well, revisiting our equation, if the value of individual terms is much larger than the magnitude of 1, a multiplicative effect results in the gradients becoming huge. This leads to a destabilization of the gradients and causes issues with learning.

Ultimately, the problem is one of unstable gradients. In practice, the vanishing gradients problem is much more common and harder to solve than the exploding gradients problem.

Fortunately, the exploding gradient problem has a robust solution: clipping. Clipping simply refers to stopping the value of gradients from growing beyond a predefined value. If the value is not clipped, you will begin seeing NaNs (Not a Number) for the gradients and weights of the network due to the representational overflow of computers. Providing a ceiling for the value will help to avoid this issue. Note that clipping only curbs the magnitude of the gradient, but not its direction. So, the learning still proceeds in the correct direction. A simple visualization of the effect of gradient clipping can be seen in the following diagram:

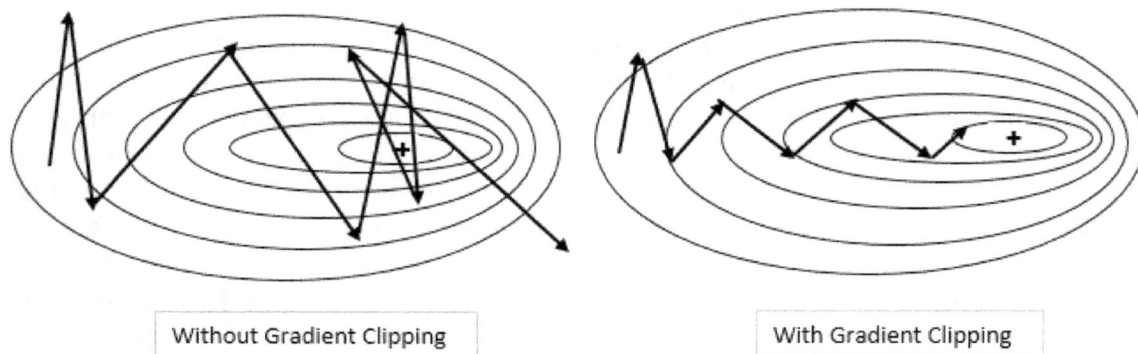

Without Gradient Clipping · With Gradient Clipping

Figure 6.5: Clipping gradients to combat the explosion of gradients

Gated Recurrent Units (GRUs)

GRUs help the network to remember long-term dependencies in an explicit manner. This is achieved by introducing more variables in the structure of a simple RNN.

So, what will help us to get rid of the vanishing gradients problem? Intuitively speaking, if we allow the network to transfer most of the knowledge from the activation function of the previous timesteps, then an error can be backpropagated more faithfully than a simple RNN case. If you are familiar with residual networks for image classification, then you will recognize this function as being similar to that of a skip connection. Allowing the gradient to backpropagate without vanishing enables the network to learn more uniformly across layers and, hence, eliminates the issue of gradient instability:

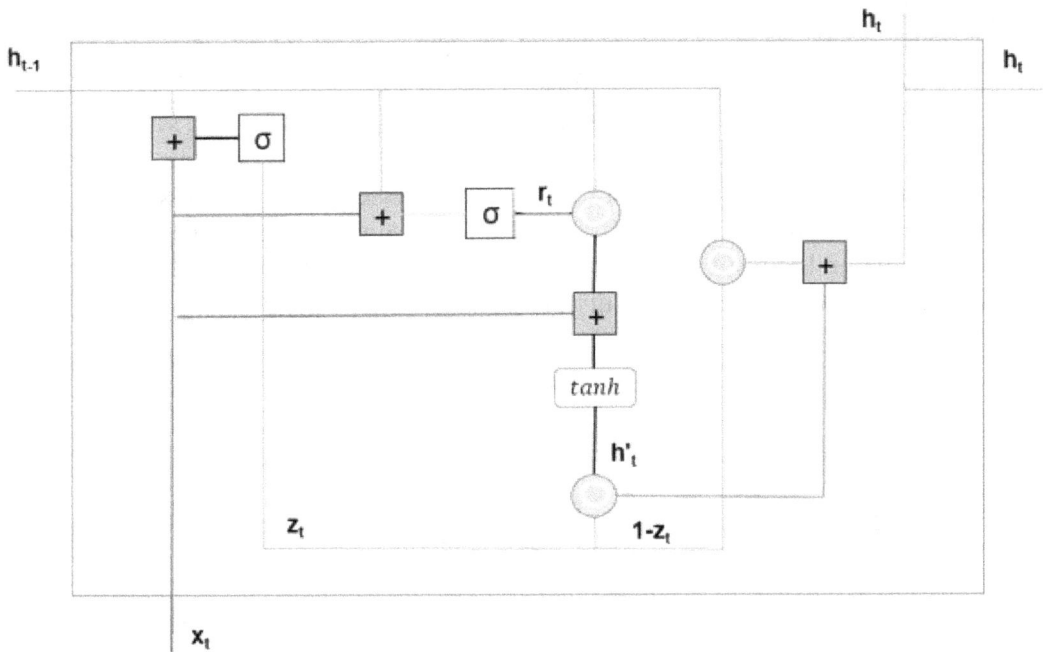

Figure 6.6: The full GRU structure

The different signs in the preceding diagram are as follows:

| "plus" operation | "sigmoid" function | "Hadamard product" operation | "tanh" function |

Figure 6.7: The meanings of the different signs in the GRU diagram

> **Note**
>
> The Hadamard product operation is an elementwise matrix multiplication.

The preceding diagram has all its components exploited by a GRU. You can observe the activation functions, h, represented at different timesteps (**h[t]**, **h[t-1]**). The **r[t]** term refers to the reset gate and **z[t]** term refers to the update gate. The **h'[t]** term refers to a candidate function, which we'll represent using the **h_candidate[t]** variable in the equation for the purpose of being explicit. The GRU layer uses the update gate to decide on the amount of previous information that can be passed onto the next activation, while it uses the reset gate to determine the amount of previous information to forget. In this section, we shall examine each of these terms in detail and explore how they help the network to remember long-term relations in the text structure.

The expression for the activation function (hidden layer) for the next layer is as follows:

$$h[t] = hadamard\{z[t], \ h[t\text{-}1]\} + hadamard\{(1 - z[t]) \ * \ h\_candidate[t]\}$$

Figure 6.8: The expression for the activation function for the next layer in terms of the candidate activation function

The activation function is, therefore, a weighing of the activation from the previous timestep and a candidate activation function for this timestep. The **z[t]** function is a sigmoid function and, hence, it takes a value between 0 and 1. In most practical cases, the value is closer to 0 or 1. Before going into the preceding expression in more depth, let's take a moment to observe the effect of the introduction of a weighted summing scheme for updating the activation function. If the value of **z[t]** remains 1 for several timesteps, then that means the value of the activation function at a very early timestep can still be propagated to a much later timestep. This, in turn, provides the network with a memory.

Additionally, observe how this is different to a simple RNN, where the value of the activation function is overwritten at every timestep without an explicit weighing of the previous timestep activation (the contribution of the previous activation in a simple RNN is present within the nonlinearity and, hence, is implicit).

Types of Gates

Let's now expand on the previous equation for the activation update in the following sections.

The Update Gate

The update gate is represented by the following diagram. As you can see from the full GRU diagram, only the relevant parts are highlighted. The purpose of the update gate is to determine the amount of information that needs to be passed on from the previous timesteps to the next step activation. To understand the diagram and the function of the update gate, consider the following expression for calculating the update gate:

$$z[t] = \text{sigmoid}(W\_z * x[t] + U\_z * h[t-1])$$

Figure 6.9: The expression for calculating the update gate

The following figure shows a graphical representation of the update gate:

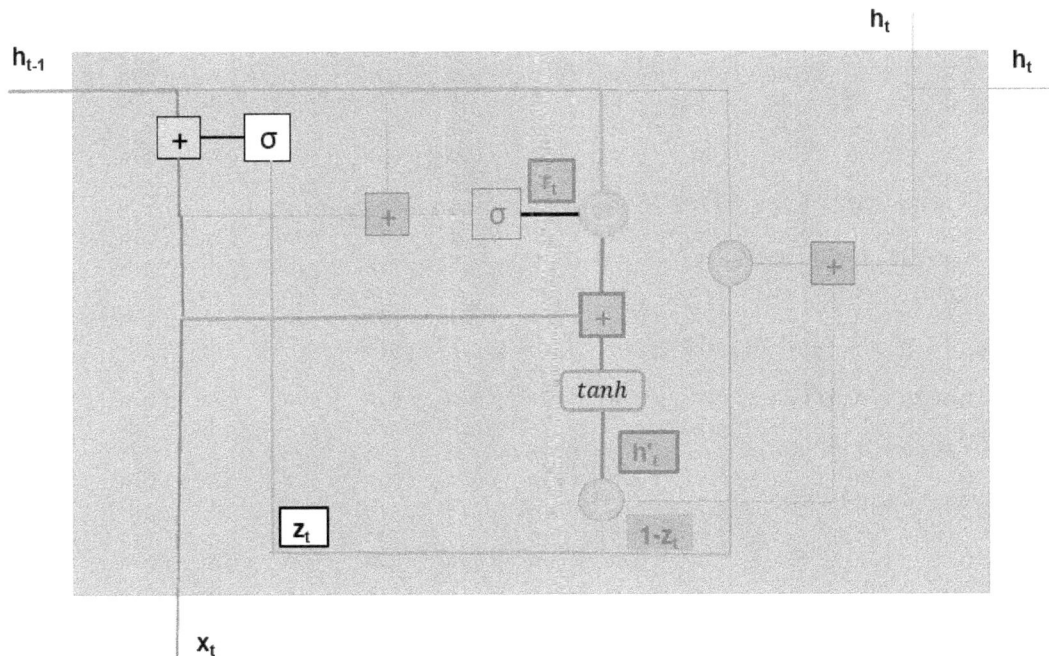

Figure 6.10: The update gate in a full GRU diagram

The number of hidden states is **n_h** (the dimensionality of **h**), while the number of input dimensions is n_x. The input at timestep t (**x[t]**), is multiplied by a new set of weights, **W_z**, using the dimensions (**n_h, n_x**). The activation function from the previous timestep, (**h[t-1]**), is multiplied by another new set of weights, **U_z**, using the dimensions (**n_h, n_h**).

Note that the multiplications here are matrix multiplications. These two terms are then added together and passed through a sigmoid function to squish the output, **z[t]**, within a range of [0,1]. The **z[t]** output has the same dimensions as the activation function, that is, (**n_h, 1**). The **W_z** and **U_z** parameters also need to be learned using BPTT. Let's write a simple Python snippet to aid in our understanding of the update gate:

```python
import numpy as np


# Write a sigmoid function to be used later in the program
def sigmoid(x):
    return 1 / (1 + np.exp(-x))


n_x = 5 # Dimensionality of input vector
n_h = 3 # Number of hidden units


# Define an input at time 't' having a dimensionality of n_x
x_t = np.random.randn(n_x, 1)


# Define W_z, U_z and h_prev (last time step activation)
W_z = np.random.randn(n_h,  n_x) # n_h = 3, n_x=5
U_z = np.random.randn(n_h, n_h) # n_h = 3
h_prev = np.random.randn(n_h, 1)
```

```
x_t

array([[-0.93576943],
        [-0.26788808],
        [ 0.53035547],
        [-0.69166075],
        [-0.39675353]])


h_prev

array([[ 0.90085595],
        [-0.68372786],
        [-0.12289023]])


W_z

array([[ 1.62434536, -0.61175641, -0.52817175, -1.07296862,  0.86540763],
        [-2.3015387 ,  1.74481176, -0.7612069 ,  0.3190391 , -0.24937038],
        [ 1.46210794, -2.06014071, -0.3224172 , -0.38405435,  1.13376944]])


U_z

array([[-1.09989127, -0.17242821, -0.87785842],
        [ 0.04221375,  0.58281521, -1.10061918],
        [ 1.14472371,  0.90159072,  0.50249434]])
```

Figure 6.11: A screenshot displaying the weights and activation functions

Following is the code snippet for update gate expression:

```
# Calculate expression for update gate

z_t = sigmoid(np.matmul(W_z, x_t) + np.matmul(U_z, h_prev))
```

In the previous code snippet, we initialised the random values for **x[t]**, **W_z**, **U_z**, and **h_prev** in order to demonstrate the calculation of **z[t]** . In a real network, these variables will have more relevant values.

The Reset Gate

The reset gate is represented by the following diagram. As you can see from the full GRU diagram, only the relevant parts are highlighted. The purpose of the reset gate is to determine the amount of information from the previous timestep that should be forgotten in order to calculate the next step activation. In order to understand the diagram and the function of the reset gate, consider the following expression for calculating the reset gate:

$$r[t] = sigmoid(W\_r * x[t] + U\_r * h[t-1])$$

Figure 6.12: The expression for calculating the reset gate

The following figure shows a graphical representation of the reset gate:

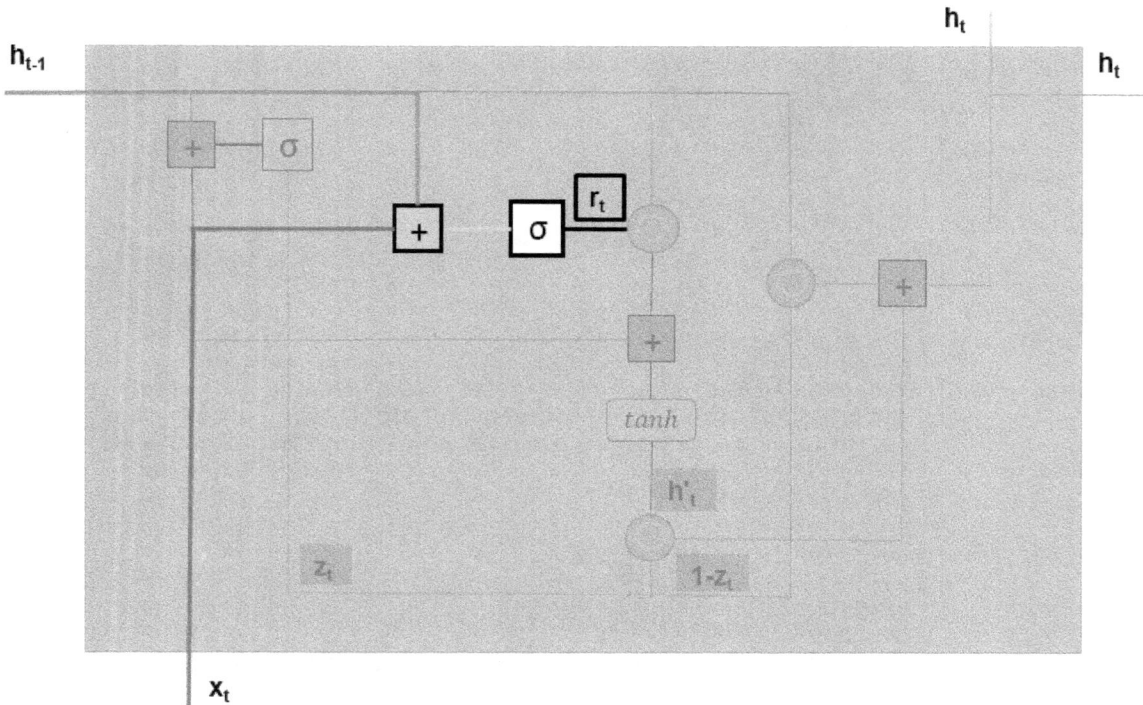

Figure 6.13: The reset gate

The input at timestep, **t**, is multiplied by the weights, **W_r**, using the dimensions (**n_h, n_x**). The activation function from the previous timestep, (**h[t-1]**), is then multiplied by another new set of weights, **U_r**, using the dimensions (**n_h, n_h**). Note that the multiplications here are matrix multiplications. These two terms are then added together and passed through a sigmoid function to squish the r[t] output within a range of **[0,1]**. The **r[t]** output has the same dimensions as the activation function, that is, (**n_h, 1**).

The **W_r** and **U_r** parameters also need to be learned using BPTT. Let's take a look at how to calculate the reset gate expression in Python:

```
# Define W_r, U_r
W_r = np.random.randn(n_h,  n_x) # n_h = 3, n_x=5
U_r = np.random.randn(n_h, n_h) # n_h = 3


# Calculate expression for update gate
r_t = sigmoid(np.matmul(W_r, x_t) + np.matmul(U_r, h_prev))
```

In the preceding snippet, the values of the **x_t**, **h_prev**, **n_h**, and **n_x** variables have been used from the update gate code snippet. Note that the values of **r_t** may not be particularly close to either 0 or 1 since it is an example. In a well-trained network, the values are expected to be close to 0 or 1:

```
W_r

array([[-0.6871727 , -0.84520564, -0.67124613, -0.0126646 , -1.11731035],
       [ 0.2344157 ,  1.65980218,  0.74204416, -0.19183555, -0.88762896],
       [-0.74715829,  1.6924546 ,  0.05080775, -0.63699565,  0.19091548]])


U_r

array([[ 2.10025514,  0.12015895,  0.61720311],
       [ 0.30017032, -0.35224985, -1.1425182 ],
       [-0.34934272, -0.20889423,  0.58662319]])
```

Figure 6.14: A screenshot displaying the values of the weights

```
r_t

array([[0.93699927],
       [0.70392511],
       [0.5971474 ]])
```

Figure 6.15: A screenshot displaying the r_t output

The Candidate Activation Function

A candidate activation function for replacing the previous timestep activation function is also calculated at every timestep. As the name suggests, the candidate activation function represents an alternative value that the next timestep activation function should take. Take a look at the expression for calculating the candidate activation function, as follows:

$$h\_candidate[t] = tanh(W * x[t] + U * hadamard\{r[t], h[t-1]\})$$

Figure 6.16: The expression for calculating the candidate activation function

The following figure shows a graphical representation of the candidate activation function:

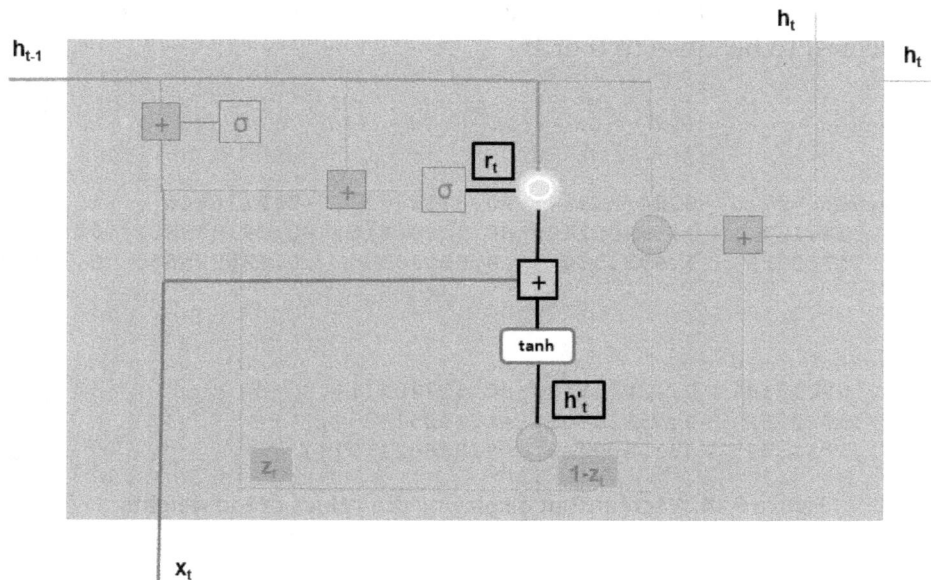

Figure 6.17: The candidate activation function

The input at timestep, t, is multiplied by the weights, W, using the dimensions (**n_h, n_x**). The W matrix serves the same purpose as the matrix that is used in a simple RNN. Then, an element-wise multiplication is carried out between the reset gate and the activation function from the previous timestep, (**h[t-1]**). This operation is referred to as 'hadamard multiplication'. The result of this multiplication is matrix-multiplied by U using the dimensions (**n_h, n_h**). The U matrix is the same matrix that is used with a simple RNN. These two terms are then added together and passed through a hyperbolic tan function to squish the output **h_candidate[t]** within a range of [-1,1]. The **h_candidate[t]** output has the same dimensions as the activation function, that is, (**n_h, 1**):

```
# Define W, U
W = np.random.randn(n_h,  n_x) # n_h = 3, n_x=5
U = np.random.randn(n_h, n_h) # n_h = 3
```

```
# Calculate h_candidate
h_candidate = np.tanh(np.matmul(W, x_t) + np.matmul(U,np.multiply(r_t, h_
prev)))
```

Again, the same values for the variables have been used as in the calculation of the update and reset gate. Note that the Hadamard matrix multiplication has been implemented using the NumPy function, 'multiply':

```
W

array([[ 0.83898341,  0.93110208,  0.28558733,  0.88514116, -0.75439794],
       [ 1.25286816,  0.51292982, -0.29809284,  0.48851815, -0.07557171],
       [ 1.13162939,  1.51981682,  2.18557541, -1.39649634, -1.44411381]])


U

array([[-0.50446586,  0.16003707,  0.57616892],
       [ 0.31563495, -2.02220122, -0.30620401],
       [ 0.82797464,  0.23009474,  0.76201118]])
```

Figure 6.18: A screenshot displaying how the W and U weights are defined

The following figure shows a graphical representation of the **h_candidate** function:

```
h_candidate

array([[-0.94284959],
       [-0.47277196],
       [ 0.9429634 ]])
```

Figure 6.19: A screenshot displaying the value of h_candidate

Now, since the values of the update gate, the reset gate, and the candidate activation function have been calculated, we can code up the expression for the current activation function that will be passed onto the next layer:

```
# Calculate h_new
h_new = np.multiply(z_t, h_prev) + np.multiply((1-z_t), h_candidate)
```

```
h_new

array([[-0.72356608],
       [-0.62428489],
       [ 0.61671542]])
```

Figure 6.20: A screenshot displaying the value of the current activation function

Mathematically speaking, the update gate serves the purpose of selecting a weighting between the previous activation function and the candidate activation function. Hence, it is responsible for the final update of the activation function for the current timestep and in determining how much of the previous activation function and candidate activation function will pass onto the next layer. The reset gate acts as a way to select or unselect the parts of the previous activation function. This is why an element-wise multiplication is carried out between the previous activation function and the reset gate vector. Consider our previous example of the poem generation sentence:

"The flowers, despite it being autumn, blooms like a star."

A reset gate will serve to remember that the word 'flowers' affect the plurality of the word 'bloom,' which occurs toward the end of the sentence. Hence, the particular value in the reset gate vector that is responsible for remembering the plurality or singularity of the word will hold a value that is closer to the values of 0 or 1. If a 0 value denotes that the word is singular, then, in our case, the reset gate will hold the value of 1 in order to remember that the word 'bloom' should now hold the plural form. Different values in the reset gate vector will remember different relations within the complex structure of the sentence.

As another example, consider the following sentence:

"The food from France was delicious, but French people were also very accommodating."

Examining the structure of the sentence, we can see that there are several complex relations that need to be kept in mind:

- The word 'food' corresponds with the word 'delicious' (here, 'delicious' can only be used in the context of 'food').

- The word 'France' corresponds with 'French' people.

- The word 'people' and 'were' are related to each other; that is, the use of the word 'people' dictates that the correct form of 'was' is used.

In a well-trained network, the reset gate will have an entry in its vector for all such relations. The value of these entries will be suitably turned 'off' or 'on' depending on which relationship needs to be remembered from the previous activations and which needs to be forgotten. In practice, it is difficult to ascribe an entry of the reset gate or hidden state to a particular function. The interpretability of deep learning networks is, hence, a hot research topic.

GRU Variations

The form of GRU just described form of a GRU is the full GRU. Several independent researchers have utilized different forms of GRU, such as by removing the reset gate entirely or by using activation functions. The full GRU is, however, still the most used approach.

Sentiment Analysis with GRU

Sentiment analysis is a popular use case for applying natural language processing techniques. The aim of sentiment analysis is to determine whether a given piece of text can be considered as conveying a 'positive' sentiment or a 'negative' sentiment. For example, consider the following text reviewing a book:

"The book had its moments of glory, but seemed to be missing the point quite frequently. An author of such calibre certainly had more in him than what was delivered through this particular work."

To a human reader, it is perfectly clear that the mentioned book review conveys a negative sentiment. So, how would you go about building a machine learning model for the classification of sentiments? As always, for using a supervised learning approach, a text corpus containing several samples is needed. Each piece of text in this corpus should have a label indicating whether the text can be mapped to a positive or a negative sentiment. The next step will be to build a machine learning model using this data.

Observing the example sentence, you can already see that such a task could be challenging for a machine learning model to solve. If a simple tokenization or TFIDF approach is used, the words such as 'glory' and 'calibre' would be easily misunderstood by the classifier as conveying a positive sentiment. To make matters worse, there is no word in the text that can be directly interpreted as negative. This observation also brings about the need to connect different parts of the text structure in order to derive a meaning out of the sentence. For instance, the first sentence can be broken into two parts:

1. "The book had its moments of glory"

2. ",but seemed to be missing the point quite frequently."

Looking at just the first part of the sentence can lead you to conclude that the remark is a positive one. It is only when the second sentence is taken into consideration that the meaning of the sentence can be truly understood as depicting negative feelings. Hence, there is a need to retain long term dependency here. A simple RNN is, therefore, not good enough for the task. Let's now apply a GRU to a sentiment classification task and see how it performs.

Exercise 25: Calculating the Model Validation Accuracy and Loss for Sentiment Classification

In this exercise, will we code up a simple sentiment classification system using the imdb dataset. The imdb dataset consists of 25,000 train text sequences and 25,000 test text sequences – each containing a review for a movie. The output variable is a binary variable having a value of 0 if the review is negative, and a value of 1 if the review is positive:

> **Note**
>
> All exercises and activities should be run in a Jupyter notebook. The requirements. txt file for creating the Python environment for running this notebook is as h5py==2.9.0, keras==2.2.4, numpy==1.16.1, tensorflow==1.12.0.

Solution:

We begin by loading the dataset, as follows:

```
from keras.datasets import imdb
```

1. Let's also define the maximum number of topmost frequent words to consider when generating the sequence for training as 10,000. We will also restrict the sequence length to 500:

```
max_features = 10000
maxlen = 500
```

2. Let's now load the data as follows:

```
(train_data, y_train), (test_data, y_test) = imdb.load_data(num_words=max_
features)
print('Number of train sequences: ', len(train_data))
print('Number of test sequences:  , len(test_data))
```

```
Number of train sequences:  25000
Number of test sequences:   25000
train_data shape: (25000, 500)
test_data shape: (25000, 500)
```

Figure 6.21: A screenshot showing the train and test sequences

3. There could be sequences having a length that is shorter than 500; therefore, we need to pad them out to have a length of exactly 500. We can use a Keras function for this purpose:

```
from keras.preprocessing import sequence
train_data = sequence.pad_sequences(train_data, maxlen=maxlen)
test_data = sequence.pad_sequences(test_data, maxlen=maxlen)
```

4. Let's examine the shapes of the train and test data, as follows:

```
print('train_data shape:', train_data.shape)
print('test_data shape:', test_data.shape)
```

Verify that the shape of both the arrays is (25,000, 500).

5. Let's now build an RNN with a GRU unit. First, we need to import the necessary packages, as follows:

```
from keras.models import Sequential
from keras.layers import Embedding
from keras.layers import Dense
from keras.layers import GRU
```

6. Since we'll use the sequential API of Keras to build the model, we need to import the sequential model API from the Keras model. The embedding layer essentially turns input vectors into a fixed size, which can then be fed to the next layer of the network. If used, it must be added as the first layer to the network. We also import a Dense layer, since it is this layer that ultimately gives a distribution over the target variable (0 or 1).

Finally, we import the GRU unit; let's initialize the sequential model API and add the embedding layer, as follows:

```
model = Sequential()
model.add(Embedding(max_features, 32))
```

The embedding layer takes max_features as input, which is defined by us to be 10,000. The 32 value is set here as the next GRU layer expects 32 inputs from the embedding layer.

7. Next, we'll add the GRU and the dense layer, as follows:

```
model.add(GRU(32))
model.add(Dense(1, activation='sigmoid'))
```

8. The 32 value is arbitrarily chosen and can function as one of the hyperparameters to tune when designing the network. It represents the dimensionality of the activation functions. The dense layer only gives out the 1 value, which is a probability of the review (that is, our target variable) to be 1. We choose sigmoid as the activation function here.

Next, we compile the model with the binary cross-entropy loss and the rmsprop optimizer:

```
model.compile(optimizer='rmsprop',
              loss='binary_crossentropy',
              metrics=['acc'])
```

9. We choose to track the accuracy (train and validation) as the metric. Next, we fit the model on our sequence data. Note that we also assign 20% of the sample from the training data as the validation dataset. We also set the number of epochs to be 10 and the batch_size to be 128 – that is, in a single forward-backward pass, we choose to pass 128 sequences in a single batch:

```
history = model.fit(train_data, y_train,
                    epochs=10,
                    batch_size=128,
                    validation_split=0.2
```

```
Train on 20000 samples, validate on 5000 samples
Epoch 1/10
20000/20000 [==============================] - 53s 3ms/step - loss: 0.5382 - acc: 0.7286 - val_loss: 0.4796 - val_ac
c: 0.7620
Epoch 2/10
20000/20000 [==============================] - 53s 3ms/step - loss: 0.3120 - acc: 0.8701 - val_loss: 0.3218 - val_ac
c: 0.8732
Epoch 3/10
20000/20000 [==============================] - 51s 3ms/step - loss: 0.2503 - acc: 0.9025 - val_loss: 0.3644 - val_ac
c: 0.8720
Epoch 4/10
20000/20000 [==============================] - 51s 3ms/step - loss: 0.2187 - acc: 0.9184 - val_loss: 0.3092 - val_ac
c: 0.8740
Epoch 5/10
20000/20000 [==============================] - 51s 3ms/step - loss: 0.1937 - acc: 0.9290 - val_loss: 0.3130 - val_ac
c: 0.8792
Epoch 6/10
20000/20000 [==============================] - 51s 3ms/step - loss: 0.1747 - acc: 0.9350 - val_loss: 0.3299 - val_ac
c: 0.8710
Epoch 7/10
20000/20000 [==============================] - 52s 3ms/step - loss: 0.1600 - acc: 0.9434 - val_loss: 0.3599 - val_ac
c: 0.8500
Epoch 8/10
20000/20000 [==============================] - 53s 3ms/step - loss: 0.1498 - acc: 0.9458 - val_loss: 0.3378 - val_ac
c: 0.8792
Epoch 9/10
20000/20000 [==============================] - 53s 3ms/step - loss: 0.1389 - acc: 0.9512 - val_loss: 0.5470 - val_ac
c: 0.8308
Epoch 10/10
20000/20000 [==============================] - 53s 3ms/step - loss: 0.1284 - acc: 0.9541 - val_loss: 0.3599 - val_ac
```

Figure 6.22: A screenshot displaying the variable history output of the training model

The variable history can be used to keep track of the training progress. The previous function will trigger a training session, which, on a local CPU, should take a couple of minutes to train.

10. Next, let's take a look at how exactly the training progressed by plotting the losses and accuracy. For this, we'll define a plotting function as follows:

```
import matplotlib.pyplot as plt

def plot_results(history):
    acc = history.history['acc']
    val_acc = history.history['val_acc']
    loss = history.history['loss']
    val_loss = history.history['val_loss']

    epochs = range(1, len(acc) + 1)
```

```
plt.plot(epochs, acc, 'bo', label='Training Accuracy')
plt.plot(epochs, val_acc, 'b', label='Validation Accuracy')

plt.title('Training and validation Accuracy')
plt.legend()
plt.figure()
plt.plot(epochs, loss, 'bo', label='Training Loss')
plt.plot(epochs, val_loss, 'b', label='Validation Loss')
plt.title('Training and validation Loss')
plt.legend()
plt.show()
```

11. Let's call our function on the history variable that us obtained as an output of the 'fit' function:

```
plot_results(history)
```

12. When run by author, the output of the preceding code looks like the following diagram:

Expected Output:

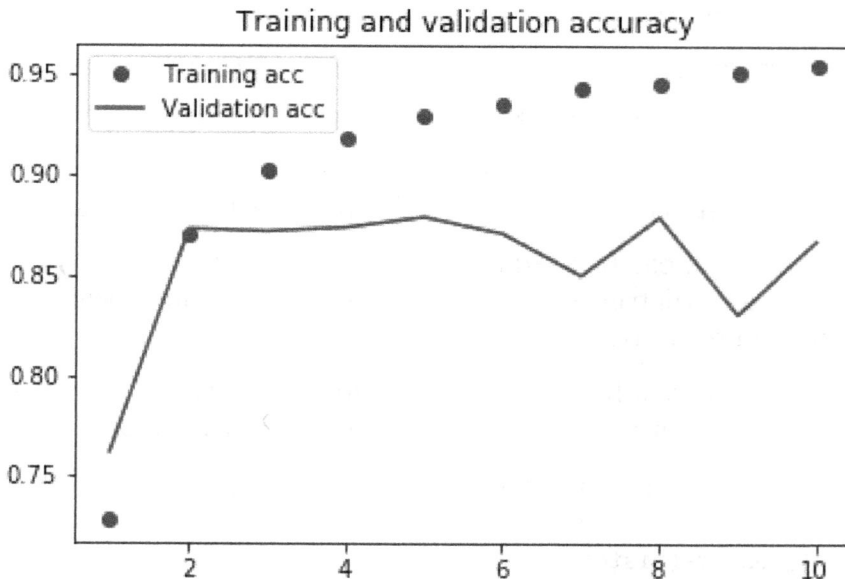

Figure 6.23: The training and validation accuracy for the sentiment classification task

The following diagram demonstrates the training and validation loss:

Figure 6.24: The training and validation loss for the sentiment classification task

> **Note**
>
> The validation accuracy is pretty high in the best epoch (~87%).

Activity 7: Developing a Sentiment Classification Model Using a Simple RNN

In this activity, we aim to generate a model for sentiment classification using a simple RNN. This is done to judge the effectiveness of GRUs over simple RNNs.

1. Load the dataset.

2. Pad the sequences out so that each sequence has the same number of characters.

3. Define and compile the model using a simple RNN with 32 hidden units.

4. Plot the validation and training accuracy and losses.

> **Note**
>
> The solution for the activity can be found on page 317.

Text Generation with GRUs

The problem of text generation requires an algorithm in order to come up with new text based on a training corpus. For example, if you feed the poems of Shakespeare into a learning algorithm, then the algorithm should be able to generate new text (character by character or word by word) in the style of Shakespeare. We will now see how to approach this problem with what we have learned in this chapter.

Exercise 26: Generating Text Using GRUs

So, let's revisit the problem that we introduced in the previous section of this chapter. That is, you wish to use a deep learning method to generate a poem. Let's go about solving this problem using a GRU. We will be using The Sonnets written by Shakespeare to train our model so that our output poem is in the style of Shakespeare:

1. Let's begin by importing the required Python packages, as follows:

```
import io
import sys
import random
import string
import numpy as np
from keras.models import Sequential
from keras.layers import Dense
from keras.layers import GRU
from keras.optimizers import RMSprop
```

   The use of each package will become clear in the code snippets that follow.

2. Next, we define a function that reads from the file that contains the Shakespearean sonnets and prints out the first 200 characters:

```
def load_text(filename):
    with open(filename, 'r') as f:
        text = f.read()
    return text

file_poem = 'shakespeare_poems.txt' # Path of the file
text = load_text(file_poem)
print(text[:200])
```

```
THE SONNETS

by William Shakespeare

From fairest creatures we desire increase,
That thereby beauty's rose might never die,
But as the riper should by time decease,
His tender heir might bear his mem
```

Figure 6.25: A screenshot of THE SONNETS

3. Next, we'll perform certain data preparation steps. First, we will get a list of the distinct characters from the file that was read in. We will then make a dictionary that maps each character to an integer index. Finally, we will create another dictionary that maps an integer index to the characters:

```
chars = sorted(list(set(text)))
print('Number of distinct characters:', len(chars))
char_indices = dict((c, i) for i, c in enumerate(chars))
indices_char = dict((i, c) for i, c in enumerate(chars))
```

4. Now, we will generate the sequences for the training data from the text. We will feed a fixed length of 40 characters per sequence for the model. The sequences will be made such that there is a sliding window of three steps with each sequence. Consider the following part of the poem:

"From fairest creatures we desire increase,

That thereby beauty's rose might never die,"

We aim to achieve the following result from the preceding snippet of text:

```
'\n\nFrom fairest creatures we desire incre',
'rom fairest creatures we desire increase',
' fairest creatures we desire increase,\nT',
'irest creatures we desire increase,\nThat',
'st creatures we desire increase,\nThat th',
'creatures we desire increase,\nThat there',
'atures we desire increase,\nThat thereby ',
'res we desire increase,\nThat thereby bea',
' we desire increase,\nThat thereby beauty',
" desire increase,\nThat thereby beauty's ",
"sire increase,\nThat thereby beauty's ros",
"e increase,\nThat thereby beauty's rose m",
"ncrease,\nThat thereby beauty's rose migh",
"ease,\nThat thereby beauty's rose might n",
"e,\nThat thereby beauty's rose might neve",
"That thereby beauty's rose might never d",
"t thereby beauty's rose might never die,",
```

Figure 6.26: A screenshot of the training sequences

These are sequences with a length of 40 characters each. Each subsequent string is shifted by three steps to the right of the previous string. This arrangement is so that we end up with enough sequences (but not too many, which would be the case with a step of 1). In general, we could have more sequences, but since this example is a demonstration and, hence, will run on a local CPU, feeding in too many sequences will make the training process much longer than desired.

Additionally, for each of these sequences, we need to have one output character that is the next character in the text. Essentially, we are teaching the model to observe 40 characters and then learn what the next most likely character will be. To understand what the output character might be, consider the following sequence:

That thereby beauty's rose might never d

The output character for this sequence will be the i character. This is because in the text, i is the next character. The following code snippet achieves the same:

```
max_len_chars = 40
step = 3
sentences = []
next_chars = []
```

```
for i in range(0, len(text) - max_len_chars, step):
    sentences.append(text[i: i + max_len_chars])
    next_chars.append(text[i + max_len_chars])
print('nb sequences:', len(sentences))
```

We now have the sequences that we wish to train on and the corresponding character output for the same. We will now need to obtain a training matrix for the samples and another matrix for the output characters, which can be fed to the model to train:

```
x = np.zeros((len(sentences), max_len_chars, len(chars)), dtype=np.bool)
y = np.zeros((len(sentences), len(chars)), dtype=np.bool)
for i, sentence in enumerate(sentences):
    for t, char in enumerate(sentence):
        x[i, t, char_indices[char]] = 1
    y[i, char_indices[next_chars[i]]] = 1
```

Here, x is the matrix that holds our input training samples. The shape of the x array is the number of sequences, the maximum number of characters, and the number of distinct characters. Therefore, x is a three-dimensional matrix. So, for each sequence, that is, for every timestep (= maximum number of characters), we have a one-hot-coded vector with the same length as the number of distinct characters in the text. This vector has a value of 1, where the character at the given step is present, and all the other entries are 0. y is a two-dimensional matrix with the shape of the number of sequences and the number of distinct characters). Thus, for every sequence, we have a one-hot-coded vector with the same length as the number of distinct characters. This vector has all the entries as 0 except for the one that corresponds to the current output character. The one-hot-encoding is accomplished using the dictionary mappings that we created in the earlier step.

1. We are now ready to define our model, as follows:

```
model = Sequential()
model.add(GRU(128, input_shape=(max_len_chars, len(chars))))
model.add(Dense(len(chars), activation='softmax'))
optimizer = RMSprop(lr=0.01)
model.compile(loss='categorical_crossentropy', optimizer=optimizer)
```

2. We make use of the sequential API, add a GRU layer with 128 hidden parameters, and then add a dense layer.

> **Note**
>
> The dense layer has the same number of outputs as the number of distinct characters. This is because we're essentially learning a distribution of the possible characters in our vocabulary. In this sense, this is essentially a multiclass classification problem, which also explains our choice of categorical cross-entropy for the cost function.

3. We will now go ahead and fit our model to the data, as follows:

```
model.fit(x, y,batch_size=128,epochs=10)
model.save("poem_gen_model.h5")
```

Here, we have selected a batch size of 128 sequences and training for 10 epochs. We will also save the model in hdf5 format file for later use:

```
Epoch 1/10
31327/31327 [==============================] - 12s 374us/step - loss: 2.2844
Epoch 2/10
31327/31327 [==============================] - 11s 335us/step - loss: 1.8985
Epoch 3/10
31327/31327 [==============================] - 11s 339us/step - loss: 1.7675
Epoch 4/10
31327/31327 [==============================] - 12s 372us/step - loss: 1.6757
Epoch 5/10
31327/31327 [==============================] - 11s 353us/step - loss: 1.5984
Epoch 6/10
31327/31327 [==============================] - 11s 341us/step - loss: 1.5479
Epoch 7/10
31327/31327 [==============================] - 12s 382us/step - loss: 1.5083
Epoch 8/10
31327/31327 [==============================] - 11s 346us/step - loss: 1.4803
Epoch 9/10
31327/31327 [==============================] - 11s 354us/step - loss: 1.4648
Epoch 10/10
31327/31327 [==============================] - 11s 356us/step - loss: 1.4428
```

Figure 6.27: A screenshot displaying epochs

> **Note**
>
> You should increase the number of the GRUs and epochs. The higher the value for these, the more time it will take to train the model and better results can be expected.

4. Next, we need to be able to use the model to actually generate some text, as follows:

```
from keras.models import load_model
model_loaded = load_model('poem_gen_model.h5')
```

5. We also define a sampling function that selects a candidate character given a probability distribution over the number of characters:

```
def sample(preds, temperature=1.0):
    # helper function to sample an index from a probability array
    preds = np.asarray(preds).astype('float64')
    preds = np.log(preds) / temperature
    exp_preds = np.exp(preds)
    preds = exp_preds / np.sum(exp_preds)
    probas = np.random.multinomial(1, preds, 1)
    return np.argmax(probas)
```

6. We are sampling using a multinomial distribution; the temperature parameter helps to add bias to the probability distribution such that the less likely words can have more or less representation. You can also simply try to return an argument argmax over the preds variable, but this will likely result in a repetition of words:

```
def generate_poem(model, num_chars_to_generate=400):
    start_index = random.randint(0, len(text) - max_len_chars - 1)
    generated = ''
    sentence = text[start_index: start_index + max_len_chars]
    generated += sentence
    print("Seed sentence: {}".format(generated))
    for i in range(num_chars_to_generate):
        x_pred = np.zeros((1, max_len_chars, len(chars)))
        for t, char in enumerate(sentence):
            x_pred[0, t, char_indices[char]] = 1.

        preds = model.predict(x_pred, verbose=0)[0]
        next_index = sample(preds, 1)
        next_char = indices_char[next_index]

        generated += next_char
        sentence = sentence[1:] + next_char
    return generated
```

7. We pass the loaded model and the number of characters that we wish to generate. We then pass a seed text for the model to use as the input (remember, we taught the model to predict the next character given a sequence length of 40 characters). This is being done before the for loop kicks in. In the first pass of the loop, we pass our seed text to the model, generate the output character, and append the output character in the 'generated' variable. In the next pass, we shift our newly updated sequence (with 41 characters after first pass) to the right by one character, so that the model can now take this 40 character input with the last character being the new character that we just generated. The function can now be called as follows:

```
generate_poem(model_loaded, 100)
```

And voila! You have a poem written in Shakespearean style. An example output is shown as follows:

```
' thou viewest,\nNow is the time that faced padince thy fete,\njevery bnuping griats I have liking dispictreessedg.\n
\nThy such thy sombeliner  h'
```

Figure 6.28: A screenshot displaying the output of the generated poem sequence

You will immediately notice that the poem does not really make sense. This can be attributed to two reasons:

- The preceding output was generated with a very small amount of data or sequences. Therefore, the model was unable to learn much. In practice, you would use a much larger dataset, make many more sequences out if it, and train the model using GPUs for a practical training time (we will learn about training on the cloud GPU in the last chapter 9- 'A practical flow NLP project workflow in an organization').

- Even if trained with a massive amount of data, there will always be some errors since a model can only learn so much.

We can still, however, see that even with this basic setup there are words that make sense despite our model being a character generation model. There are phrases such as 'I have liking' that are valid as standalone phrases.

Note

White space, newline characters, and more are also being learned by the model.

Activity 8: Train Your Own Character Generation Model Using a Dataset of Your Choice

We just used some of Shakespeare's work to generate our own poem. You don't need to restrict yourself to poem generation but you can use any piece of text to start generating your own piece of writing. The basic steps and setup remains same as discussed in the previous example.

> **Note**
>
> Create a conda environment using the requirements file and activate it. Then, run the code in a Jupyter notebook. Don't forget to input a text file containing the text from an author in whose style you wish to generate new text.

1. Load the text file.

2. Create dictionaries mapping the characters to indices and vice versa.

3. Create sequences from the text.

4. Make input and output arrays to feed to the model.

5. Build and train the model using GRU.

6. Save the model.

7. Define the sampling and generation functions.

8. Generate the text.

> **Note**
>
> The solution for the activity can be found on page 320.

Summary

A GRU is an extension of a simple RNN, which helps to combat the vanishing gradient problem by allowing the model to learn long-term dependencies in the text structure. A variety of use cases can benefit from this architectural unit. We discussed a sentiment classification problem and learned how GRUs perform better than simple RNNs. We then saw how text can be generated using GRUs.

In the next chapter, we talk about another advancement over a simple RNN – Long Short-Term Memory (LSTM) networks, and explore what advantages they bring with their new architecture.

7

Long Short-Term Memory (LSTM)

Learning Objectives

By the end of this chapter, you will be able to:

- Describe the purpose of an LSTM

- Evaluate the architecture of an LSTM in detail

- Develop a simple binary classification model using LSTMs

- Implement neural language translation and develop an English-to-German translation model

This chapter briefly introduces you to the LSTM architecture and its applications in the world of natural language processing.

Introduction

In the previous chapters, we studied Recurrent Neural Networks (RNNs) and a specialized architecture called the Gated Recurrent Unit (GRU), which helps combat the vanishing gradient problem. LSTMs offer yet another way to tackle the vanishing gradient problem. In this chapter, we will take a look at the architecture of LSTMs and see how they enable a neural network to propagate gradients in a faithful manner.

Additionally, we will look at an interesting application of LSTMs in the form of neural language translation, which will empower us to build a model that can be used to translate text given in one language to another language.

LSTM

The vanishing gradient problem makes it difficult for the gradient to propagate from the later layers in the network to the early layers, causing the initial weights of the network to not change much from the initial values. Thus, the model doesn't learn well and leads to poor performance. LSTMs solve the issue by introducing a "memory" to the network, which leads to the retention of long-term dependencies in the text structure. However, LSTMs add memory in a way that is different from the GRU's method. In the following sections, we will see how LSTMs accomplish this task.

An LSTM helps a network to remember long-term dependencies in an explicit manner. As in the case of the GRU, this is achieved by introducing more variables in the structure of a simple RNN.

Using LSTMs, we allow the network to transfer most of the knowledge from the activation of previous timesteps, a feat difficult to achieve with simple RNNs.

Recall the structure of the simple RNN; it's essentially an unfolding of the same unit and can be represented by the following diagram:

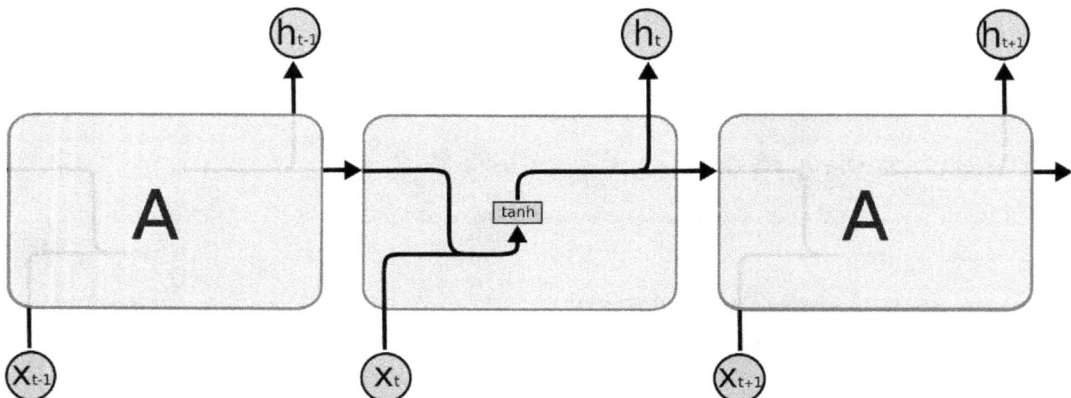

Figure 7.1: The repeating module in a standard RNN

The recurrence of block "**A**"in the diagram signifies that it is the same structure that is repeated over time. The input to each unit is an activation from the previous timestep (represented by the letter "**h**"). Another input is the sequence value at time "**t**" (represented by the letter "**x**").

Similar to the case with a simple RNN, LSTMs also have a fixed, time-unfolding, repeating structure, but the repeated unit itself has a different structure. Each unit of an LSTM has several different kinds of modules that interoperate to impart memory to the model. An LSTM's structure can be represented by the following diagram:

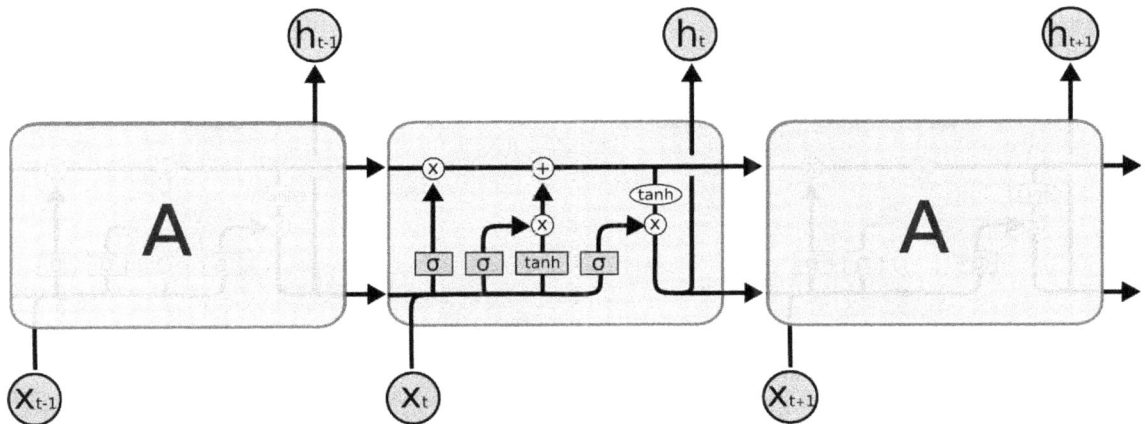

Figure 7.2: The LSTM unit

Let's also get familiar with the notations we'll be using for the diagrams:

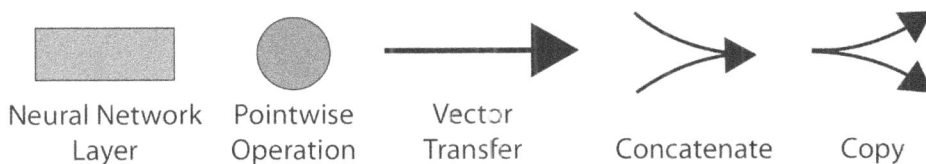

Figure 7.3: Notations used in the model

The most essential component of an LSTM is the cell state, henceforth represented by the letter "**C**". The cell state can be depicted by a constant bold line on the upper end of the boxes in the following diagram. It is often convenient to think of this line as a conveyor belt running through different time instances and carrying some information. Although there are several operations that can affect the value that propagates through the cell state, in practice, it is very easy for the information from previous cell states to reach the next cell state.

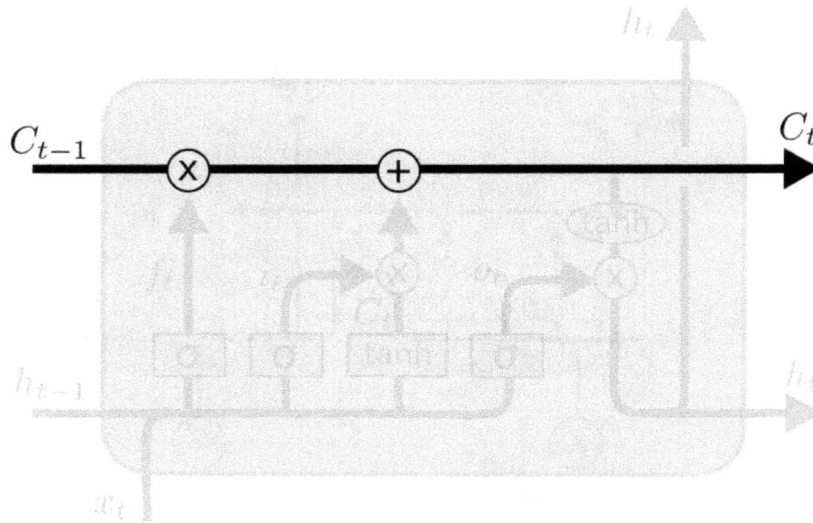

Figure 7.4: Cell state

It would be useful to understand LSTMs as seen from the perspective of the modification of this cell state. As with GRUs, the components of LSTMs that allow the modification of the cell state are called "*gates*".

An LSTM operates over several steps, which are described in the sections that follow.

The Forget Gate

The forget gate is responsible for determining the cell state content that should be forgotten from the previous timestep. The expression for the forget gate is as follows:

$$f[t] = \text{sigmoid}\left(w\_f * x[t] + U\_f * h[t-1]\right)$$

Figure 7.5: Expression for the forget gate

The input at timestep **t** is multiplied by a new set of weights, **W_f**, with the dimensions (**n_h**, **n_x**). The activation from the previous timestep (**h[t-1]**) is multiplied by another new set of weights, **U_f**, with the dimensions (**n_h**, **n_h**). Note that the multiplications are matrix multiplications. These two terms are then added and passed through a sigmoid function to squish the output, **f[t]**, within a range of [0,1]. The output has the same number of dimensions as there are in cell state vector C (**n_h**,1). The forget gate outputs a '1' or a '0' for each dimension. A value of '1' signifies that all information from the previous cell state for this dimension should pass, retained, while a value '0' indicates that all information from the previous cell state for this dimension should be forgotten. Diagrammatically, it can be represented as shown:

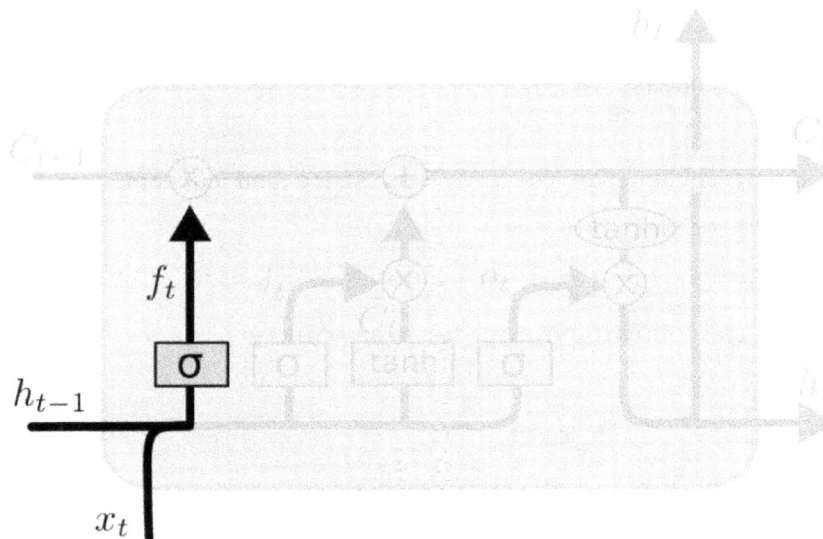

Figure 7.6: The Forget gate

So, how does the output of the forget gate impact the sentence construction? Let's take a look at the generated sentence:

"Jack goes for a walk when his daughter goes to bed."

The first subject in the sentence is 'Jack,' which connotes the male gender. The cell state representing the gender of the subject has a value corresponding to 'Male' (this could be 0 or 1). Now, up to the word 'his' in the sentence, the subject of the sentence does not change, and the cell state for the subject's gender continues having the 'male' value. The next word, however, 'daughter,' is a new subject and hence there is a need to forget the old value in the cell state that represents the gender. Note that even if the old gender state was female, there is still a need to forget this value so that a value corresponding to the new subject can be used.

The forget gate accomplishes the 'forget' operation by setting the subject gender value to 0 (that is, f[t] will output 0 for the said dimension).

In Python, the forget gate can be calculated with the following code snippet:

```
# Importing packages and setting the random seed to have a fixed output


import numpy as np
np.random.seed(0)


# A sigmoid needs to be defined to be used later
def sigmoid(x):
    return 1 / (1 + np.exp(-x))


# Simulating dummy values for the previous state and current input
h_prev = np.random.randn(3, 1)
x = np.random.randn(5, 1)
```

This code produces the following output for **h_prev** and **x**:

```
h_prev

array([[1.76405235],
       [0.40015721],
       [0.97873798]])


x

array([[ 2.2408932 ],
       [ 1.86755799],
       [-0.97727788],
       [ 0.95008842],
       [-0.15135721]])
```

Figure 7.7: Output for the previous state, 'h_prev,' and the current input, 'x'

We can initialize some dummy values for `W_f` and `U_f`:

```
# Initialize W_f and U_f with dummy values


W_f = np.random.randn(3, 5) # n_h = 3, n_x=5
U_f = np.random.randn(3, 3) # n_h = 3
```

This produces the following values:

```
W_f

array([[-0.10321885,  0.4105985 ,  0.14404357,  1.45427351,
0.76103773],
        [ 0.12167502,  0.44386323,  0.33367433,  1.49407907, -
0.20515826],
        [ 0.3130677 , -0.85409574, -2.55298982,  0.6536186 ,
0.8644362 ]])
```

```
U_f

array([[-0.74216502,  2.26975462, -1.45436567],
        [ 0.04575852, -0.18718385,  1.53277921],
        [ 1.46935877,  0.15494743,  0.37816252]])
```

Figure 7.8: Output of the matrix values

Now the forget gate can be calculated:

```
f = sigmoid(np.matmul(W_f, x) + np.matmul(U_f, h_prev))
```

This produces the following values for `f[t]`:

```
f

array([[0.45930054],
        [0.97661676],
        [0.99403442]])
```

Figure 7.9: Output of the forget gate, f[t]

The Input Gate and the Candidate Cell State

At each timestep, a new candidate cell state is also calculated using the following expression:

$$C\_candidate = tanh(W\_c * h[t-1] + U\_c * x[t])$$

Figure 7.10: Expression for candidate cell state

The input at timestep **t** is multiplied by a new set of weights, **W_c**, with the dimensions (**n_h, n_x**). The activation from the previous timestep (**h[t-1]**) is multiplied by another new set of weights, **U_c**, with the dimensions (**n_h, n_h**). Note that the multiplications are matrix multiplications. These two terms are then added and passed through a hyperbolic tan function to squish the output, **f[t]**, within a range of [-1,1]. The output, **C_candidate**, has the dimensions (**n_h,1**). In the diagram that follows, the candidate cell state is represented by C tilde:

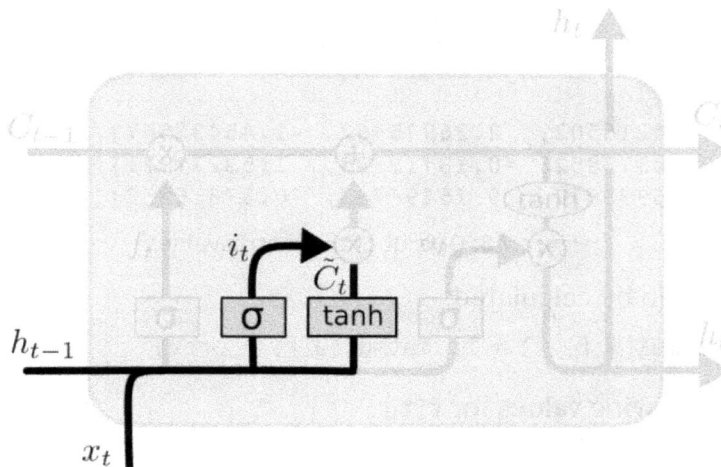

Figure 7.11: Input gate and candidate state

The candidate aims at calculating the cell state that it deduces from the current timestep. In our example sentence, this corresponds to calculating the new subject gender value. This candidate cell state is not passed as is to update the next cell state but is regulated by an input gate.

The input gate determines which values of the candidate cell state get passed on to the next cell state. The following expression can be used to calculate the input gate value:

$$i[t] = sigmoid(W\_i * x[t] + U\_i * h[t-1])$$

Figure 7.12: Expression for the input gate value

The input at timestep **t** is multiplied by a new set of weights, **W_i**, with the dimensions (**n_h, n_x**). The activation from the previous timestep (**h[t-1]**) is multiplied by another new set of weights, **U_i**, with the dimensions (**n_h, n_h**). Note that the multiplications are matrix multiplications. These two terms are then added and passed through a sigmoid function to squish the output, **i[t]**, within a range of **[0,1]**. The output has the same number of dimensions as there are in cell state vector **C (n_h, 1)**. In our example sentence, after reaching the word 'daughter,' there is a need to update the cell state for the values that correspond to the gender of the subject. After having calculated the new candidate value for the subject gender through the candidate cell state, only the dimension corresponding to the subject gender is set to 1 in the input gate vector.

The Python code snippet for the candidate cell state and input gate is as follows:

```
# Initialize W_i and U_i with dummy values


W_i = np.random.randn(3, 5) # n_h = 3, n_x=5
U_i = np.random.randn(3, 3) # n_h = 3
```

This produces the following values for the matrices:

```
W_i

array([[-0.88778575, -1.98079647, -0.34791215,  0.15634897,
1.23029068],
       [ 1.20237985, -0.38732682, -0.30230275, -1.04855297, -
1.42001794],
       [-1.70627019,  1.9507754 , -0.50965218, -0.4380743 , -
1.25279536]])
```

```
U_i

array([[ 0.77749036, -1.61389785, -0.21274028],
       [-0.89546656,  0.3869025 , -0.51080514],
       [-1.18063218, -0.02818223,  0.42833187]])
```

Figure 7.13: Screenshot of values of matrices for candidate cell state and input gate

The input gate can be calculated as shown:

```
i = sigmoid(np.matmul(W_i, x) + np.matmul(U_i, h_prev))
```

This outputs the following value for **i**:

```
i
```

```
array([[0.00762368],
       [0.39184172],
       [0.17027909]])
```

Figure 7.14: Screenshot of output of input gate

To calculate the candidate cell state, we first initialize the **W_c** and **U_c** matrices:

```
# Initialize W_c and U_c with dummy values
W_c = np.random.randn(3, 5) # n_h = 3, n_x=5
U_c = np.random.randn(3, 3) # n_h = 3
```

The values produced for these matrices are as given:

```
W_c
```

```
array([[ 0.06651722,  0.3024719 , -0.63432209, -0.36274117, -
0.67246045],
       [-0.35955316, -0.81314628, -1.7262826 ,  0.17742614, -
0.40178094],
       [-1.63019835,  0.46278226, -0.90729836,  0.0519454 ,
0.72909056]])
```

```
U_c
```

```
array([[ 0.12898291,  1.13940068, -1.23482582],
       [ 0.40234164, -0.68481009, -0.87079715],
       [-0.57884966, -0.31155253,  0.05616534]])
```

Figure 7.15: Screenshot for values of matrices W_c and U_c

We can now use the update equation for the candidate cell state:

```
c_candidate = np.tanh(np.matmul(W_c, x) + np.matmul(U_c, h_prev))
```

The candidate cell state produces the following value:

```
c_candidate

array([[ 0.51233992],
       [-0.67747899],
       [-0.99555958]])
```

Figure 7.16: Screenshot of the candidate cell state

Cell State Update

At this point, we know what should be forgotten from the old cell state (forget gate), what should be allowed to affect the new cell state (input gate), and what value the candidate cell change should have (candidate cell state). Now, the cell state for the current timestep can be calculated as follows:

$$C[t]=hadamard(f[t], C[t-1]) + hadamard(i[t], C\_candidate[t])$$

Figure 7.17: Expression for cell state update

In the preceding expression, '**hadamard**' represents element-wise multiplications. So, the forget gate gets multiplied element wise with the old cell state, allowing it to forget the gender of the subject in our example sentence. On the other hand, the input gate allows the new candidate value for the gender of the subject to affect the new cell state. These two terms are then added element-wise so that the current cell state now has a subject gender that corresponds to a value that corresponds to 'female.'

The next diagram depicts the operation

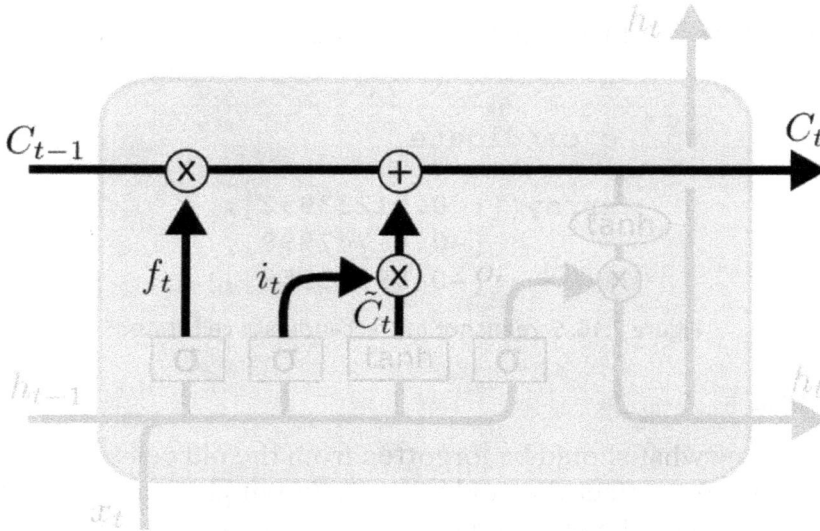

Figure 7.18: Updated cell state

Here is the code snippet for producing the current cell state.

First, initialize a value for the previous cell state:

```
# Initialize c_prev with dummy value
c_prev = np.random.randn(3,1)
c_new = np.multiply(f, c_prev) + np.multiply(i, c_candidate)
```

The value becomes the following:

```
c_new

array([[-0.53124803],
       [ 0.61429771],
       [ 0.29336152]])
```

Figure 7.19: Screenshot for output of updated cell state

Output Gate and Current Activation

Note that all we have done is update the cell state until now. We need to generate the activation for the current state as well; that is, (**h[t]**). This is done using an output gate that is calculated as given:

$$o[t] = sigmoid(W\_o*x[t] + U\_o*h[t-1])$$

Figure 7.20: Expression for output gate.

The input at timestep **t** is multiplied by a new set of weights, **W_o**, with the dimensions (**n_h, n_x**). The activation from the previous timestep (**h[t-1]**) is multiplied by another new set of weights, **U_o**, with the dimensions (**n_h, n_h**). Note that the multiplications are matrix multiplications. These two terms are then added and passed through a sigmoid function to squish the output, **o[t]**, within a range of [0,1]. The output has the same number of dimensions as there are in cell state vector **h (n_h, 1)**.

The output gate is responsible for regulating the amount by which the current cell state is allowed to affect the activation value for the timestep. In our example sentence, it is worth propagating the information that depicts whether the subject is singular or plural such that the correct verb form may be used. For example, if the word following the word 'daughter' is a verb such as 'goes,' it is important to use the correct form of the word, 'go'. Hence, the output gate allows relevant information to be passed on to the activation, which then goes as an input to the next timestep. In the next diagram, the output gate is represented as **o_t**:

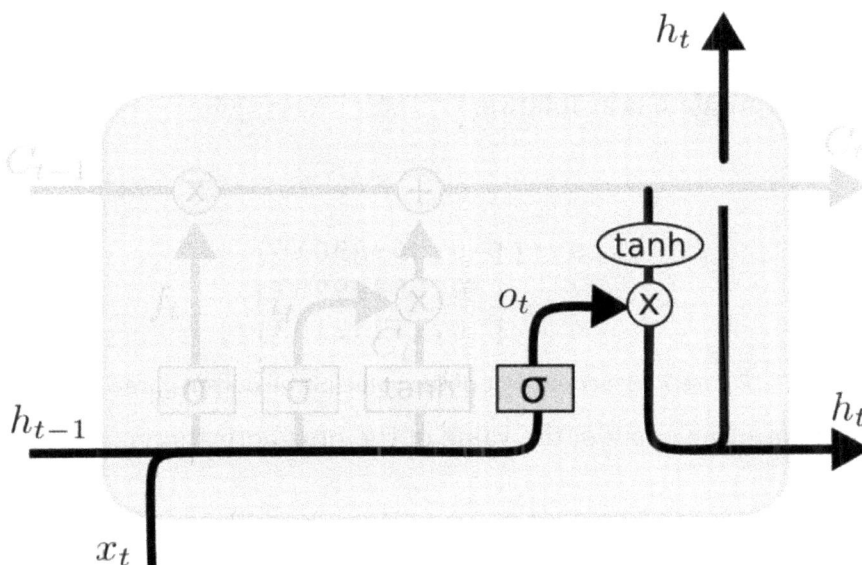

Figure 7.21: Output gate and current activation

The following code snippet shows how the value for the output gate can be calculated:

```
# Initialize dummy values for W_o and U_o

W_o = np.random.randn(3, 5) # n_h = 3, n_x=5
U_o = np.random.randn(3, 3) # n_h = 3
```

This produces the following output:

```
W_o

array([[-1.16514984,  0.90082649,  0.46566244, -1.53624369,
1.48825219],
       [ 1.89588918,  1.17877957, -0.17992484, -1.07075262,
1.05445173],
       [-0.40317695,  1.22244507,  0.20827498,  0.97663904,
0.3563664 ]])


U_o

array([[ 0.70657317,  0.01050002,  1.78587049],
       [ 0.12691209,  0.40198936,  1.8831507 ],
       [-1.34775906, -1.270485  ,  0.96939671]])
```

Figure 7.22: Screenshot for output of matrices W_o and U_o

Now the output can be calculated:

```
o = np.tanh(np.matmul(W_o, x) + np.matmul(U_o, h_prev))
```

The value of the output gate is as follows:

```
o

array([[-0.06989015],
       [ 0.99999957],
       [ 0.11232103]])
```

Figure 7.23: Screenshot of the value of the output gate

Once the output gate is evaluated, the value of the next activation can be calculated:

$$h[t] = hadamard(o[t], tanh\ (C[t]))$$

Figure 7.24: Expression to calculate the value of the next activation

First, a hyperbolic tangent function is applied to the current cell state. This limits the values in the vector between -1 and 1. Then, an element-wise product of this value is done with the output gate value that was just calculated.

Let's see the code snippet for calculating the current timestep activation:

```
h_new = np.multiply(o, np.tanh(c_new))
```

This finally produces the following:

```
h_new
array([[-0.04695679],
       [ 0.12468345],
       [ 0.07479682]])
```

Figure 7.25: Screenshot for the current timestep activation

Now let's build a very simple binary classifier to demonstrate the use of an LSTM.

Exercise 27: Building an LSTM-Based Model to Classify an Email as Spam or Not Spam (Ham)

In this exercise, we will be building an LSTM-based model that will help us classify emails as spam or genuine:

1. We will start by importing the required Python packages:

```
import pandas as pd
import numpy as np
from keras.models import Model, Sequential
from keras.layers import LSTM, Dense,Embedding
from keras.preprocessing.text import Tokenizer
from keras.preprocessing import sequence
```

Note:

The LSTM unit has been imported the same way as you would for a simple RNN or GRU.

2. We can now read the input file containing a column that contains text and another column that contains the label for the text depicting whether the text is spam or not.

> **Note**
>
> For the input file, go to the repository link at
>
> https://github.com/TrainingByPackt/Deep-Learning-for-Natural-Language-Processing/tree/master/Lesson%2007/exercise

```
df = pd.read_csv("spam.csv", encoding="latin")
df.head()
```

3. The data looks as depicted here:

`df.head()`

	v1	v2	Unnamed: 2	Unnamed: 3	Unnamed: 4
0	ham	Go until jurong point, crazy.. Available only ...	NaN	NaN	NaN
1	ham	Ok lar... Joking wif u oni...	NaN	NaN	NaN
2	spam	Free entry in 2 a wkly comp to win FA Cup fina...	NaN	NaN	NaN
3	ham	U dun say so early hor... U c already then say...	NaN	NaN	NaN
4	ham	Nah I don't think he goes to usf, he lives aro...	NaN	NaN	NaN

Figure 7.26: Screenshot of the output for spam classification

4. There are some irrelevant columns as well, but we only need the columns containing the text data and labels:

```
df = df[["v1","v2"]]
df.head()
```

5. The output should be as follows:

```
df.head()
```

	v1	v2
0	ham	Go until jurong point, crazy.. Available only ...
1	ham	Ok lar... Joking wif u oni...
2	spam	Free entry in 2 a wkly comp to win FA Cup fina...
3	ham	U dun say so early hor... U c already then say...
4	ham	Nah I don't think he goes to usf, he lives aro...

Figure 7.27: Screenshot for columns with text and labels

6. We can check the label distribution:

```
df["v1"].value_counts()
```

The label distribuiton would look like this:

```
df["v1"].value_counts()

ham      4825
spam      747
Name: v1, dtype: int64
```

Figure 7.28: Screenshot for label distribution

7. We can now map the label distribution to 0/1 so that it can be fed to a classifier. Also, an array is created to contain the texts:

```
lab_map = {"ham":0, "spam":1}
Y = df["v1"].map(lab_map).values
X = df["v2"].values
```

8. This produces output X and Y as follows:

```
X

array(['Go until jurong point, crazy.. Available only in bugi
s n great world la e buffet... Cine there got amore wat...',
       'Ok lar... Joking wif u oni...',
       "Free entry in 2 a wkly comp to win FA Cup final tkts
21st May 2005. Text FA to 87121 to receive entry question(std
txt rate)T&C's apply 08452810075over18's",
       ..., 'Pity, * was in mood for that. So...any other sug
gestions?',
       "The guy did some bitching but I acted like i'd be int
erested in buying something else next week and he gave it to
us for free",
       'Rofl. Its true to its name'], dtype=object)
```

Figure 7.29: Screenshot for output X

```
Y

array([0, 0, 1, ..., 0, 0, 0])
```

Figure 7.30: Screenshot for output Y

9. Next, we will restrict the maximum number of tokens to be generated for the 100 most frequent words. We will initialize a tokenizer that assigns an integer value to each word being used in the text corpus:

```
max_words = 100
mytokenizer = Tokenizer(nb_words=max_words,lower=True, split=" ")
mytokenizer.fit_on_texts(X)
text_tokenized = mytokenizer.texts_to_sequences(X)
```

10. This will produce a **text_tokenized** value:

```
In [24]:  text_tokenized

Out[24]:  [[50, 64, 8, 89, 67, 58],
          [46, 6],
          [47, 8, 19, 4, 2, 71, 2, 2, 73],
          [6, 23, 6, 57],
          [1, 98, 69, 2, 69],
          [67, 21, 7, 38, 87, 55, 3, 44, 12, 14, 85, 46, 2, 68, 2],
          [11, 9, 25, 55, 2, 36, 10, 10, 55],
          [72, 13, 72, 13, 12, 51, 2, 13],
          [72, 4, 3, 17, 2, 2, 16, 64],
          [13, 96, 26, 6, 81, 2, 2, 5, 36, 12, 47, 16, 5, 96, 47, 18],
          [30, 32, 77, 7, 1, 98, 70, 2, 80, 40, 93, 88],
          [2, 48, 2, 73, 7, 68, 2, 65, 92, 42],
          [3, 17, 4, 47, 8, 91, 73, 5, 2, 38],
          [12, 5, 2, 3, 12, 40, 1, 1, 97, 13, 12, 7, 33, 11, 3, 17, 7,
          4, 29, 51],
          [1, 17, 4, 18, 36, 33],
          [2, 13, 5, 8, 5, 73, 26, 89],
          [93, 30],
          [6, 49, 19, 1, 69, 1],
          [34   5   6   5   61]
```

Figure 7.31: Screenshot for the output of tokenized values

Note that since we restricted the maximum number words to be 100, only the words in the text that fall within the top 100 most frequent words will be assigned an integer index. The rest of the works will be ignored. So, even though the first sequence in X has 20 words, there are 6 indices in the tokenized representation of this sentence.

11. Next, we will allow a maximum sequence length of 50 words per sequence and pad the sequences that are shorter than this length. The longer sequences, on the other hand, get truncated:

```
max_len = 50
sequences = sequence.pad_sequences(text_tokenized, maxlen=max_len)
```

The output is as follows:

```
sequences
```

```
array([[ 0,   0,   0, ...,  89,  67,  58],
       [ 0,   0,   0, ...,   0,  46,   6],
       [ 0,   0,   0, ...,   2,   2,  73],
       ...,
       [ 0,   0,   0, ...,  12,  20,  23],
       [ 0,   0,   0, ...,   2,  12,  47],
       [ 0,   0,   0, ...,  61,   2,  61]], dtype=int32)
```

Figure 7.32: Screenshot for padded sequences

Note that the padding was done in the 'pre' mode, meaning that the initial part of the sequences get padded to make the sequence length equal to max_len.

12. Next, we define the model with the LSTM layer having 64 hidden units and fit it to our sequence data with the respective target values:

```
model = Sequential()
model.add(Embedding(max_words, 20, input_length=max_len))
model.add(LSTM(64))
model.add(Dense(1, activation="sigmoid"))
model.compile(loss='binary_crossentropy',
              optimizer='adam',
              metrics=['accuracy'])
model.fit(sequences,Y,batch_size=128,epochs=10,
          validation_split=0.2)
```

Here, we start with an embedding layer, which ensures a fixed size for input to the network (20). We have a dense layer with a single sigmoid output, which indicates whether the target variable is 0 or 1. We then compile the model with binary cross-entropy as the loss function and use Adam as the optimization strategy. After that, we fit the model to our data with a batch size of 128 and an epoch count of 10. Note that we also keep aside 20% of the training data as validation data. This starts a training session:

```
model.fit(sequences,Y,batch_size=128,epochs=10,
        validation_split=0.2)

Train on 4457 samples, validate on 1115 samples
Epoch 1/10
4457/4457 [==============================] - 2s 539us/step -
loss: 0.4885 - acc: 0.8548 - val_loss: 0.3700 - val_acc: 0.87
00
Epoch 2/10
4457/4457 [==============================] - 2s 374us/step -
loss: 0.3425 - acc: 0.8652 - val_loss: 0.2649 - val_acc: 0.87
71
Epoch 3/10
4457/4457 [==============================] - 2s 381us/step -
loss: 0.2028 - acc: 0.9226 - val_loss: 0.1489 - val_acc: 0.95
34
Epoch 4/10
4457/4457 [==============================] - 2s 367us/step -
loss: 0.1348 - acc: 0.9547 - val_loss: 0.1271 - val_acc: 0.95
16
Epoch 5/10
4457/4457 [==============================] - 2s 404us/step -
loss: 0.1157 - acc: 0.9605 - val_loss: 0.1073 - val_acc: 0.95
78
Epoch 6/10
4457/4457 [==============================] - 2s 368us/step -
loss: 0.1061 - acc: 0.9632 - val_loss: 0.1027 - val_acc: 0.96
14
Epoch 7/10
4457/4457 [==============================] - 2s 371us/step -
loss: 0.0998 - acc: 0.9657 - val_loss: 0.1046 - val_acc: 0.95
78
Epoch 8/10
4457/4457 [==============================] - 2s 372us/step -
loss: 0.0955 - acc: 0.9672 - val_loss: 0.1004 - val_acc: 0.95
96
```

Figure 7.33: Screenshot of model fitting to 10 epochs

After 10 epochs, a validation accuracy of 96% is achieved. This is remarkably good performance.

We can now try some test sequences and obtain the probability of the sequence being spam:

```
inp_test_seq = "WINNER! U win a 500 prize reward & free entry to FA cup
final tickets! Text FA to 34212 to receive award"
test_sequences = mytokenizer.texts_to_sequences(np.array([inp_test_seq]))
test_sequences_matrix = sequence.pad_sequences(test_sequences,maxlen=max_
len)
model.predict(test_sequences_matrix)
```

Expected output:

```
model.predict(test_sequences_matrix)
array([[0.96648586]], dtype=float32)
```

Figure 7.34: Screenshot of the output of model prediction

There is a very high probability of the test text being spam.

Activity 9: Building a Spam or Ham Classifier Using a Simple RNN

We will be building a spam-or-ham classifier using a simple RNN with the same hyperparameters as earlier and compare the performance with that of our LSTM-based solution. For a simple dataset such as this, a simple RNN would perform very close to an LSTM. However, this is usually not the case with more complex models, as we will see in the next section.

> **Note**
>
> Find the input file at https://github.com/TrainingByPackt/Deep-Learning-for-Natural-Language-Processing/tree/master/Lesson%2007/exercise.

1. Import the required Python packages.

2. Read the input file containing a column that contains text and another column that contains the label for the text depicting whether the text is spam or not.

3. Convert to sequences.

4. Pad the sequences.

5. Train the sequences.

6. Build the model.

7. Predict the mail category on the new test data.

   Expected output:

```
array([[0.979119]], dtype=float32)
```

Figure 7.35: Output for mail category prediction

> **Note**
>
> The solution for the activity can be found on page 324.

Neural Language Translation

The simple binary classifier described in the previous section is a basic use case for the area of natural language processing (NLP) and doesn't fully justify the use of any techniques that are more complex than using a simple RNN or even simpler techniques. However, there are many complex use cases for which it is imperative to use more complex units such as LSTMs. Neural language translation is one such application.

The goal of a neural language translation task is to build a model that can translate a piece of text from a source language to a target language. Before starting with the code, let's discuss the architecture of this system.

Neural language translation represents a many-to-many NLP application, which means that there are many inputs to the system and the system produces many outputs as well.

Additionally, the number of inputs and outputs could be different as the same text can have a different number of words in the source and target language. The area of NLP that solves such problems is referred to as sequence-to-sequence modeling. The architecture consists of an encoder block and a decoder block. The following diagram represents the architecture:

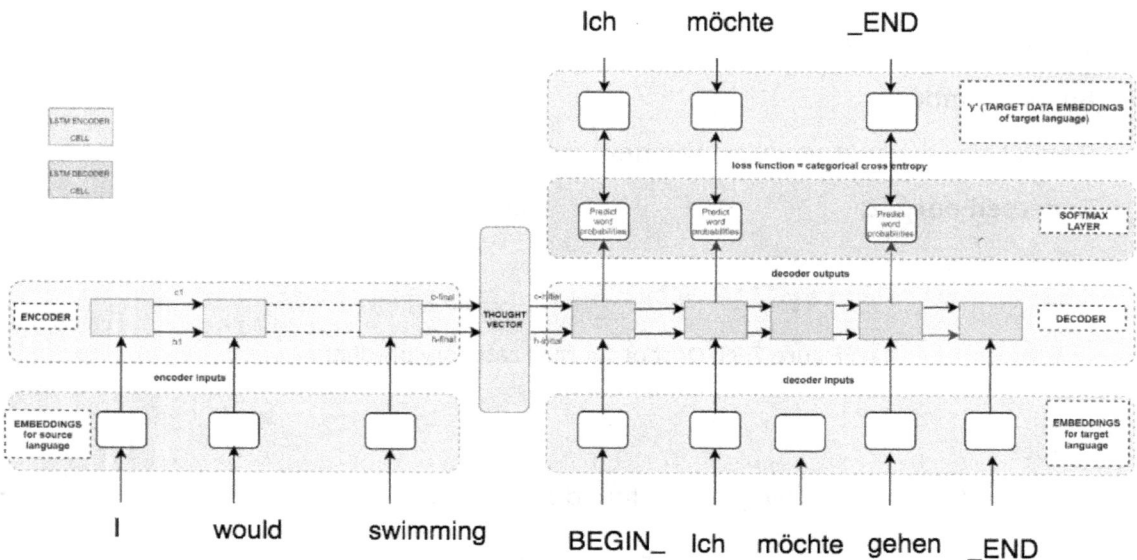

Figure 7.36: Neural translation model

The left part of the architecture is the encoder block, and the right part is the decoder block. The diagram attempts to translate an English sentence to German, as here:

English: I would like to go swimming

German: Ich möchte schwimmen gehen

> **Note**
>
> Periods have been dropped from the preceding sentences for demonstration purposes only. Periods are also considered valid tokens.

The encoder block takes each word of the English (source language) sentence as input at a given timestep. Each unit of the encoder block is an LSTM. The only outputs for the encoder block are the final cell state and activations. These are jointly referred to as the thought vector. The thought vector is used to initialize the activation and cell state for the decoder block, which is another LSTM block. During the training phase, at each timestep, the decoder output is the next word in the sentence. This is represented by a dense softmax layer that has a value 1 for the next word token and 0 for all the other entries in the vector.

The English sentence is fed to the encoder word by word, producing a final cell state and activation. During the training phase, the real output of the decoder at each timestep is known. This is simply the next German word in the sentence. Note that there is a '**BEGIN_**' token inserted at the sentence beginning and an '**_END**' token at the end of the sentence. The output for the '**BEGIN_**' token is the first word in the German sentence. This can be seen in the last diagram. At the time of training, the network is made to learn the translation word by word.

In the inference phase, the English input sentence is fed to the encoder block, producing a final cell state and activation. The decoder has the '**BEGIN_**' token as the input at the first timestep, along with the cell state and activations. Using these three inputs, a softmax output is produced for this timestep. In a well-trained network, the softmax value is the highest for the entry corresponding to the correct word. This next word is then fed as the input to the next timestep. This process is continued until an '**_END**' token is sampled or a maximum sentence length is reached.

Now let's go through the code for the model.

We read in the file containing sentence pairs first. We also keep the number of pairs restricted to 20,000 for demonstration purposes:

```
import os
import re
import numpy as np


with open("deu.txt", 'r', encoding='utf-8') as f:
    lines = f.read().split('\n')


num_samples = 20000 # Using only 20000 pairs for this example
lines_to_use = lines[: min(num_samples, len(lines) - 1)]
print(lines_to_use)
```

Output:

lines_to_use

```
['Hi.\tHallo!',
 'Hi.\tGrüß Gott!',
 'Run!\tLauf!',
 'Wow!\tPotzdonner!',
 'Wow!\tDonnerwetter!',
 'Fire!\tFeuer!',
 'Help!\tHilfe!',
 'Help!\tZu Hülf!',
 'Stop!\tStopp!',
 'Wait!\tWarte!',
 'Go on.\tMach weiter.',
 'Hello!\tHallo!',
 'I ran.\tIch rannte.',
 'I see.\tIch verstehe.',
 'I see.\tAha.',
 'I try.\tIch probiere es.',
 'I won!\tIch hab gewonnen!',
```

Figure 7.37: Screenshot for the English-to-German translation of sentence pairs

Each line has first the English sentence, followed by a tab character, and then the German translation of the sentence. Next, we'll map all the numbers to a placeholder word, '**NUMBER_PRESENT**', and append the '**BEGIN_** ' and ' **_END**' tokens to each German sentence, as discussed previously:

```
for l in range(len(lines_to_use)):
    lines_to_use[l] = re.sub("\d", " NUMBER_PRESENT ",lines_to_use[l])


input_texts = []
target_texts = []
input_words = set()
target_words = set()
for line in lines_to_use:
    input_text, target_text = line.split('\t')
    target_text = 'BEGIN_ ' + target_text + ' _END'
    input_texts.append(input_text)
    target_texts.append(target_text)
    for word in input_text.split():
```

```
        if word not in input_words:
            input_words.add(word)
    for word in target_text.split():
        if word not in target_words:
            target_words.add(word)
```

In the previous snippet, we obtained the input and output texts. They look as depicted:

```
input_texts

['Hi.',
 'Hi.',
 'Run!',
 'Wow!',
 'Wow!',
 'Fire!',
 'Help!',
 'Help!',
 'Stop!',
 'Wait!',
 'Go on.',
 'Hello!',
 'I ran.',
 'I see.',
 'I see.',
 'I try.',
 'I won!',
 'I won!',
 'Smile.',
 'Cheers!'
```

```
target_texts

['BEGIN_ Hallo! _END',
 'BEGIN_ Grüß Gott! _END',
 'BEGIN_ Lauf! _END',
 'BEGIN_ Potzdonner! _END',
 'BEGIN_ Donnerwetter! _END',
 'BEGIN_ Feuer! _END',
 'BEGIN_ Hilfe! _END',
 'BEGIN_ Zu Hülf! _END',
 'BEGIN_ Stopp! _END',
 'BEGIN_ Warte! _END',
 'BEGIN_ Mach weiter. _END',
 'BEGIN_ Hallo! _END'
```

Figure 7.38: Screenshot for input and output texts after mapping

Next, we get the maximum length of the input and output sequences and get a list of all the words in the input and output corpus:

```
max_input_seq_length = max([len(i.split()) for i in input_texts])
max_target_seq_length = max([len(i.split()) for i in target_texts])


input_words = sorted(list(input_words))
target_words = sorted(list(target_words))
num_encoder_tokens = len(input_words)
num_decoder_tokens = len(target_words)
```

input_words and target_words look as shown in the following figure:

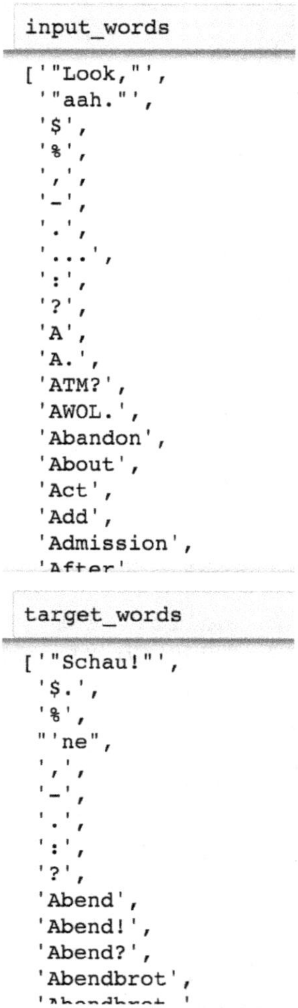

```
input_words

['"Look,"',
 '"aah."',
 '$',
 '%',
 ',',
 '-',
 '.',
 '...',
 ':',
 '?',
 'A',
 'A.',
 'ATM?',
 'AWOL.',
 'Abandon',
 'About',
 'Act',
 'Add',
 'Admission',
 'After'
```

```
target_words

['"Schau!"',
 '$.',
 '%',
 "'ne",
 ',',
 '-',
 '.',
 ':',
 '?',
 'Abend',
 'Abend!',
 'Abend?',
 'Abendbrot',
 'Abendbrot'
```

Figure 7.39: Screenshot for input text and target words

Next, we generate an integer index for each token in the input and output words:

```
input_token_index = dict(
    [(word, i) for i, word in enumerate(input_words)])
target_token_index = dict([(word, i) for i, word in enumerate(target_words)])
```

The values of these variables are as follows:

```
input_token_index

{'"Look,"': 0,
 '"aah."': 1,
 '$': 2,
 '%': 3,
 ',': 4,
 '-': 5,
 '.': 6,
 '...': 7,
 ':': 8,
 '?': 9,
 'A': 10,
 'A.': 11,
 'ATM?': 12,
 'AWOL.': 13,
 'Abandon': 14,
 'About': 15,
 'Act': 16,
 'Add': 17,
 'Admission': 18,
 'After': 19
```

```
target_token_index

{'"Schau!"': 0,
 '$.': 1,
 '%': 2,
 "'ne": 3,
 ',': 4,
 '-': 5,
 '.': 6,
 ':': 7,
 '?': 8,
 'Abend': 9,
 'Abend!': 10,
 'Abend?': 11,
 'Abendbrot': 12,
```

Figure 7.40: Screenshot for output of integer index for each token

We now define the arrays for the encoder input data, which is a 2-dimensional matrix with as many rows as sentence pairs and as many columns as the maximum input sequence length. Similarly, the decoder input data is also a 2-dimensional matrix with as many rows as sentence pairs and as many columns as the maximum sequence length in the target corpus. We also need target output data, which is required during the training phase. This is a 3-dimensional matrix where the first dimension has the same value as the number of sentence pairs. The second dimension has the same number of elements as the maximum target sequence length. The third dimension represents the number of decoder tokens (the number of distinct words in the target corpus). We initialize these variables with zeros:

```
encoder_input_data = np.zeros(
    (len(input_texts), max_input_seq_length),
    dtype='float32')
decoder_input_data = np.zeros(
    (len(target_texts), max_target_seq_length),
    dtype='float32')
decoder_target_data = np.zeros(
    (len(target_texts), max_target_seq_length, num_decoder_tokens),
    dtype='float32')
```

We now populate these matrices:

```
for i, (input_text, target_text) in enumerate(zip(input_texts, target_
texts)):
    for t, word in enumerate(input_text.split()):
        encoder_input_data[i, t] = input_token_index[word]
    for t, word in enumerate(target_text.split()):
        decoder_input_data[i, t] = target_token_index[word]
        if t > 0:
            # decoder_target_data is ahead of decoder_input_data by one
timestep
            decoder_target_data[i, t - 1, target_token_index[word]] = 1.
```

The values look as follows:

```
encoder_input_data
array([[ 283.,      0.,      0., ...,     0.,     0.,     0.],
       [ 283.,      0.,      0., ...,     0.,     0.,     0.],
       [ 505.,      0.,      0., ...,     0.,     0.,     0.],
       ...,
       [ 696.,   3001.,   4502., ...,     0.,     0.,     0.],
       [ 696.,   3001.,   4682., ...,     0.,     0.,     0.],
       [ 696.,   3004.,   3008., ...,     0.,     0.,     0.]], dtyp
e=float32)

decoder_input_data
array([[ 175.,   1172.,   3665., ...,     0.,     0.,     0.],
       [ 175.,   1140.,   1113., ...,     0.,     0.,     0.],
       [ 175.,   1706.,   3665., ...,     0.,     0.,     0.],
       ...,
       [ 175.,   3405.,   8432., ...,     0.,     0.,     0.],
       [ 175.,   3405.,   6239., ...,     0.,     0.,     0.],
       [ 175.,   3405.,   6239., ...,     0.,     0.,     0.]], dtyp
e=float32)

decoder_target_data
array([[[0., 0., 0., ..., 0., 0., 0.],
        [0., 0., 0., ..., 0., 0., 0.],
        [0., 0., 0., ..., 0., 0., 0.],
        ...,
        [0., 0., 0., ..., 0., 0., 0.],
        [0., 0., 0., ..., 0., 0., 0.],
        [0., 0., 0., ..., 0., 0., 0.]],

       [[0., 0., 0., ..., 0., 0., 0.],
        [0., 0., 0., ..., 0., 0., 0.],
```

Figure 7.41: Screenshot of matrix population

We will now define a model. For this exercise, we'll use the functional API of Keras:

```
from keras.layers import Input, LSTM, Embedding, Dense
from keras.models import Model


embedding_size = 50 # For embedding layer
```

Let's see the encoder block:

```
encoder_inputs = Input(shape=(None,))
encoder_after_embedding =  Embedding(num_encoder_tokens, embedding_size)
(encoder_inputs)
encoder_lstm = LSTM(50, return_state=True)
_, state_h, state_c = encoder_lstm(encoder_after_embedding)
encoder_states = [state_h, state_c]
```

First, an Input layer with a flexible number of inputs is defined (with the None attribute). Then, an embedding layer is defined and applied to the encoder inputs. Next, an LSTM unit is defined with 50 hidden units and applied to the embedding layer. Note that the return_state parameter in the LSTM definition is set to True since we would like to obtain the final encoder states to be used for initializing decoder cell state and activations. The encoder LSTM is then applied to the embeddings and the states are collected back into variables.

Now let's define the decoder block:

```
decoder_inputs = Input(shape=(None,))
decoder_after_embedding = Embedding(num_decoder_tokens, embedding_size)
(decoder_inputs)
decoder_lstm = LSTM(50, return_sequences=True, return_state=True)
decoder_outputs, _, _ = decoder_lstm(decoder_after_embedding,
                                initial_state=encoder_states)
decoder_dense = Dense(num_decoder_tokens, activation='softmax')
decoder_outputs = decoder_dense(decoder_outputs)
```

The decoder takes in inputs and defines embedding layers in a way similar to that of the encoder. An LSTM block is then defined with the return_sequences and return_state parameters set to True. This is done since we wish to use the sequences and states for the decoder. A dense layer is then defined with a softmax activation and a number of outputs equal to the number of distinct tokens in the target corpus. We can now define a model that takes in the encoder and decoder inputs as its input and produces the decoder outputs as final outputs:

```
model = Model([encoder_inputs, decoder_inputs], decoder_outputs)
model.compile(optimizer='rmsprop', loss='categorical_crossentropy',
metrics=['acc'])
model.summary()
```

The following model summary is seen:

Layer (type) Connected to	Output Shape	Param #
input_1 (InputLayer)	(None, None)	0
input_2 (InputLayer)	(None, None)	0
embedding_1 (Embedding) input_1[0][0]	(None, None, 50)	286200
embedding_2 (Embedding) input_2[0][0]	(None, None, 50)	456300
lstm_1 (LSTM) embedding_1[0][0]	[(None, 50), (None,	20200
lstm_2 (LSTM) embedding_2[0][0] lstm_1[0][1] lstm_1[0][2]	[(None, None, 50), (	20200
dense_1 (Dense) lstm_2[0][0]	(None, None, 9126)	465426

Total params: 1,248,326
Trainable params: 1,248,326
Non-trainable params: 0

Figure 7.42: Screenshot of model summary

We can now fit the model for our inputs and outputs:

```
model.fit([encoder_input_data, decoder_input_data], decoder_target_data,
          batch_size=128,
          epochs=20,
          validation_split=0.05)
```

We set a batch size of 128 with 20 epochs:

```
Train on 19000 samples, validate on 1000 samples
Epoch 1/20
19000/19000 [==============================] - 310s 16ms/step
- loss: 1.6492 - acc: 0.0787 - val_loss: 1.8068 - val_acc: 0.
0674
Epoch 2/20
19000/19000 [==============================] - 303s 16ms/step
- loss: 1.5174 - acc: 0.0908 - val_loss: 1.6923 - val_acc: 0.
0822
Epoch 3/20
19000/19000 [==============================] - 304s 16ms/step
- loss: 1.4060 - acc: 0.1040 - val_loss: 1.6107 - val_acc: 0.
1065
Epoch 4/20
19000/19000 [==============================] - 292s 15ms/step
- loss: 1.3343 - acc: 0.1157 - val_loss: 1.5683 - val_acc: 0.
1100
Epoch 5/20
19000/19000 [==============================] - 292s 15ms/step
- loss: 1.2860 - acc: 0.1212 - val_loss: 1.5299 - val_acc: 0.
1197
Epoch 6/20
19000/19000 [==============================] - 291s 15ms/step
- loss: 1.2510 - acc: 0.1241 - val_loss: 1.5037 - val_acc: 0.
1145
Epoch 7/20
19000/19000 [==============================] - 291s 15ms/step
```

Figure 7.43: Screenshot of model fitting with 20 epochs

The model is now trained. Now, as described in our section on neural language translation, the inference phase follows a slightly different architecture from the one used during training. We first define the encoder model, which takes encoder_inputs (with embedding) as input and produces encoder_states as output. This makes sense as the output of the encoder block is the cell state and activations:

```
encoder_model = Model(encoder_inputs, encoder_states)
```

Next, a decoder inference model is defined:

```
decoder_state_input_h = Input(shape=(50,))
decoder_state_input_c = Input(shape=(50,))
decoder_states_inputs = [decoder_state_input_h, decoder_state_input_c]
decoder_outputs_inf, state_h_inf, state_c_inf = decoder_lstm(decoder_after_
embedding, initial_state=decoder_states_inputs)
```

The initial states of decoder_lstm, which was trained earlier, are set to the decoder_ states_inputs variable, which will be set to encoder state output later on. Then, we pass decoder outputs through a dense softmax layer for getting the index of the predicted word and define the decoder inference model:

```
decoder_states_inf = [state_h_inf, state_c_inf]
decoder_outputs_inf = decoder_dense(decoder_outputs_inf)
# Multiple input, multiple output
decoder_model = Model(
    [decoder_inputs] + decoder_states_inputs,
    [decoder_outputs_inf] + decoder_states_inf)
```

The decoder model takes multiple inputs in the form of decoder_input (with embedding) and decoder states. The output is also a multivariable where the dense layer output and decoder states are returned. The states are required here as they need to passed on as input states for the sampling of the word at the next timestep.

Since the output of the dense layer will return a vector, we need a reverse lookup dictionary to map the index for the generated word to an actual word:

```
# Reverse-lookup token index to decode sequences

reverse_input_word_index = dict(
    (i, word) for word, i in input_token_index.items())
reverse_target_word_index = dict(
    (i, word) for word, i in target_token_index.items())
```

The values in the dictionaries are as follows:

```
reverse_input_word_index

 3:  '%',
 4:  ',',
 5:  '-',
 6:  '.',
 7:  '...',
 8:  ':',
 9:  '?',
10:  'A',
11:  'A.',
12:  'ATM?',
13:  'AWOL.',
14:  'Abandon',
15:  'About',
16:  'Act',
17:  'Add',
18:  'Admission',
19:  'After',
20:  'Aim.',
21:  "Ain't",
22:  'Air'.
```

```
reverse_target_word_index

{0:  '"Schau!"',
 1:  '$.',
 2:  '%',
 3:  "'ne",
 4:  ',',
 5:  '-',
 6:  '.',
 7:  ':',
 8:  '?',
 9:  'Abend',
10:  'Abend!',
11:  'Abend?',
12:  'Abendbrot',
```

Figure 7.44: Screenshot of dictionary values

We now need to develop a sampling logic. Given a token representation for every word in an input sentence, we first get the output from encoder_model using these word tokens as inputs for the encoder. We also initialize the first input word to the decoder to be a **'BEGIN_'** token. We then sample a new word token using these values. The input to the decoder for the next timestep is this newly generated token. We continue in this fashion until we either sample the **'_END'** token or reach the maximum allowed output sequence length.

The first step is encoding the input as a state vector:

```
def decode_sequence(input_seq):
states_value = encoder_model.predict(input_seq)
```

Then, we generate an empty target sequence of length 1:

```
target_seq = np.zeros((1,1))
```

Next, we populate the first character of the target sequence with the start character:

```
target_seq[0, 0] = target_token_index['BEGIN_']
```

Then, we create a sampling loop for a batch of sequences:

```
stop_condition = False
decoded_sentence = ''

while not stop_condition:
    output_tokens, h, c = decoder_model.predict(
        [target_seq] + states_value)
```

Next, we sample a token:

```
sampled_token_index = np.argmax(output_tokens)
sampled_word = reverse_target_word_index[sampled_token_index]
decoded_sentence += ' ' + sampled_word
```

Then, we state the exit condition "**either hit max length**":

```
# or find stop character.
if (sampled_word == '_END' or
    len(decoded_sentence) > 60):
    stop_condition = True

# Update the target sequence (of length 1).
target_seq = np.zeros((1,1))
target_seq[0, 0] = sampled_token_index
```

Then, we update the states:

```
        states_value = [h, c]
```

```
    return decoded_sentence
```

In this instance, you can test the model by translating a user-defined English sentence to German:

```
text_to_translate = "Where is my car?"
```

```
encoder_input_to_translate = np.zeros(
    (1, max_input_seq_length),
    dtype='float32')
```

```
for t, word in enumerate(text_to_translate.split()):
    encoder_input_to_translate[0, t] = input_token_index[word]
```

```
decode_sequence(encoder_input_to_translate)
```

The output is depicted in this screenshot:

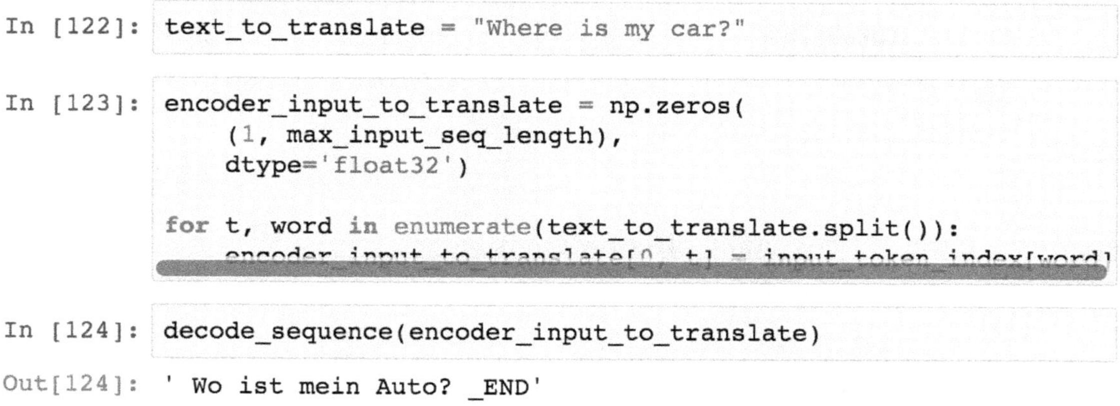

```
In [122]:   text_to_translate = "Where is my car?"

In [123]:   encoder_input_to_translate = np.zeros(
                (1, max_input_seq_length),
                dtype='float32')

            for t, word in enumerate(text_to_translate.split()):
                encoder_input_to_translate[0, t] = input_token_index[word]

In [124]:   decode_sequence(encoder_input_to_translate)

Out[124]:   ' Wo ist mein Auto? _END'
```

Figure 7.45: Screenshot of English-to-German translator

This is, indeed, the correct translation.

So, even a model trained on just 20,000 sequences for only 20 epochs is capable of producing good translations. With the current settings, the training session ran for about 90 minutes.

Activity 10: Creating a French-to-English translation model

In this activity, we aim to generate a language translator model that converts French text into English.

> **Note**
>
> You can find the related files to the activity at https://github.com/TrainingByPackt/Deep-Learning-for-Natural-Language-Processing/tree/master/Lesson%2007/activity.

1. Read in the sentence pairs (check the GitHub repository for the file).

2. Generate input and output texts with the '**BEGIN_**' and '**_END**' words attached to the output sentences.

3. Convert the input and output texts into input and output sequence matrices.

4. Define the encoder and decoder training models and train the network.

5. Define the encoder and decoder architecture for inference.

6. Create the user input text (French: ' *Où est ma voiture?*'). The sample output text in English should be '*Where is my car?*'. Refer to the '*French.txt*' file from the GitHub repository for some sample French words.

Expected output:

```
' Get a lot. _END'
```

Figure 7.46: Output for French to English translator model

> **Note**
>
> The solution for the activity can be found on page 327.

Summary

We introduced LSTM units as a possible remedy to the vanishing gradient problem. We then discussed the LSTM architecture in detail and built a simple binary classifier using it. We then delved into a neural nanguage translation application that utilizes LSTM units, and we built a French-to-English translator model using the techniques we explored. In the next chapter, we will discuss the current state of the art in the NLP sphere.

8

State-of-the-Art Natural Language Processing

Learning Objectives

By the end of this chapter, you will be able to:

- Evaluate vanishing gradients in long sentences
- Describe an attention mechanism model as a state-of-the-art NLP domain
- Assess one specific attention mechanism architecture
- Develop a neural machine translation model using an attention mechanism
- Develop a text summarization model using an attention mechanism

This chapter aims to acquaint you with the current practices and technologies in the NLP domain.

Introduction

In the last chapter, we studied Long Short Term Memory units (LSTMs), which help combat the vanishing gradient problem. We also studied GRU in detail, which has its own way of handling vanishing gradients. Although LSTM and GRU reduce this problem in comparison to simple recurrent neural networks, the vanishing gradient problem still manages to prevail in many practical cases. The issue essentially remains the same: longer sentences with complex structural dependences are challenging for deep learning algorithms to encapsulate. Therefore, one of the most prevalent research areas represents the community's attempts to mitigate the effects of the vanishing gradient problem.

Attention mechanisms, in the last few years, have attempted to provide a solution to the vanishing gradient problem. The basic concept of an attention mechanism relies on having access to all parts of the input sentence when arriving at an output. This allows the model to lay varying amounts of weight (attention) to different parts of the sentence, which allows dependencies to be deduced. Due to their uncanny ability to learn such dependencies, attention mechanism-based architectures represent the current state of the art in the NLP domain.

In this chapter, we will learn about attention mechanisms and solve a neural machine translation task using a specific architecture based on an attention mechanism. We will also mention some other related architectures that are being used in the industry today.

Attention Mechanisms

In the last chapter, we solved a *Neural Language Translation* task. The architecture for the translation model adopted by us consists of two parts: *Encoder and Decoder*. Refer to the following diagram for the architecture:

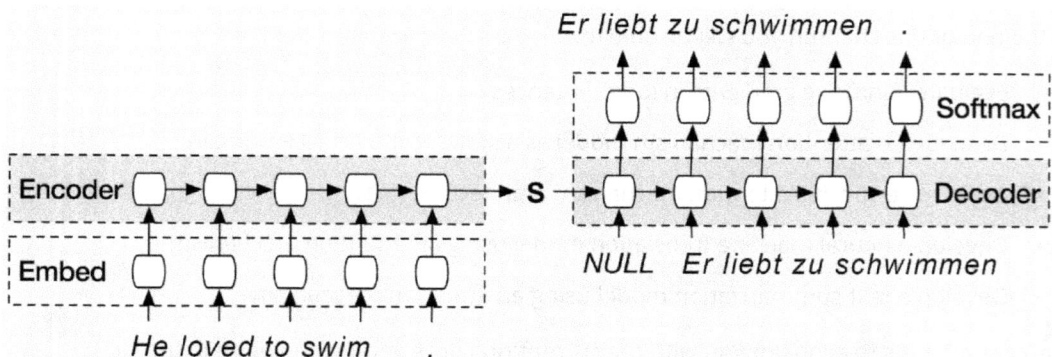

Figure 8.1: Neural language translation model

For a neural machine translation task, a sentence is passed into an encoder word by word, which produces a single *thought* vector (represented in the preceding image as **'S'**), which embeds the meaning of the entire sentence into a single representation. The decoder then uses this vector to initialize the hidden states and produce a translation word by word.

In the simple encoder-decoder regime, only 1 vector (the thought vector) contains the representation of the entire sentence. The longer the sentence, the more difficult it becomes for the single thought vector to retain long-term dependencies. The use of LSTM units reduces the problem only to some extent. A new concept was developed to mitigate the vanishing gradient problem further, and this concept is called **Attention mechanisms**.

An attention mechanism aims to mimic a human's way of learning dependencies. Let's illustrate this with an example sentence:

"There have been many incidents of thefts lately in our neighborhood, which has forced me to consider hiring a security agency to install a burglar-detection system in my house so that I can keep myself and my family safe."

Note the use of the words 'my', 'I', 'me', 'myself,' and 'our'. These occur at distant positions within the sentence but are tightly coupled to each other to represent the meaning of the sentence.

When trying to translate the previous sentence, a traditional encoder-decoder functions as follows:

1. Pass the sentence word by word to the encoder.

2. The encoder produces a single thought vector, which represents the entire sentence encoding. For a long sentence, such as the previous one, even with the use of LSTMs, it would be difficult for the encoder to embed all the dependencies. Therefore, the earlier part of the sentence is not as strongly encoded as the later part of the sentence, which means the later part of the sentence ends up having a dominant influence over the encodings.

3. The decoder uses the thought vector to initialize the hidden state vector to generate the output translation.

A more intuitive way to translate the sentence would be to pay attention to the correct positions of words in the input sentence when determining a particular word in the target language. As an example, consider the following sentence:

'The animal could not walk on the street because it was badly injured.'

In this sentence, whom does the word 'it' refer to? Is it the animal or the street? An answer to this question would be possible if the entire sentence were considered together and different parts of the sentence were weighed differently to determine the answer to the question. An attention mechanism accomplishes this, as depicted here:

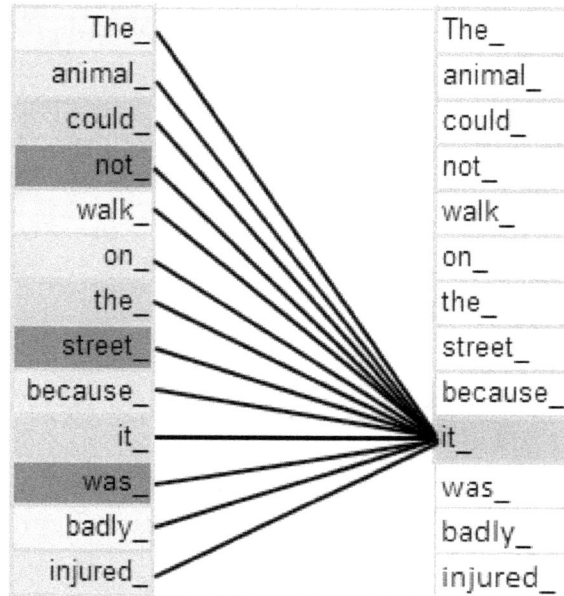

Figure 8.2: An example of an attention mechanism

The diagram shows how much weight each word receives in understanding every word in a sentence. As can be seen, the word '**it_**' receives a very strong weighting from '**animal_**' and a relatively weaker weighting from '**street_**'. Thus, the model can now answer the question of which entity 'it' refers to in the sentence.

For a translation encoder-decoder model, while generating word-by-word output, at a given point in time, not all the words in the input sentence are important for the determination of the output word. An attention mechanism implements a scheme that does exactly that: weighs different parts of the input sentence with all of the input words at each point in the determination of the output. A well-trained network with an attention mechanism would learn to apply an appropriate amount of weighting to different parts of the sentence. This regime allows the entire part of the input sentence to be always available for use at every point of determining the output. Thus, instead of one thought vector, the decoder has access to the "thought" vector specific for the determination of each word in the output sentence. This ability of an attention mechanism is in stark contrast to a traditional LSTM/GRU/RNN-based encoder-decoder.

An attention mechanism is a general concept. It can be realized in several architectural flavors, which are discussed in the later part of the chapter.

An Attention Mechanism Model

Let's see how an encoder-decoder architecture could look with an attention mechanism in place:

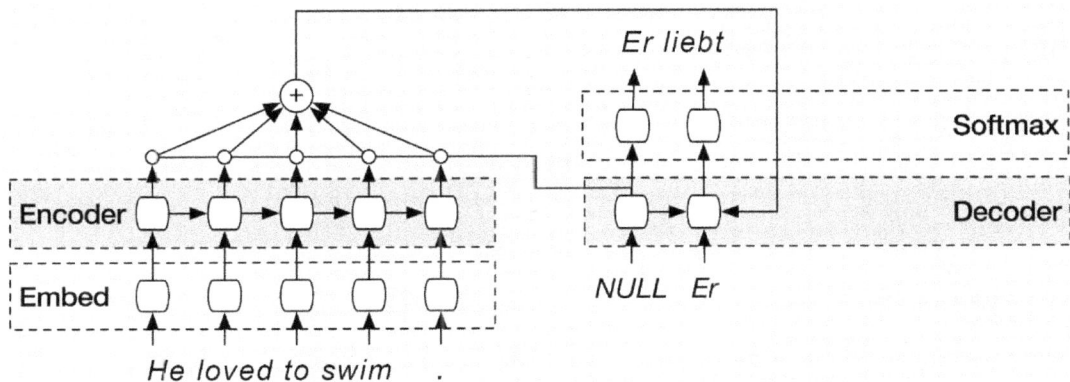

Figure 8.3: An attention mechanism model

The preceding diagram depicts the training phase of a language translation model with an attention mechanism. We can note a few differences compared to a basic encoder-decoder regime, as follows:

- The initial states of the decoder get initialized with the encoder output state from the last encoder cell. An initial **NULL** word is used to start the translation, and the first word is produced as '**Er**'. This is the same as the previous encoder-decoder model.

- For the second word, in addition to the input from the previous word and the hidden state of the preceding decoder timestep, another vector is fed as input to the cell. This vector, generally regarded as '**Context vector**', is a function of all the encoder hidden states. From the preceding diagram, it is a weighted summation of the hidden states of the encoder for all the timesteps.

- During the training phase, since the output of each decoder timestep is known, we can learn all the parameters of the network. In addition to the usual parameters, corresponding to whichever RNN flavor is being used, the parameters specific to the attention function are also learned. If the attention function is just a simple summation of the hidden state encoder vectors, the weights of the hidden states at each encoder timestep can be learned.

- At inference time, at every timestep, the decoder cell can take as input the predicted word from the last timestep, the hidden states from the previous decoder cell, and the context vector.

Let's look at one specific realization of an attention mechanism for neural machine translation. In the previous chapter, we built a neural language translation model, which is a subproblem area of a more general area of NLP called neural machine translation. In the following section, we attempt to solve a date-normalization problem.

Data Normalization Using an Attention Mechanism

Let's say you're maintaining a database that has a table containing a column for date. The input for the date is taken from your customers, who fill in a form and enter the date in a **date** field. The frontend engineer somehow forgot to enforce a scheme upon the field, such that only dates in a "YYYY-MM-DD" format are accepted. You are now tasked with normalizing the **date** column of database table, such that the user inputs in several formats get converted to a standard "YYYY-MM-DD" format.

As an example, the user inputs for date and the corresponding correct normalization are shown here:

User Input	Normalized Date
3-May-79	5/3/1979
5-Apr-09	5/5/2009
21th of August 2016	8/21/2016
Tue 10 Jul 2007	7/10/2007

Figure 8.4: Table for date normalization

You can see that there is a lot of variation in the way a user can input a date. There are many more ways in which the date could be specified apart from the examples in the table.

This problem is a good candidate to be solved by a neural machine translation model as the input has a sequential structure, wherein the meanings of the different components in the input need to be learned. This model will have the following components:

- Encoder
- Decoder
- Attention mechanisms

Encoder

This is a bidirectional LSTM that takes each character of the date as input. Thus, at each timestep, the input to the encoder is a single character of the input date. Apart from this, the hidden state and memory state is also taken as an input from the previous encoder cell. Since this is a bidirectional architecture, there are two sets of parameters pertaining to the LSTM: one in the forward direction and the other in the backward direction.

Decoder

This is a unidirectional LSTM. It takes as input the context vector for this timestep. Since each output character is not strictly dependent upon the last output character in the case of date normalization, we don't need to feed the previous timestep output as an input to the current timestep. Additionally, since it is an LSTM unit, the hidden states and memory state from the previous decoder timestep are also fed to the current timestep unit for the determination of the decoder output at this timestep.

Attention mechanisms

Attention mechanisms are explained in this section. For determination of a decoder input at a given timestep, a context vector is calculated. A context vector is a weighted summation of all the hidden state of an encoder from all timesteps. This is as follows:

$$context[t] = dot(H, alpha[t])$$

Figure 8.5: Expression for the context vector

The dot operation is a dot product operation that multiplies weights (represented by **alpha**) with the corresponding hidden state vector for all timesteps and sums them up. The value of the alpha vector is calculated separately for each decoder output timestep. The alphas encapsulate the essence of an attention mechanism, that is, determining how much 'attention' to be given to which part of the input to figure out the current timestep output. This can be realized in a diagram, as follows:

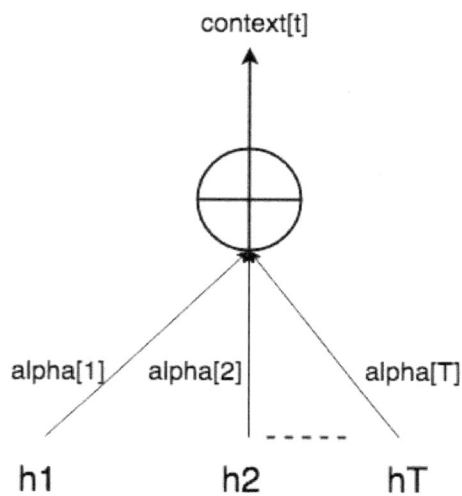

Figure 8.6: Determination of attention to inputs

As an example, let's say that the encoder input has a fixed length of 30 characters, and the decoder output has a fixed output length of 10 characters. For the date normalization problem, this means that the user input is fixed to be a maximum of 30 characters, while the model output is fixed at 10 characters (the number of characters in the YYYY-MM-DD format, including the hyphens).

Let's say that we wish to determine the decoder output at the output timestep=4 (an arbitrary number chosen to explain the concept; it just needs to be <=10, which is the output timestep count). At this step, the weight vector alpha is computed. This vector has a dimensionality equal to the number of timesteps of the encoder input (as a weight needs to be computed for every encoder input timestep). So, in our case, alpha has a dimensionality of 30.

Now, we already have the hidden state vector from each of the encoder timesteps, so there are a total of 30 hidden state vectors available. The dimensionality of the hidden state vector accounts for both the forward and backward components of the bidirectional encoder LSTM. For a given timestep, we combine the forward hidden state and backward hidden state into a single vector. So, if the dimensionality of forward and backward hidden states is 32 each, we put them in a single vector of 64 dimensions as [**h_forward**, **h_backward**]. This is a simple concatenation function. Let's call this the encoder hidden state vector.

We now have a single 30-dimensional weight vector alpha, and 30 vectors of 64-dimensional hidden states. So, we can now multiply each of the 30 hidden state vectors with a corresponding entry in the alpha vector. Furthermore, we can sum up these scaled representations of hidden states to receive a single 64-dimensional context vector. This is essentially the operation performed by the dot operator.

The Calculation of Alpha

The weights can be modeled by a multilayer perceptron (MLP), which is a simple neural network consisting of multiple hidden layers. We choose to have two dense layers with a **softmax** output. The number of dense layers and units can be treated as hyperparameters. The input to this MLP consists of two components: these are the hidden state vectors for all timesteps from the encoder bidirectional LSTM, as explained in the last point, and the hidden states from the previous timestep of the decoder. These are concatenated to form a single vector. So, the input to the MLP is: [*encoder hidden state vector, previous state vector from decoder*]. This is a concatenation operation of tensors: [**H**, **S_prev**]. **S_prev** refers to the decoder's hidden state output from the previous timestep. If the dimensionality of **S_prev** is 64 (denoting a hidden state dimensionality of 64 for the decoder LSTM) and the dimensionality of the encoder's hidden state vector is 64 (from the last point), a concatenation of these two vectors produces a vector of size 128.

Thus, the MLP receives a 128-dimension input for a single encoder timestep. As we have fixed the encoder input length to 30 characters, we will have a matrix (more accurately, a tensor) of size [30, 128]. The parameters of this MLP are learned using the same BPTT regime that is used to learn all the other parameters of the model. So, all the parameters of the entire model (encoder + decoder + attention function MLP) are learned together. This can be seen in the following diagram:

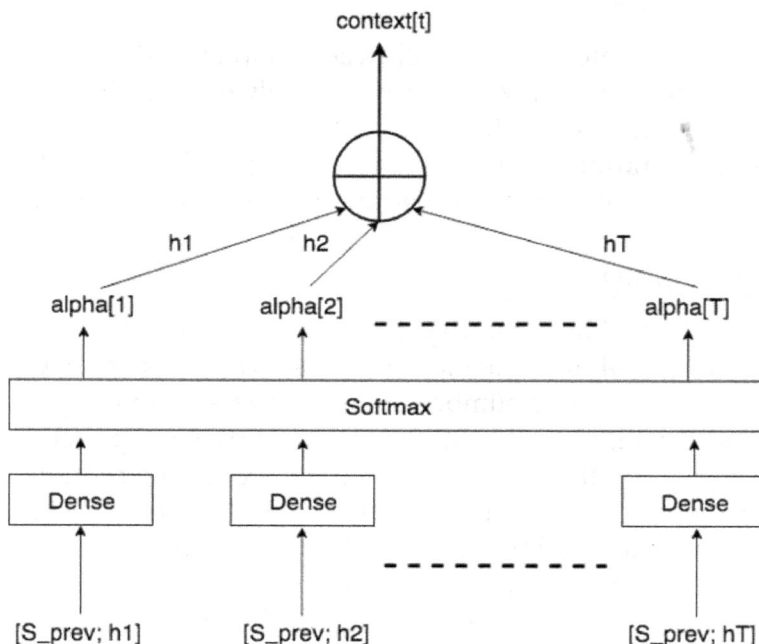

Figure 8.7: The calculation of alpha

In the previous step, we learned the weights (alpha vector) for determining only one step of the decoder output (we had assumed this timestep to be 4 in an earlier point). So, the determination of a single step decoder output requires the inputs: **S_prev** and encoder hidden states for calculating the context vector, decoder hidden states, and decoder previous timestep memory, which goes as input to the decoder unidirectional LSTM. Proceeding to the next decoder timestep requires a calculation of a new alpha vector since, for this next step, various parts of the input sequence will most likely be weighted differently compared to the previous timestep.

Due to the architecture of the model, the training and inference steps are the same. The only difference is that, during training, we know the output for each decoder timestep and use that to train the model parameters (this technique is referred to as 'Teacher Forcing').

In contrast, during inference time, we predict the output character. Note that both during training and inference, we do not feed the previous timestep decoder output character as input to the current timestep decoder cell. It should be noted that the architecture proposed here is specific to this problem. There are a lot of architectures and ways to define an attention function. We will take a brief look at some of these in later sections of the chapter.

Exercise 28: Build a Date Normalization Model for a Database Column

A database column accepts date inputs from various users in multiple formats. In this exercise, we aim to normalize the date column of the database table such that the user inputs in several formats get converted to a standard "YYYY-MM-DD" format:

> **Note**
>
> The Python requirements for running the code are as follows:
>
> Babel==2.6.0
>
> Faker==1.0.2
>
> Keras==2.2.4
>
> numpy==1.16.1
>
> pandas==0.24.1
>
> scipy==1.2.1
>
> tensorflow==1.12.0
>
> tqdm==4.31.1
>
> Faker==1.0.2

1. We import all the necessary modules:

```
from keras.layers import Bidirectional, Concatenate, Permute, Dot, Input,
LSTM, Multiply
from keras.layers import RepeatVector, Dense, Activation, Lambda
from keras.optimizers import Adam
from keras.utils import to_categorical
from keras.models import load_model, Model
import keras.backend as K
import numpy as np
from babel.dates import format_date
from faker import Faker
import random
from tqdm import tqdm
```

2. Next, we define some helper functions. We first use the '**faker**' and **babel** modules to generate data for training. The **format_date** function from **babel** generates date in a specific format (using **FORMATS**). Additionally, dates are also returned in a human-readable format that emulates the informal user input date that we wish to normalize:

```
fake = Faker()
fake.seed(12345)
random.seed(12345)
```

3. Define the format of the data we would like to generate:

```
FORMATS = ['short',
           'medium',
           'long',
           'full',
           'full',
           'full',
           'full',
           'full',
           'full',
           'full',
           'full',
           'full',
           'full',
           'full',
           'd MMM YYY',
           'd MMMM YYY',
           'dd MMM YYY',
           'd MMM, YYY',
```

```
                    'd MMMM, YYY',
                    'dd, MMM YYY',
                    'd MM YY',
                    'd MMMM YYY',
                    'MMMM d YYY',
                    'MMMM d, YYY',
                    'dd.MM.YY']

    # change this if you want it to work with another language
    LOCALES = ['en_US']

    def load_date():
        """
            Loads some fake dates
            :returns: tuple containing human readable string, machine readable
        string, and date object
        """
        dt = fake.date_object()

        human_readable = format_date(dt, format=random.choice(FORMATS),
    locale='en_US') # locale=random.choice(LOCALES))
            human_readable = human_readable.lower()
            human_readable = human_readable.replace(',','')
            machine_readable = dt.isoformat()
        return human_readable, machine_readable, dt
```

4. Next, we generate and write a function to load the dataset. In this function,
   examples are created using the **load_date()** function defined earlier. In addition to
   this dataset, the function also returns dictionaries for mapping human-readable
   and machine-readable tokens along with the inverse machine vocabulary:

```
    def load_dataset(m):
        """
            Loads a dataset with m examples and vocabularies
            :m: the number of examples to generate
        """

        human_vocab = set()
        machine_vocab = set()
        dataset = []
        Tx = 30
```

```
for i in tqdm(range(m)):
    h, m, _ = load_date()
    if h is not None:
        dataset.append((h, m))
        human_vocab.update(tuple(h))
        machine_vocab.update(tuple(m))

human = dict(zip(sorted(human_vocab) + ['<unk>', '<pad>'],
              list(range(len(human_vocab) + 2))))
inv_machine = dict(enumerate(sorted(machine_vocab)))
machine = {v:k for k,v in inv_machine.items()}

return dataset, human, machine, inv_machine
```

The previous helper functions are used to generate a dataset using the **babel** Python package. Additionally, it returns the input and output vocab dictionaries, as we have been doing in past exercises.

5. Next, we generate a dataset having 10,000 samples using these helper functions:

```
m = 10000
dataset, human_vocab, machine_vocab, inv_machine_vocab = load_dataset(m)
```

The variables hold values, as depicted:

```
m = 10000
dataset, human_vocab, machine_vocab, inv_machine_vocab = load_dataset(m)

100%|███████████| 10000/10000 [00:00<00:00, 23983.69it/s]
```

```
dataset
```

```
[('9 may 1998', '1998-05-09'),
 ('10.09.70', '1970-09-10'),
 ('4/28/90', '1990-04-28'),
 ('thursday january 26 1995', '1995-01-26'),
 ('monday march 7 1983', '1983-03-07'),
```

Figure 8.8: Screenshot displaying variable values

The **human_vocab** is a dictionary that maps input characters to integers. The following is the mapping of values for **human_vocab**:

```
human_vocab
'9': 12,
'a': 13,
'b': 14,
'c': 15,
'd': 16,
'e': 17,
'f': 18,
```

Figure 8.9: Screenshot for human_vocab dictionary

The **machine_vocab** dictionary contains the mapping of the output character to integers.

```
machine_vocab
{'-': 0,
 '0': 1,
 '1': 2,
 '2': 3,
 '3': 4,
 '4': 5,
 '5': 6,
 '6': 7,
 '7': 8,
 '8': 9,
 '9': 10}
```

Figure 8.10: Screenshot for the machine_vocab dictionary

`inv_machine_vocab` is an inverse mapping of `machine_vocab` to map predicted integers back to characters:

```
inv_machine_vocab

{0:  '-',
  1:  '0',
  2:  '1',
  3:  '2',
  4:  '3',
  5:  '4',
  6:  '5',
  7:  '6',
  8:  '7',
  9:  '8',
 10:  '9'}
```

Figure 8.11: Screenshot for the inv_machine_vocab dictionary

6. Next, we preprocess data such that the input sequences have shape (**10000, 30, len(human_vocab)**). Thus, every row in this matrix represents 30 timesteps and the one-coded vector, having a value of 1 corresponding to the character at a given timestep. Similarly, the Y output gets the shape (**10000, 10, len(machine_vocab)**). This corresponds to 10 output timesteps and the corresponding one-hot-coded output vector. We first define a function named '**string_to_int**' that takes as input a single user date and returns a sequence of integers that can be fed to the model:

```
def string_to_int(string, length, vocab):
    """

    Converts all strings in the vocabulary into a list of integers
    representing the positions of the
        input string's characters in the "vocab"

    Arguments:
    string -- input string, e.g. 'Wed 10 Jul 2007'
    length -- the number of timesteps you'd like, determines if the output
    will be padded or cut
```

vocab -- vocabulary, dictionary used to index every character of your "string"

```
    Returns:
    rep -- list of integers (or '<unk>') (size = length) representing the
position of the string's character in the vocabulary
    """
```

7. Change the case to lowercase to standardize the text

```
string = string.lower()
string = string.replace(',','')

if len(string) > length:
    string = string[:length]

rep = list(map(lambda x: vocab.get(x, '<unk>'), string))

if len(string) < length:
    rep += [vocab['<pad>']] * (length - len(string))

return rep
```

8. We can now utilize this helper function to generate input and output integer sequences, as explained previously:

```
def preprocess_data(dataset, human_vocab, machine_vocab, Tx, Ty):

    X, Y = zip(*dataset)
    print("X shape before preprocess: {}".format(X))
    X = np.array([string_to_int(i, Tx, human_vocab) for i in X])
    Y = [string_to_int(t, Ty, machine_vocab) for t in Y]
    print("X shape from preprocess: {}".format(X.shape))
    print("Y shape from preprocess: {}".format(Y))

    Xoh = np.array(list(map(lambda x: to_categorical(x, num_
classes=len(human_vocab)), X)))
    Yoh = np.array(list(map(lambda x: to_categorical(x, num_
classes=len(machine_vocab)), Y)))
```

```
        return X, np.array(Y), Xoh, Yoh

    Tx = 30
    Ty = 10
    X, Y, Xoh, Yoh = preprocess_data(dataset, human_vocab, machine_vocab, Tx,
    Ty)
```

9. Print the shape of the matrices.

```
    print("X.shape:", X.shape)
    print("Y.shape:", Y.shape)
    print("Xoh.shape:", Xoh.shape)
    print("Yoh.shape:", Yoh.shape)
```

The output of this step is as follows:

```
        X.shape: (10000, 30)
        Y.shape: (10000, 10)
        Xoh.shape: (10000, 30, 37)
        Yoh.shape: (10000, 10, 11)
```

Figure 8.12: Screenshot for the shape of matrices

10. We can further inspect the shapes of the **X,Y, Xoh**, and **Yoh** vectors:

```
    index = 0
    print("Source date:", dataset[index][0])
    print("Target date:", dataset[index][1])
    print()
    print("Source after preprocessing (indices):", X[index].shape)
    print("Target after preprocessing (indices):", Y[index].shape)
    print()
    print("Source after preprocessing (one-hot):", Xoh[index].shape)
    print("Target after preprocessing (one-hot):", Yoh[index].shape)
```

The output should be as follows:

```
index = 0
print("Source date:", dataset[index][0])
print("Target date:", dataset[index][1])
print()
print("Source after preprocessing (indices):", X[index].shape)
print("Target after preprocessing (indices):", Y[index].shape)
print()
print("Source after preprocessing (one-hot):", Xoh[index].shape)
print("Target after preprocessing (one-hot):", Yoh[index].shape)
```

```
Source date: 9 may 1998
Target date: 1998-05-09

Source after preprocessing (indices): (30,)
Target after preprocessing (indices): (10,)

Source after preprocessing (one-hot): (30, 37)
Target after preprocessing (one-hot): (10, 11)
```

Figure 8.13: Screenshot for the shape of matrices after processing

11. We now start defining some functions that we need to build the model. First, we define a function that calculates a softmax value given a tensor as input:

```
def softmax(x, axis=1):
    """Softmax activation function.
    # Arguments
        x : Tensor.
        axis: Integer, axis along which the softmax normalization is
applied.
    # Returns
        Tensor, output of softmax transformation.
    # Raises
        ValueError: In case 'dim(x) == 1'.
    """
    ndim = K.ndim(x)
    if ndim == 2:
        return K.softmax(x)
    elif ndim > 2:
        e = K.exp(x - K.max(x, axis=axis, keepdims=True))
        s = K.sum(e, axis=axis, keepdims=True)
        return e / s
    else:
        raise ValueError('Cannot apply softmax to a tensor that is 1D')
```

12. Next, we can start to put the model together:

```
# Defined shared layers as global variables
repeator = RepeatVector(Tx)
concatenator = Concatenate(axis=-1)
densor1 = Dense(10, activation = "tanh")
densor2 = Dense(1, activation = "relu")

activator = Activation(softmax, name='attention_weights')
dotor = Dot(axes = 1)
```

13. **RepeatVector** serves the purpose of repeating a given tensor multiple times. In our case, this is done **Tx** times, which is 30 input timesteps. The repeator is used to repeat **S_prev** 30 times. Recall that to calculate the context vector for determining one timestep decoder output, **S_prev** needs to be concatenated with each of the input encoder timesteps. The **Concatenate keras** function accomplishes the next step, that is, concatenating the repeated **S_prev** and encoder hidden state vector for each timestep. We have also defined MLP layers, which are two dense layers (**densor1**, **densor2**). Next, the output of MLP is passed through a **softmax** layer. This **softmax** distribution is an alpha vector with each entry corresponding to the weight for each concatenated vector. In the end, a **dotor** function is defined, which is responsible for calculating the context vector. The entire flow corresponds to one step attention (since it is for one decoder output timestep):

```
def one_step_attention(h, s_prev):
    """
    Performs one step of attention: Outputs a context vector computed as a
dot product of the attention weights
    "alphas" and the hidden states "h" of the Bi-LSTM.

    Arguments:
    h -- hidden state output of the Bi-LSTM, numpy-array of shape (m, Tx,
2*n_h)
    s_prev -- previous hidden state of the (post-attention) LSTM, numpy-
array of shape (m, n_s)

    Returns:
    context -- context vector, input of the next (post-attetion) LSTM cell
    """
```

14. Use **repeator** to repeat **s_prev** to be of shape (**m**, **Tx**, **n_s**) so that you can concatenate it with all hidden states, '**h**':

```
s_prev = repeator(s_prev)
```

15. Use **concatenator** to concatenate **a** and **s_prev** on the last axis:

```
concat = concatenator([h, s_prev])
```

16. Use **densor1** to propagate **concat** through a small fully-connected neural network to compute the intermediate energies variable, **e**:

```
e = densor1(concat)
```

17. Use **densor2** to propagate **e** through a small fully-connected neural network to compute the variable energies:

```
energies = densor2(e)
```

18. Use **activator** on **energies** to compute the attention weights **alphas**:

```
alphas = activator(energies)
```

19. Use **dotor** along with **alphas** and **a** to compute the context vector to be given to the next (post-attention) LSTM-cell:

```
context = dotor([alphas, h])


return context
```

20. Up to this point, we still haven't defined the number of hidden state units for the encoder and decoder LSTMs. We also need to define the decoder LSTM, which is a unidirectional LSTM:

```
n_h = 32
n_s = 64
post_activation_LSTM_cell = LSTM(n_s, return_state = True)
output_layer = Dense(len(machine_vocab), activation=softmax)
```

21. We now define the encoder and decoder model:

```
def model(Tx, Ty, n_h, n_s, human_vocab_size, machine_vocab_size):
    """

    Arguments:
    Tx -- length of the input sequence
    Ty -- length of the output sequence
    n_h -- hidden state size of the Bi-LSTM
```

```
    n_s -- hidden state size of the post-attention LSTM
    human_vocab_size -- size of the python dictionary "human_vocab"
    machine_vocab_size -- size of the python dictionary "machine_vocab"

    Returns:
    model -- Keras model instance
    """
```

22. Define the inputs of your model with a shape (Tx,). Define s0 and c0, and the initial hidden state for the decoder LSTM of shape (n_s,):

```
    X = Input(shape=(Tx, human_vocab_size), name="input_first")
    s0 = Input(shape=(n_s,), name='s0')
    c0 = Input(shape=(n_s,), name='c0')
    s = s0
    c = c0
```

23. Initialize an empty list of **outputs**:

```
    outputs = []
```

24. Define your pre-attention Bi-LSTM. Remember to use **return_sequences=True**:

```
    h = Bidirectional(LSTM(n_h, return_sequences=True))(X)
```

25. Iterate for **Ty** steps:

```
    for t in range(Ty):
```

26. Perform one step of the attention mechanism to get back the context vector at step **t**:

```
        context = one_step_attention(h, s)
```

27. Apply the post-attention LSTM cell to the **context** vector. Also, pass **initial_state = [hidden state, cell state]**:

```
        s, _, c = post_activation_LSTM_cell(context, initial_state =
    [s,c])
```

28. Apply the **Dense** layer to the hidden state output of the post-attention LSTM:

```
        out = output_layer(s)

        # Append "out" to the "outputs" list
        outputs.append(out)
```

29. Create a model instance by taking three inputs and returning the list of outputs:

```
model = Model(inputs=[X, s0, c0], outputs=outputs)

return model
```

```
model = model(Tx, Ty, n_h, n_s, len(human_vocab), len(machine_vocab))
model.summary()
```

The output could be as shown in the following figure:

```
model.summary()


dense_3 (Dense)                   (None, 11)           715           lstm_1[0][0]
                                                                     lstm_1[1][0]
                                                                     lstm_1[2][0]
                                                                     lstm_1[3][0]
                                                                     lstm_1[4][0]
                                                                     lstm_1[5][0]
                                                                     lstm_1[6][0]
                                                                     lstm_1[7][0]
                                                                     lstm_1[8][0]
                                                                     lstm_1[9][0]
==================================================================================
======
Total params: 52,960
Trainable params: 52,960
Non-trainable params: 0
```

Figure 8.14: Screenshot for model summary

30. We will now compile the model with **categorical_crossentropy** as the loss function and **Adam** optimizer as the optimization strategy:

```
opt = Adam(lr = 0.005, beta_1=0.9, beta_2=0.999, decay = 0.01)
model.compile(loss='categorical_crossentropy', optimizer=opt,
metrics=['accuracy'])
```

31. We need to initialize the hidden state vector and memory state for decoder LSTM before fitting the model:

```
s0 = np.zeros((m, n_s))
c0 = np.zeros((m, n_s))
outputs = list(Yoh.swapaxes(0,1))
model.fit([Xoh, s0, c0], outputs, epochs=1, batch_size=100)
```

This starts the training:

```
Epoch 1/1
10000/10000 [==============================] - 15s 1ms/step - loss: 17.0066 - dense_3_loss:
2.5402 - dense_3_acc: 0.4576 - dense_3_acc_1: 0.7088 - dense_3_acc_2: 0.3134 - dense_3_acc_3:
0.0748 - dense_3_acc_4: 0.8606 - dense_3_acc_5: 0.3337 - dense_3_acc_6: 0.0510 - dense_3_acc_
7: 0.8976 - dense_3_acc_8: 0.2671 - dense_3_acc_9: 0.1082
```

Figure 8.15: Screenshot for epoch training

32. The model is now trained and can be called for inference:

```
EXAMPLES = ['3 May 1979', '5 April 09', '21th of August 2016', 'Tue 10 Jul
2007', 'Saturday May 9 2018', 'March 3 2001', 'March 3rd 2001', '1 March
2001']
for example in EXAMPLES:

    source = string_to_int(example, Tx, human_vocab)
    source = np.array(list(map(lambda x: to_categorical(x, num_
classes=len(human_vocab)), source)))#.swapaxes(0,1)
    source = source[np.newaxis, :]
    prediction = model.predict([source, s0, c0])
    prediction = np.argmax(prediction, axis = -1)
    output = [inv_machine_vocab[int(i)] for i in prediction]

    print("source:", example)
    print("output:", ''.join(output))
```

Expected output:

```
source: 3 May 1979
output: 1979-05-03
source: 5 April 09
output: 2009-05-05
source: 21th of August 2016
output: 2016-08-21
source: Tue 10 Jul 2007
output: 2007-07-10
source: Saturday May 9 2018
output: 2018-05-09
source: March 3 2001
output: 2001-03-03
source: March 3rd 2001
output: 2001-03-03
source: 1 March 2001
output: 2001-03-01
```

Figure 8.16: Screenshot for normalized date output

Other Architectures and Developments

The attention mechanism architecture described in the last section is only a way of building attention mechanism. In recent times, several other architectures have been proposed, which constitute a state of the art in the deep learning NLP world. In this section, we will briefly mention some of these architectures.

Transformer

In late 2017, Google came up with an attention mechanism architecture in their seminal paper titled "Attention is all you need." This architecture is considered state-of-the-art in the NLP community. The transformer architecture makes use of a special multi-head attention mechanism to generate attention at various levels. Additionally, it is also employs residual connections to further ensure that the vanishing gradient problem has a minimal impact on learning. The special architecture of transformers also allows a massive speed up of the training phase while providing better quality results.

The most commonly used package with transformer architecture is **tensor2tensor**. The Keras code for transformer tends to be very bulky and untenable, while **tensor2tensor** allows the use of both a Python package and a simple command-line utility that can be used to train a transformer model.

> **Note**
>
> For more information on tensor2tensor, refer to https://github.com/tensorflow/tensor2tensor/#t2t-overview
>
> Readers interested in learning more about the architecture should read the mentioned paper and the associated Google blogpost at this link: https://ai.googleblog.com/2017/08/transformer-novel-neural-network.html

BERT

In late 2018, Google open sourced yet another groundbreaking architecture, called **BERT** (**Bidirectional Encoder Representations from Transformers**). The deep learning community for NLP has been missing the transfer-learning regime for training models for a long time. The transfer learning approach to deep learning has been state-of-the-art with image-related tasks such as image classification. Images are universal in their basic structure, as they do not differ regardless of geographical locations. This allows the training of deep learning models on generic images. These pre-trained models can then be fine-tuned for a specific task. This saves training time and the need for massive amounts of data to achieve a respectable model performance.

Languages, unfortunately, vary a lot depending upon geographical locations and tend to not share basic structures. Hence, transfer learning is not a viable option when it comes to NLP tasks. BERT has now made it possible with its new attention mechanism architecture, which builds on top of the basic transformer architecture.

> **Note**
>
> For more information on BERT, refer to https://github.com/google-research/bert
>
> Readers interested in learning more about BERT should take a look at the Google blog on it at https://ai.googleblog.com/2018/11/open-sourcing-bert-state-of-art-pre.html.

Open AI GPT-2

Open AI also open sourced an architecture called **GPT-2**, which builds upon their previous architecture called GPT. The mainstay of the GPT-2 architecture is its ability to perform well on text-generation tasks. The GPT-2 model is also a transformer-based model containing around 1.5 billion parameters.

> **Note**
>
> Readers interested in learning more can refer to the blogpost by OpenAI at https://blog.openai.com/better-language-models/.

Activity 11: Build a Text Summarization Model

We will use the attention mechanism model architecture we built for neural machine translation to build a text summarization model. The goal of text summarization is to write a summary of a given large text corpus. You can imagine using text summarizers for the summarization of books or the generation of headlines for news articles.

As an example, use the given input text:

"Celebrating its 25th year, Mercedes-Benz India is set to redefine India's luxury space in the automotive segment by launching the new V-Class. The V-Class is powered by a 2.1-litre BS VI diesel engine that generates 120kW power, 380Nm torque, and can go from 0-100km/h in 10.9 seconds. It features LED headlamps, a multi-functional steering wheel, and 17-inch alloy wheels."

A good text summarization model should be able to produce a meaningful summary, such as:

"Mercedes-Benz India launches the new V-Class"

From an architectural viewpoint, a text summarization model is exactly the same as a translation model. The input to the model is text that is fed character by character (or word by word) to an encoder, while the decoder produces output characters in the same language as the source text.

> **Note**
>
> The input text can be found at https://github.com/TrainingByPackt/Deep-Learning-for-Natural-Language-Processing/tree/master/Lesson%2008.

The following steps will help you with the solution:

1. Import the required Python packages and make the human and machine vocab dictionaries.

2. Define the length of the input and output characters and the model functions (*Repeator*, *Concatenate*, *Densors*, and *Dotor*).

3. Define a one-step-attention function and the number of hidden states for the decoder and encoder.

4. Define the model architecture and run it to obtain a model.

5. Define model loss functions and other hyperparameters. Also, initialize the decoder state vectors.

6. Fit the model to our data.

7. Run the inference step for the new text.

    Expected Output:

```
source: Last night a meteorite was seen flying near the earth's moon.
output: aaaaa           <pad><pad><pad><pad><pad><pad><pad><pad><pad><pad><pad><pad><pad><pad><pad><pad>
```

Figure 8.17: Output for text summarization

> **Note**
>
> The solution for the activity can be found on page 333.

Summary

In this chapter, we learned about the concept of attention mechanisms. Based on attention mechanisms, several architectures have been proposed that constitute the state of the art in the NLP world. We learned about one specific model architecture to perform a neural machine translation task. We also briefly mentioned other state-of-the-art architectures such as transformers and BERT.

Up to now, we have seen many different NLP models. In the next chapter, we will look at the flow of a practical NLP project in an organization and related technology.

9

A Practical NLP Project Workflow in an Organization

Learning Objectives

By the end of this chapter, you will be able to:

- Identify the requirements of a natural language processing project

- Understand how different teams in an organization might be involved

- Use Google Colab notebooks to leverage a GPU to train Deep Learning models

- Deploy a model on AWS to be used as Software as a Service (SaaS)

- Get acquainted with a simple tech stack for deployment

In this chapter, we will be looking at a real-time NLP project and its flow in an organization, right till the final stage through the entire chapter.

Introduction

Up to this point in the book, we have studied several deep learning techniques that can be applied to solve specific problems in the NLP domain. Having knowledge of these techniques has empowered us to build good models and deliver high-quality performance. However, when it comes to delivering a working machine learning product in an organization, several other aspects need to be considered.

In this chapter, we will go through a practical project workflow when delivering a working deep learning system in an organization. Specifically, you will be introduced to the possible roles of various teams within your organization, building a deep learning pipeline and, finally, delivering your product in the form of SaaS.

General Workflow for the Development of a Machine Learning Product

Today, there are several ways of working with data science in an organization. Most organizations have a workflow that is specific to their environment. Some example workflows are as follows:

Figure 9.1: General workflow for the development of a machine learning product

The Presentation Workflow:

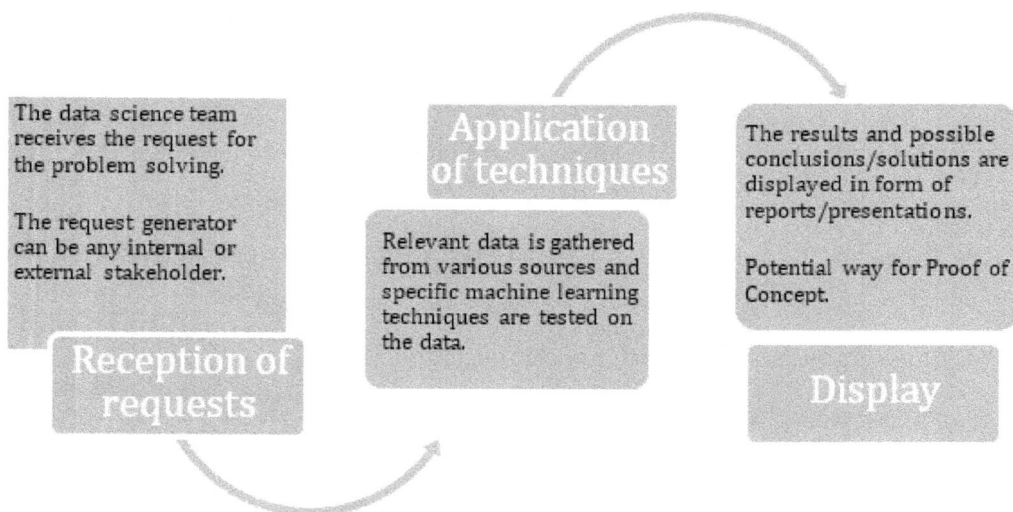

Figure 9.2: General presentation workflow

The presentation workflow can be elaborated as follows:

1. The data science team receives a request to solve a problem using machine learning. The requester could be some other team within the organization or some other company that has hired you as consultants.

2. You obtain the relevant data and apply specific machine learning techniques.

3. You showcase the results and insights in the form of a report/presentation to the stakeholders. This could also be a potential way to approach the *Proof of Concept* (PoC) phase of a project.

The Research Workflow:

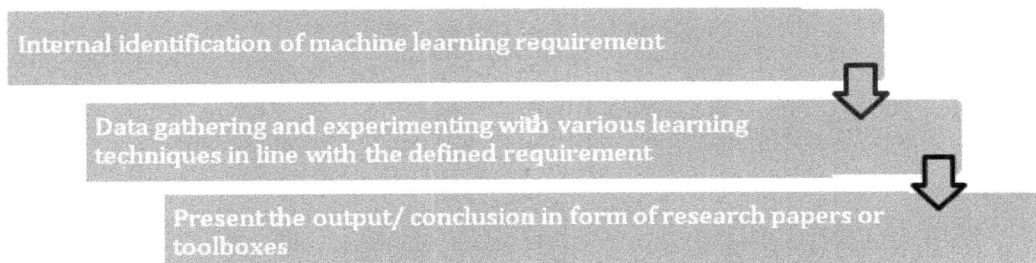

Figure 9.3: Research workflow

The main focus of this approach is to conduct research to solve a particular problem that caters to a use case. The solution can be leveraged both by the organization as well as the community in general. Other factors that distinguish this workflow from the presentation workflow are as follows:

- The timelines for such projects are typically longer than those imposed on presentation workflows.

- The deliverable is in the form of research papers and/or toolboxes.

The workflow can be broken down as follows:

1. Your organization has a research wing that wishes to enhance the existing machine learning state in the community, while also allowing your company to leverage the results.

2. Your team goes through the existing research that caters to the problem you are being asked to solve. This involves reading research papers in detail and implementing them to establish the baseline performance on some datasets suggested in the research papers.

3. You then either try to tailor the existing research to solve your problem or come up with novel ways to solve it yourself.

4. The end product could be research papers and/or toolboxes.

The Production-Oriented Workflow

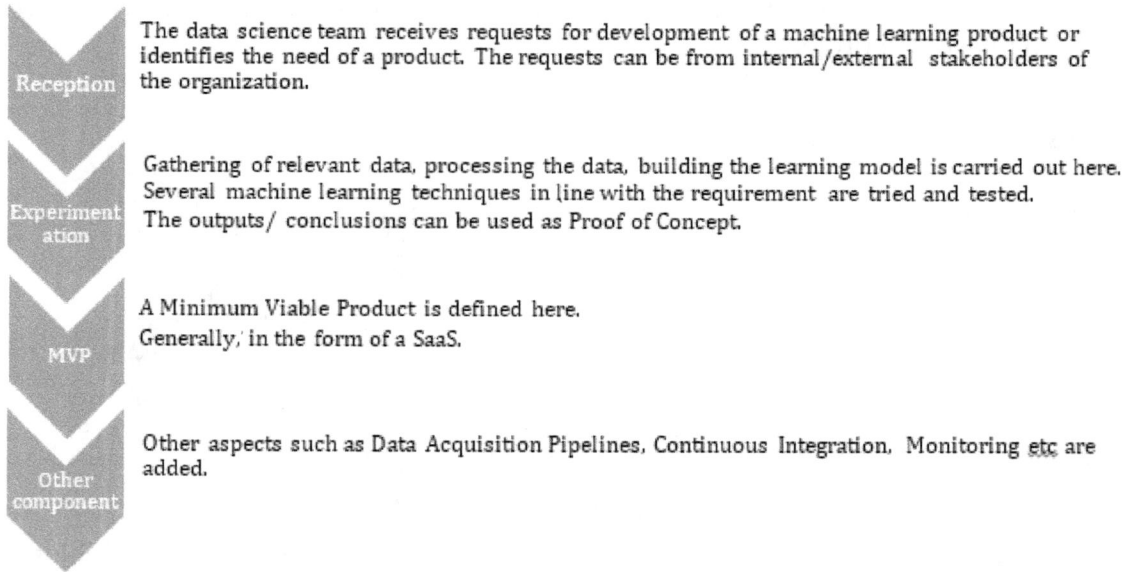

Reception

The data science team receives requests for development of a machine learning product or identifies the need of a product. The requests can be from internal/external stakeholders of the organization.

Experimentation

Gathering of relevant data, processing the data, building the learning model is carried out here. Several machine learning techniques in line with the requirement are tried and tested. The outputs/ conclusions can be used as Proof of Concept.

MVP

A Minimum Viable Product is defined here. Generally, in the form of a SaaS.

Other component

Other aspects such as Data Acquisition Pipelines, Continuous Integration, Monitoring etc are added.

Figure 9.4: Production-oriented workflow

The workflow can be elaborated on as follows:

1. The data science team receives a request to solve a problem using machine learning. The requester could be some other team within the organization or another company that has hired you as consultants. It could also be that the data science team wishes to build a product that they think will bring value to the organization.

2. You obtain the data, do the necessary research, and build the machine learning model. The data could be obtained either from within the organization or, if the problem is general enough (for example: language translation), it could also be an open source dataset. The model built could, hence, qualify as PoC to be shown to the stakeholders.

3. You define a Minimum Viable Product (MVP): for example, a machine learning model in the form of SaaS.

Once MVP is achieved, you iteratively add other aspects, such as *Data Acquisition Pipelines, Continuous Integration, Monitoring* and so on.

You will notice that even the sample workflows share components. In this chapter, our focus will be on part of *The Production Workflow*. We will build a Minimum Viable Product for a specific problem.

Problem Definition

Let's say that you work for an e-commerce platform, through which your customers can purchase a variety of products. The merchandising department of your company comes up with a request to add a feature to the website – '**Addition of a slider that contains the 5 items that received the most positive reviews in a given calendar week**'.

This request is first made to the web development department since, ultimately, they are the ones responsible for displaying the website contents. The web development department realizes that, to get a review rating, the data science team needs to be involved. The data science team receives the request from the web development team – '**We need a web service that takes a string of text as input and returns a score that indicates the degree to which the text represents a positive sentiment**'.

The data science team then refines the requirements and agrees upon the definition of a Minimum Viable Product (MVP) with the web development team:

1. The deliverable will be a web service deployed on an AWS EC2 instance.

2. The input to the web service will be a post request containing four reviews (that is, a single post request to the service will contain four reviews).

3. The output of the web service will be a set of four scores that correspond to each input text.

4. The output score will be on a scale from 1 to 5, with 1 being the least and 5 being the most positive review.

Data Acquisition

A big contribution toward determining the performance of any machine learning model is the quality and quantity of the data.

Usually, a data warehousing team/infrastructure team (DWH) is responsible for maintaining the data-related infrastructure at a company. The team takes care that data is never lost, that the underlying infrastructure is stable, and that data is always available for any team that might be interested in using it. The data science team, being one of the consumers of the data, contacts the DWH team, which grants them access to a database that contains all the reviews for various items in the product catalog of the company.

Typically, there are multiple data fields/tables in the database, some of which may not be important for the machine learning model development.

A data engineer (a part of the DWH team/member of another team/member of your team) then connects to the database, processes the data into a tabular format, and generates a flat file in the **csv** format. A discussion between the data scientist and the data engineer at this point results in the retention of only three columns from the database table:

- 'Rating': A score on the scale of 1 to 5 that indicates the degree to which a positive sentiment is represented

- 'Review Title': A simple title for the review

- 'Review': Actual review text

Notice that all three fields are inputs from customers (users of your e-commerce platform). Additionally, fields such as *item id* are not retained since they are not required to build this machine learning model for sentiment classification. The removal and retention of such information is also a product of discussions between the DS team, data engineers, and the DWH team.

It might have been the case that the current data is devoid of sentiment ratings. In such a case, one common solution is to manually go through each review and assign it a sentiment score for the purpose of obtaining training data for the model. However, as you can imagine, doing so for millions of reviews is a daunting task. Thus, crowdsourcing services such as *Amazon Mechanical Turk* can be utilized to annotate the data and get training labels for it.

> **Note**
>
> For more information on Amazon Mechanical Turk, refer to https://www.mturk.com/.

Google Colab

You are familiar with the intense computational requirements of deep learning models. On a CPU, it would take a remarkably long time to train a deep learning model with lots of training data. Hence, to keep training times practical, it is common practice to use cloud-based services that offer Graphics Processing Units (GPU) to speed up computations. You can expect a speedup of 10-30 times when compared to running the training session on a CPU. The exact amount of speedup, of course, depends upon the power of the GPU, the amount of data involved, and the processing steps.

There are many vendors offering such cloud services, such as **Amazon Web Services (AWS)**, **Microsoft Azure** and others. Google offers an environment/IDE called **Google Colab**, which offers up to 12 hours of free GPU usage per day for anyone looking to train deep learning models. Additionally, the code is run on a **Jupyter**-like notebook. In this chapter, we will leverage the power of Google Colab to develop our deep learning-based sentiment classifier.

In order to familiarize yourself with Google Colab, you are urged to go through a tutorial for it.

> **Note**
>
> Before proceeding further, refer to the tutorial at https://colab.research.google.com/notebooks/welcome.ipynb#recent=true

The following steps should acquaint you well with Google Colab:

1. To open a new blank **colab** notebook, go to https://colab.research.google.com/notebooks/welcome.ipynb, select **'File'** from the menu, and then select the **'New Python 3 notebook'** option, as shown in the screenshot:

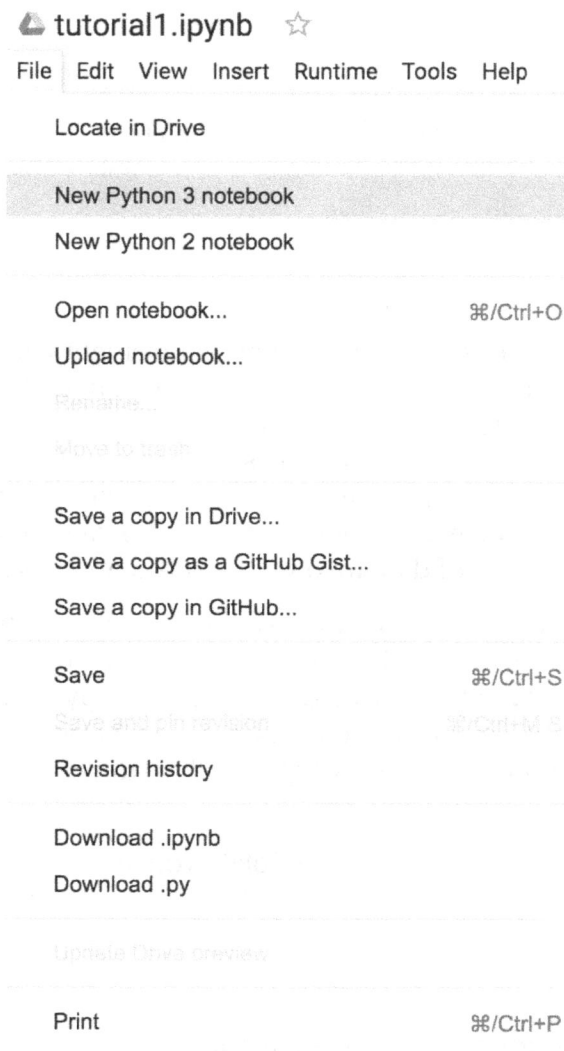

Figure 9.5: A new Python notebook on Google Colab

2. Next, rename the notebook any name of your choice. Then, to use a **GPU** for training, we need to select a **GPU** as the runtime. To do so, choose the '**Edit**' option from the menu and select '**Notebook Settings**'.

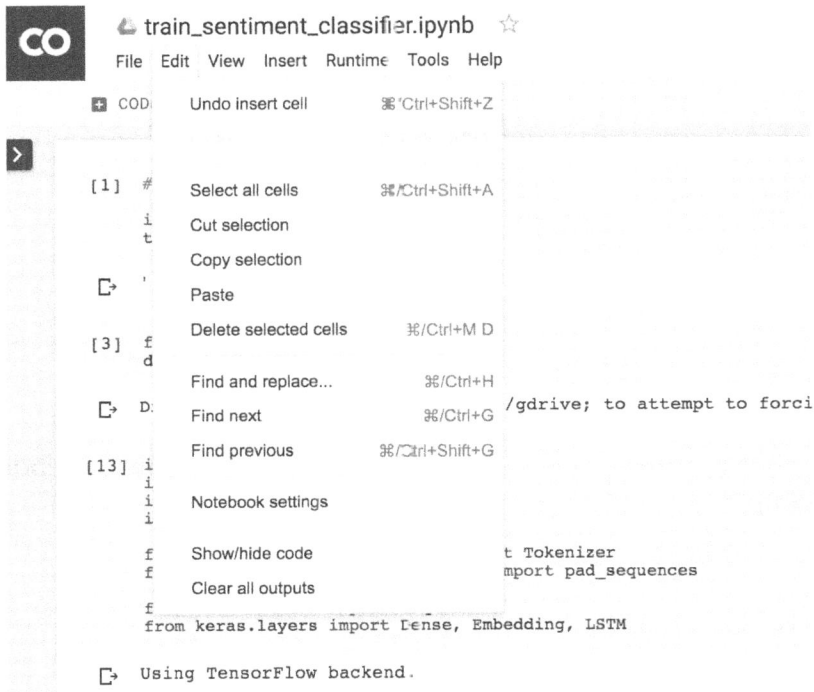

Figure 9.6: Edit dropdown in Google Colab

3. A menu pops up with a '**Hardware Accelerator**' field, which is set to '**None**' by default:

Figure 9.7: Notebook settings for Google Colab

4. A dropdown can be used at this point to select '**GPU**' as the option:

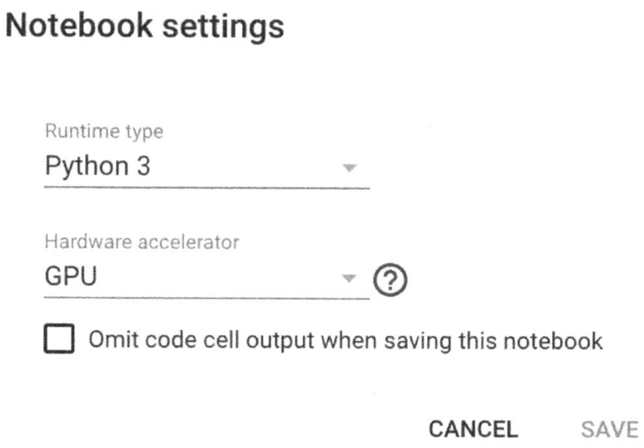

Notebook settings

Runtime type
Python 3 ▾

Hardware accelerator
GPU ▾ ⑦

☐ Omit code cell output when saving this notebook

CANCEL   SAVE

Figure 9.8: GPU hardware accelerator

5. To check whether the GPU has, in fact, been allotted to your notebook, run the following snippet:

```
# Check if GPU is detected

import tensorflow as tf
tf.test.gpu_device_name()
```

The output of running this snippet should indicate the GPU's availability:

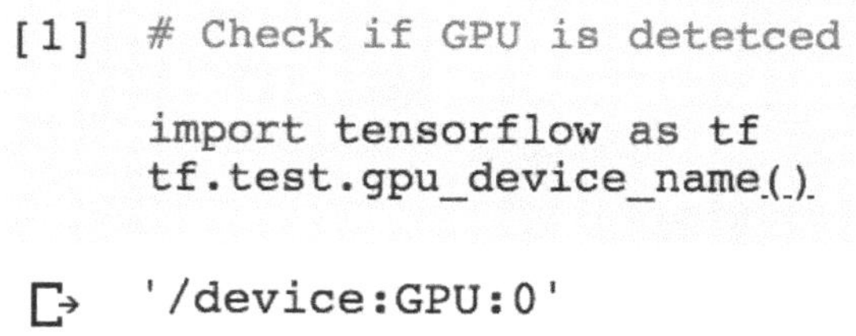

```
[1]  # Check if GPU is detetced

     import tensorflow as tf
     tf.test.gpu_device_name()
```

⇨ '/device:GPU:0'

Figure 9.9: Screenshot for GPU device name

The output is the GPU device name.

6. Next, the data needs to be made accessible within the notebook. There are a number of ways to do this. One way to accomplish this task is by moving the data to a personal Google Drive location. It's better to move the data in a zipped format to avoid using up too much space on the drive. Go ahead and create a new folder on Google Drive and move the zipped CSV data file within the folder. Next, we mount the Google Drive onto the Colab notebook machine to make the drive data available for use within the Colab notebook:

```
from google.colab import drive
drive.mount('/content/gdrive')
```

The snippet we just mentioned would return a weblink for authorization. Upon clicking on that link, a new browser tab opens up containing an authorization code that should be copied and pasted onto the notebook prompt:

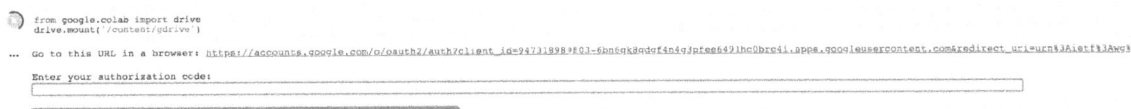

Figure 9.10: Screenshot for importing data from Google Drive

At this point, all the data within your Google Drive is available for use within the Colab notebook.

7. Next, navigate to the folder location where the zipped data is present:

```
cd "/content/gdrive/My Drive/Lesson-9/"
```

8. Confirm that you have navigated to the desired location by issuing a 'pwd' command in the notebook cell:

```
[ ]  pwd
```

```
    '/content/gdrive/My Drive/Lesson-9'
```

Figure 9.11: Data imported on the Colab notebook from Google Drive

9. Next, unzip the zipped data file using the **unzip** command:

```
!unzip data.csv.zip
```

This will result in the following output:

```
[ ]  !unzip data.csv.zip

 ⊳   Archive:  data.csv.zip
        inflating: data.csv
         creating: __MACOSX/
        inflating: __MACOSX/._data.csv
```

Figure 9.12: Unzipping a data file on a Colab notebook

The '**MACOSX**' output lines are operating system-specific and may not be the same for everyone. Anyhow, an unzipped data file, '**data.csv**' is now available for use within the Colab notebook.

10. Now that we have the data available and the environment to use the GPU is set, we can start coding up the model. We will import the required packages first:

```
import os
import re
import pandas as pd

from keras.preprocessing.text import Tokenizer
from keras.preprocessing.sequence import pad_sequences

from keras.models import Sequential
from keras.layers import Dense, Embedding, LSTM
```

11. Next, we will write a preprocessing function that turns all the text to lowercase and removes any numbers:

```
def preprocess_data(data_file_path):
    data = pd.read_csv(data_file_path, header=None) # read the csv
    data.columns = ['rating', 'title', 'review'] # add column names
    data['review'] = data['review'].apply(lambda x: x.lower()) # change
all text to lower
    data['review'] = data['review'].apply((lambda x: re.sub('[^a-zA-z0-
9\s]','',x))) # remove all numbers
    return data
```

12. Note that we are using pandas for reading and processing texts. Let's run this function with the path of our CSV file:

```
df = preprocess_data('data.csv')
```

13. We can now examine the contents of the dataframe:

```
df.head()
```

	rating	title	review
0	3	more like funchuck	gave this to my dad for a gag gift after direc...
1	5	Inspiring	i hope a lot of people hear this cd we need mo...
2	5	The best soundtrack ever to anything.	im reading a lot of reviews saying that this i...
3	4	Chrono Cross OST	the music of yasunori misuda is without questi...
4	5	Too good to be true	probably the greatest soundtrack in history us...

Figure 9.13: Screenshot of dataframe contents

14. As expected, we have three fields. Also, we see that the 'review' column has much more text than the 'title' column. So, we choose to use only the 'review' column for developing the model. We'll now proceed with tokenizing the text:

```
# initialize tokenization

max_features = 2000
maxlength = 250

tokenizer = Tokenizer(num_words=max_features, split=' ')

# fit tokenizer

tokenizer.fit_on_texts(df['review'].values)
X = tokenizer.texts_to_sequences(df['review'].values)

# pad sequences
X = pad_sequences(X, maxlen=maxlength)
```

Here, we have restricted the feature count to 2,000 words. We then apply the tokenizer with the maximum features to the 'review' column of the data. We also pad the sequence length to 250 words.

The **X** variable looks as follows:

```
X

array([[   0,    0,    0, ...,   40,    7,    6],
       [   0,    0,    0, ...,   23, 1694,    2],
       [   0,    0,    0, ...,   24,  171,  170],
       ...,
       [   0,    0,    0, ...,   42,  712, 1358],
       [   0,    0,    0, ...,  580,  290, 1722],
       [   0,    0,    0, ...,    1,   38, 1840]], dtype=int32)
```

Figure 9.14: Screenshot of the X variable array

The X variable is a **NumPy** array with 3,000,000 rows and 250 columns. This is because there are 3,000,000 reviews available and each review has a fixed length of 250 words after padding.

15. We'll now prepare the target variable for training. We define the problem as a five-class classification problem where each class corresponds to a rating. Since the rating (sentiment score) is on a scale of 1-5, there are 5 outputs of the classifier. (You could also model this as a regression problem). We use the **get_dummies** function from pandas to get the five outputs:

```
# get target variable

y_train = pd.get_dummies(df.rating).values
```

The **y_train** variable is a **NumPy** array with 3,000,000 rows and 5 columns with values, as shown:

```
y_train

array([[0, 0, 1, 0, 0],
       [0, 0, 0, 0, 1],
       [0, 0, 0, 0, 1],
       ...,
       [0, 1, 0, 0, 0],
       [0, 0, 1, 0, 0],
       [1, 0, 0, 0, 0]], dtype=uint8)
```

Figure 9.15: y_train output

16. We have now preprocessed the text and prepared the target variable. Let's now define the model:

```
embed_dim = 128
hidden_units = 100
n_classes = 5

model = Sequential()
model.add(Embedding(max_features, embed_dim, input_length = X.shape[1]))
model.add(LSTM(hidden_units))
model.add(Dense(n_classes, activation='softmax'))
model.compile(loss = 'categorical_crossentropy', optimizer='adam',metrics
= ['accuracy'])
print(model.summary())
```

We choose 128 embedding dimensions for input. We also choose an LSTM as the RNN unit with 100 hidden dimensions. The model summary is printed as follows:

```
Layer (type)                    Output Shape                Param #
===============================================================
embedding_1 (Embedding)         (None, 250, 128)            256000

lstm_1 (LSTM)                   (None, 100)                 91600

dense_1 (Dense)                 (None, 5)                   505
===============================================================
Total params: 348,105
Trainable params: 348,105
Non-trainable params: 0
```

None

Figure 9.16: Screenshot of the model summary

17. We can now fit the model:

```
# fit the model

model.fit(X[:100000, :], y_train[:100000, :], batch_size = 128, epochs=15,
validation_split=0.2)
```

Note that we fit 100,000 reviews instead of 3,000,000. Running the training session with this configuration takes around 90 minutes. It would take much longer with a complete amount of data:

```
# fit the model

model.fit(X[:100000, :], y_train[:100000, :], batch_size = 128, epochs=15, validation_split=0.2)

Train on 80000 samples, validate on 20000 samples
Epoch 1/15
80000/80000 [==============================] - 320s 4ms/step - loss: 1.1106 - acc: 0.5231 - val_loss: 1.1261 - val_acc: 0.5171
Epoch 2/15
80000/80000 [==============================] - 319s 4ms/step - loss: 1.0786 - acc: 0.5385 - val_loss: 1.1099 - val_acc: 0.5192
Epoch 3/15
80000/80000 [==============================] - 318s 4ms/step - loss: 1.0482 - acc: 0.5533 - val_loss: 1.1256 - val_acc: 0.5164
Epoch 4/15
80000/80000 [==============================] - 311s 4ms/step - loss: 1.0226 - acc: 0.5660 - val_loss: 1.1226 - val_acc: 0.5172
Epoch 5/15
80000/80000 [==============================] - 315s 4ms/step - loss: 1.0014 - acc: 0.5771 - val_loss: 1.1348 - val_acc: 0.5087
Epoch 6/15
80000/80000 [==============================] - 319s 4ms/step - loss: 0.9754 - acc: 0.5873 - val_loss: 1.1455 - val_acc: 0.5078
Epoch 7/15
80000/80000 [==============================] - 320s 4ms/step - loss: 0.9496 - acc: 0.6015 - val_loss: 1.1708 - val_acc: 0.5051
Epoch 8/15
80000/80000 [==============================] - 322s 4ms/step - loss: 0.9244 - acc: 0.6099 - val_loss: 1.1870 - val_acc: 0.5028
Epoch 9/15
80000/80000 [==============================] - 317s 4ms/step - loss: 0.8978 - acc: 0.6226 - val_loss: 1.2118 - val_acc: 0.5002
Epoch 10/15
80000/80000 [==============================] - 313s 4ms/step - loss: 0.8678 - acc: 0.6383 - val_loss: 1.2304 - val_acc: 0.4975
Epoch 11/15
80000/80000 [==============================] - 319s 4ms/step - loss: 0.8391 - acc: 0.6508 - val_loss: 1.2817 - val_acc: 0.4953
Epoch 12/15
80000/80000 [==============================] - 320s 4ms/step - loss: 0.8089 - acc: 0.6655 - val_loss: 1.3062 - val_acc: 0.4907
Epoch 13/15
80000/80000 [==============================] - 319s 4ms/step - loss: 0.7753 - acc: 0.6810 - val_loss: 1.3529 - val_acc: 0.4883
Epoch 14/15
80000/80000 [==============================] - 315s 4ms/step - loss: 0.7442 - acc: 0.6958 - val_loss: 1.3931 - val_acc: 0.4814
Epoch 15/15
80000/80000 [==============================] - 316s 4ms/step - loss: 0.7081 - acc: 0.7134 - val_loss: 1.4570 - val_acc: 0.4803
<keras.callbacks.History at 0x7fcba53a00f0>
```

Figure 9.17: Screenshot of the training session

The validation accuracy for this 5-class problem is 48%. This isn't a good result, but for the purpose of demonstration, we can go ahead and deploy it.

18. We now have the model that we wish to deploy. Now, we need to save the model file and the tokenizer that will be used in the production environment to get predictions on the new reviews:

```
# save model and tokenizer

model.save('trained_model.h5')  # creates a HDF5 file 'trained_model.h5'

with open('trained_tokenizer.pkl', 'wb') as f: # creates a pickle file
'trained_tokenizer.pkl'
    pickle.dump(tokenizer, f)
```

19. These files now need to be downloaded from the Google Colab environment to the local drive:

```
from google.colab import files
files.download('trained_model.h5')
files.download('trained_tokenizer.pkl')
```

This snippet will download the tokenizer and model files to the local computer. We are now ready to use the model for predictions.

Flask

In this section, we will use the Flask microserver framework provided by Python to make a web application that provides predictions. We will get a RESTful API that we can query to get our results. Before commencing, we need to install Flask (use **pip**):

1. Let's begin by importing the packages:

```
import re
import pickle
import numpy as np

from flask import Flask, request, jsonify
from keras.models import load_model
from keras.preprocessing.sequence import pad_sequences
```

2. Now, let's write a function that loads the trained model and **tokenizer**:

```
def load_variables():
    global model, tokenizer
    model = load_model('trained_model.h5')
    model._make_predict_function()  #https://github.com/keras-team/keras/
issues/6462
    with open('trained_tokenizer.pkl', 'rb') as f:
        tokenizer = pickle.load(f)
```

The **make_predict_function()** is a hack that allows using **keras** models with Flask.

3. Now, we'll define preprocessing functions similar to the training code:

```
def do_preprocessing(reviews):
    processed_reviews = []
    for review in reviews:
        review = review.lower()
        processed_reviews.append(re.sub('[^a-zA-z0-9\s]', '', review))
    processed_reviews = tokenizer.texts_to_sequences(np.array(processed_
reviews))
    processed_reviews = pad_sequences(processed_reviews, maxlen=250)
    return processed_reviews
```

Similar to the training phase, the reviews are first lowercased. Then, numbers are replaced with blanks. Next, the loaded tokenizer is applied and the sequences are padded to have a fixed length of 250 to make them consistent with the training input.

4. We will now define a Flask app instance:

```
app = Flask(__name__)
```

5. We now define an endpoint that displays a fixed message:

```
@app.route('/')
def home_routine():
    return 'Hello World!'
```

It is good practice to have a root endpoint to check whether the web service is up.

6. Next, we'll have a prediction endpoint, to which we can send our review strings. The kind of HTTP request we will use is a **'POST'** request:

```
@app.route('/prediction', methods=['POST'])
def get_prediction():
    # get incoming text
    # run the model
    if request.method == 'POST':
        data = request.get_json()
    data = do_preprocessing(data)
    predicted_sentiment_prob = model.predict(data)
    predicted_sentiment = np.argmax(predicted_sentiment_prob, axis=-1)
    return str(predicted_sentiment)
```

7. We can now start the web server:

```
if __name__ == '__main__':
    # load model
    load_variables()
    app.run(debug=True)
```

8. We could save this file as **app.py** (any name could be used). Run this code from the terminal using **app.py**:

```
python app.py
```

An output such as the one shown here will be produced in the terminal window:

```
Using TensorFlow backend.
2019-03-24 23:08:25.948604: I tensorflow/core/platform/cpu_feature_guard.cc:141] Your CPU supports instructions
that this TensorFlow binary was not compiled to use: AVX2 FMA
 * Serving Flask app "app" (lazy loading)
 * Environment: production
   WARNING: Do not use the development server in a production environment.
   Use a production WSGI server instead.
 * Debug mode: on
 * Running on http://127.0.0.1:5000/ (Press CTRL+C to quit)
 * Restarting with stat
Using TensorFlow backend.
2019-03-24 23:08:31.730337: I tensorflow/core/platform/cpu_feature_guard.cc:141] Your CPU supports instructions
that this TensorFlow binary was not compiled to use: AVX2 FMA
 * Debugger is active!
 * Debugger PIN: 150-665-765
```

Figure 9.18: Output for Flask

9. At this point, go to your browser window and enter the **http://127.0.0.1:5000/** address. The 'Hello World!' message will be displayed on the screen. The output produced corresponds to the root endpoint we set in the code. Now, we send our review texts to the 'prediction' endpoint of our Flask web service. Let's send the following four reviews:

10. "The book was very poor"

11. "Very nice!"

12. "The author could have done more"

13. "Amazing product!"

14. We can send post requests to a web service using **curl** requests. For the four reviews mentioned, the **curl** request can be sent through the terminal, as follows:

```
curl -X POST \
127.0.0.1:5000/prediction \
-H 'Content-Type: application/json' \
-d '["The book was very poor", "Very nice!", "The author could have done
more", "Amazing product!"]'
```

The list of four reviews is posted to the prediction endpoint of the web service.

The web service replies with a list of four ratings:

```
[0 4 2 4]
```

So, the sentiment ratings are as follows:

15. "The book was very poor"- 0

16. "Very nice!"- 4

17. "The author could have done more" - 2

18. "Amazing product!" - 4

The ratings actually make sense!

Deployment

Up to this point, the data science team has a Flask web service that works on a local system. However, the web development team is still not in a position to use the service, since it only runs on a local system. So, we need to host this web service somewhere on a cloud platform so that it is also available for the web development team to use. This section provides a basic pipeline for the deployment to work, which can be broken down into the following steps:

1. Make changes to the Flask web app so that it can be deployed.

2. Use Docker to wrap the flask web application into a container.

3. Host the container on an Amazon Web Services (AWS) EC2 instance.

Let's look at each of these steps in detail.

Making Changes to a Flask Web App

The flask application that was coded in the FLASK section ran on a local web address: `http://127.0.0.1:5000`. Since our intention is to host it on the internet, this address needs to be changed to: 0.0.0.0. Additionally, since the default HTTP port is 80, the port also needs to be changed from 5000 to 80. So, the address that needs to be queried now becomes: 0.0.0.0:80.

In the code snippet, this change can be accomplished simply by modifying the call to the `app.run` function, as shown here:

```
app.run(host=0.0.0.0, port=80)
```

Notice that the **'debug'** flag has also vanished (the default value of **'debug'** flag is *'False'*). This is because the application is past the debugging phase and is ready to be deployed to production.

> **Note**
>
> The rest of the code remains exactly the same as before.

The application should be run again using the same command as earlier, and it should be verified that the same responses as earlier are received. The address in the curl request needs to be changed to reflect the updated web address:

```
curl -X POST \
0.0.0.0:80/prediction \
-H 'Content-Type: application/json' \
-d '["The book was very poor", "Very nice!", "The author could have done
more", "Amazing product!"]'
```

> **Note**
>
> If a permission error is received at this point, change the port number to 5000 in the **app.run()** command in app.py. (Port 80 is a privileged port, so change it to a port that isn't, for example, 5000). However, be sure to change the port back to 80 once it is verified that the code works.

Use Docker to Wrap the Flask Web Application into a Container

The DS team intends to run the web service on a virtual machine hosted on a cloud platform (that is, AWS EC2). To isolate the EC2 operating system from the code environment, Docker offers containerization as a solution. We'll be using that here.

> **Note**
>
> For a quick tutorial on the basics of Docker and how to install and use it, refer to https://docker-curriculum.com/.

Follow these steps to deploy the application onto the container:

1. We first need a *requirements.txt* file that lists the specific packages that are needed to run the Python code:

    ```
    Flask==1.0.2
    numpy==1.14.1
    keras==2.2.4
    tensorflow==1.10.0
    ```

2. We need a **Dockerfile** containing instructions so that the Docker daemon can build the docker image:

    ```
    FROM python:3.6-slim
    COPY ./app.py /deploy/
    COPY ./requirements.txt /deploy/
    COPY ./trained_model.h5 /deploy/
    COPY ./trained_tokenizer.pkl /deploy/
    WORKDIR /deploy/
    RUN pip install -r requirements.txt
    EXPOSE 80
    ENTRYPOINT ["python", "app.py"]
    ```

The Docker image is pulled from the Python dockerhub repository. Here, the Dockerfile is executed. The *app.py*, *requirements.txt*, *tokenizer pickle* file, and *trained model* are copied over to the Docker image using the COPY command. To change the working directory to the 'deploy' directory (in which the files were copied), the WORKDIR command is used. The **RUN** command then installs the Python packages mentioned in the Dockerfile. Since port 80 is required to be accessed outside the container, the **EXPOSE** command is used.

> **Note**
>
> The Docker Hub link can be found at https://hub.docker.com/_/python.

3. The Docker image should next be made using the **docker build** command:

```
docker build -f Dockerfile -t app-packt .
```

Don't forget the period in this command. The output of the command is as follows:

```
Sending build context to Docker daemon  115.6MB
Step 1/9 : FROM python:3.6-slim
 ---> 5d4dd7f71a65
Step 2/9 : COPY ./app.py /deploy/
 ---> f71341666654
Step 3/9 : COPY ./requirements.txt /deploy/
 ---> 688538f2682c
Step 4/9 : COPY ./trained_model.h5 /deploy/
 ---> 89af21aa696e
Step 5/9 : COPY ./trained_tokenizer.pkl /deploy/
 ---> 9cba42121f49
Step 6/9 : WORKDIR /deploy/
 ---> Running in 204358b07798
Removing intermediate container 204358b07798
 ---> 33241b6c6015
Step 7/9 : RUN pip install -r requirements.txt
 ---> Running in d19156053f1d
Collecting Flask==1.0.2 (from -r requirements.txt (line 1))
  Downloading https://files.pythonhosted.org/packages/7f/e7/08578774ed4536d3242b14dacb4696386634607af824ea99
7202cd0edb4b/Flask-1.0.2-py2.py3-none-any.whl (91kB)
Collecting numpy==1.14.1 (from -r requirements.txt (line 2))
  Downloading https://files.pythonhosted.org/packages/ce/7d/348c5d8d44443656e76285aa97b828b6dbd9c10e5b9c0f7f
98eff0ff70e4/numpy-1.14.1-cp36-cp36m-manylinux1_x86_64.whl (12.2MB)
Collecting keras==2.2.4 (from -r requirements.txt (line 3))
  Downloading https://files.pythonhosted.org/packages/5e/10/aa32dad071ce52b5502266b5c65945l1cfd6ffcbf14e6c8c4
f16c0ff5aaab/Keras-2.2.4-py2.py3-none-any.whl (312kB)
Collecting tensorflow==1.10.0 (from -r requirements.txt (line 4))
  Downloading https://files.pythonhosted.org/packages/ea/e6/a6d371306c23c2b01cd2cb38909673d17ddd388d9e4b3c0f
6602bfd972c8/tensorflow-1.10.0-cp36-cp36m-manylinux1_x86_64.whl (58.4MB)
```

Figure 9.19: Output screenshot for docker build

'**app-packt**' is the name of the Docker image generated.

4. The Docker image can now be run as a container by issuing the **docker run** command:

```
docker run -p 80:80 app-packt
```

The **p flag** is used to do port mapping between port 80 of the local system to port 80 of the Docker container. (Change the port mapping part of the command to 5000:80 if 5000 is used locally. Please change the mapping back to 80:80 after verifying that the Docker container works, as explained.)

The following screenshot depicts the output of the **docker run** command:

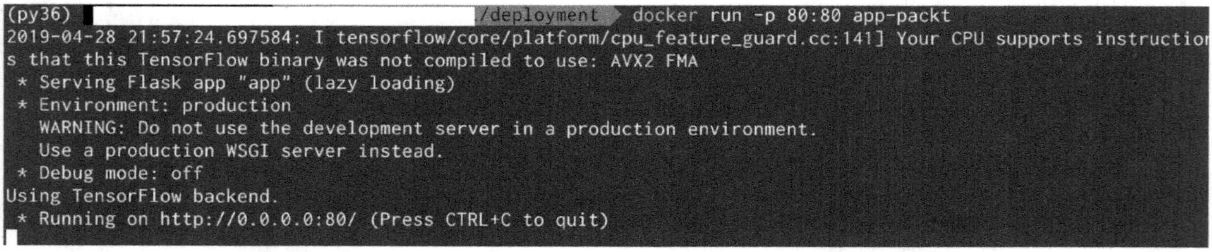

```
(py36)                              /deployment   docker run -p 80:80 app-packt
2019-04-28 21:57:24.697584: I tensorflow/core/platform/cpu_feature_guard.cc:141] Your CPU supports instructio
s that this TensorFlow binary was not compiled to use: AVX2 FMA
 * Serving Flask app "app" (lazy loading)
 * Environment: production
   WARNING: Do not use the development server in a production environment.
   Use a production WSGI server instead.
 * Debug mode: off
Using TensorFlow backend.
 * Running on http://0.0.0.0:80/ (Press CTRL+C to quit)
```

Figure 9.20: Output screenshot for the docker run command

The exact same curl request from the last section can now be issued to verify that the application works.

The application code is now ready to be deployed onto AWS EC2.

Host the Container on an Amazon Web Services (AWS) EC2 instance

The DS team now has a containerized application that works on their local system. The web development team is still not in a position to use it, as it is still local. As per the initial MVP definition, the DS team now goes on to use the AWS EC2 instance to deploy the application. The deployment will ensure that the web service is available for the web development team to use.

As a prerequisite, you need to have an AWS account to use the EC2 instance. For the purpose of demonstration, we will be using a 't2.*small*' EC2 instance type. This instance costs around 2 cents (USD) per hour at the time of writing. Note that this instance is not free-tier eligible. By default, this instance will not be available in your AWS region and a request needs to be raised for this instance to be added to your account. This usually takes a couple of hours. Alternatively, check the instance limits for your AWS region and select another instance with a minimum of 2GB RAM. A simple 't2.*micro*' instance will not work for us here, as it has only 1GB of memory.

> **Note**
>
> The link for the AWS account can be found at https://aws.amazon.com/premiumsupport/knowledge-center/create-and-activate-aws-account/
>
> To add instances and check instance limits, refer to https://docs.aws.amazon.com/AWSEC2/latest/UserGuide/ec2-resource-limits.html.

Let's start with the deployment process:

1. After logging into the AWS Management Console, search for '**ec2**' in the search bar. This takes you to the EC2 dashboard, as shown here:

AWS Management Console

AWS services

Find Services
You can enter names, keywords or acronyms.

Q ec2	✕

EC2
Virtual Servers in the Cloud

ECS
Run and Manage Docker Containers

EFS
Managed File Storage for EC2

Figure 9.21: AWS services in the AWS Management Console

2. A key pair needs to be created to access AWS resources. To create one, look for the following pane and select '**Key Pairs**'. This allows you to create a new key pair:

NETWORK & SECURITY

Security Groups

Elastic IPs

Placement Groups

Key Pairs

Network Interfaces

Figure 9.22: Network and security on the AWS console

3. A '.pem' file is downloaded, which is the key file. Be sure to save the pem file safely and change its mode using the following command:

```
chmod 400 key-file-name.pem
```

This is required to change file permissions to private.

4. To configure the instance, select '**Launch Instance**' on the EC2 dashboard:

Resources

You are using the following Amazon EC2 resources in the EU Central (Frankfurt) region:

0	Running Instances	0	Elastic IPs
0	Dedicated Hosts	0	Snapshots
1	Volumes	0	Load Balancers
2	Key Pairs	6	Security Groups
0	Placement Groups		

Learn more about the latest in AWS Compute from AWS re:Invent by viewing the EC2 Videos.

Create Instance

To start using Amazon EC2 you will want to launch a virtual server, known as an Amazon EC2 instance.

Launch Instance ▼

Note: Your instances will launch in the EU Central (Frankfurt) region

Service Health   ↻ Scheduled Events

Figure 9.23: Resources on the AWS console

5. Next, select the **Amazon Machine Instance** (**AMI**), which selects the OS that EC2 instance runs. We will work with '**Amazon Linux 2 AMI**':

> **Note**
>
> For more information on Amazon Linux 2 AMI, refer to https://aws.amazon.com/amazon-linux-2/.

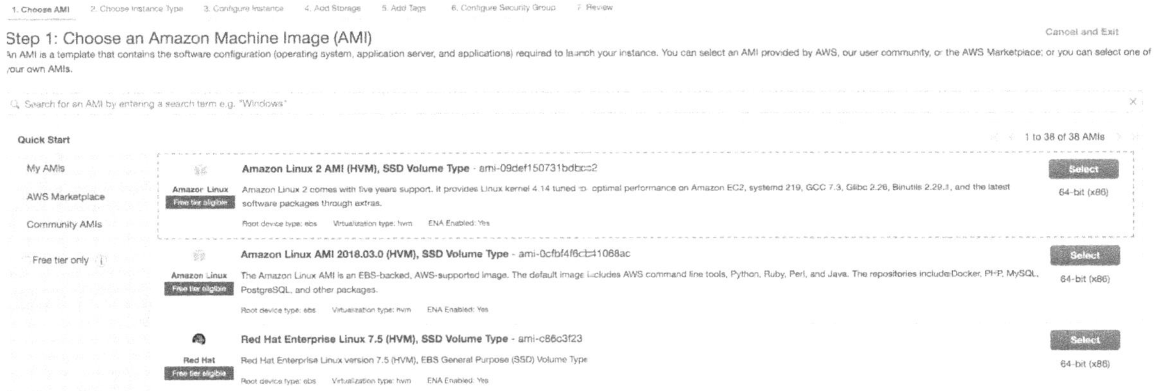

Figure 9.24: Amazon Machine Instance (AMI)

6. Now, we select the hardware part of EC2, which is the '**t2.small**' instance:

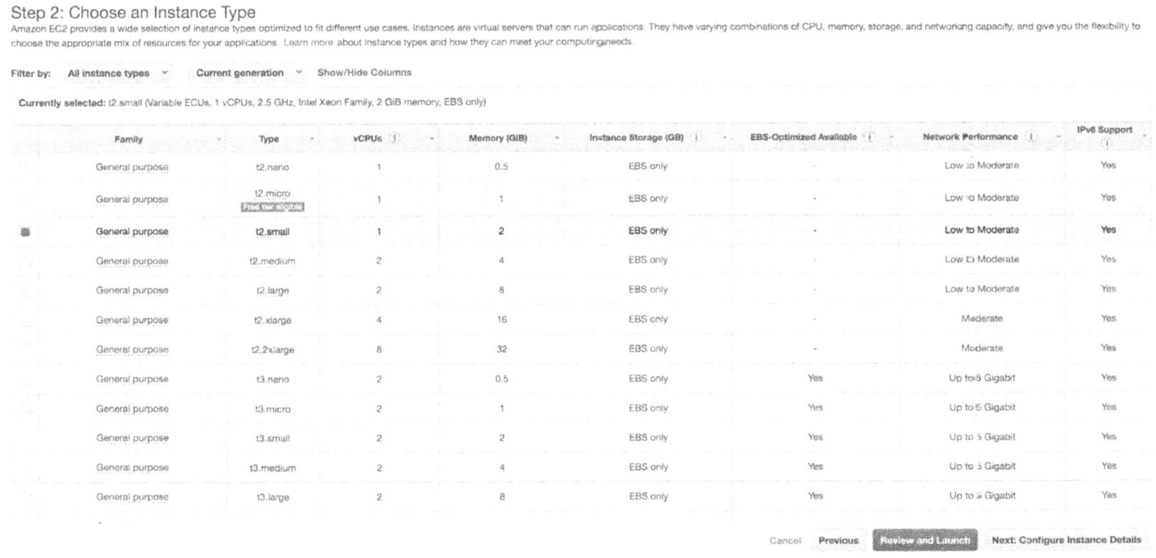

Family	Type	vCPUs	Memory (GiB)	Instance Storage (GB)	EBS-Optimized Available	Network Performance	IPv6 Support
General purpose	t2.nano	1	0.5	EBS only	-	Low to Moderate	Yes
General purpose	t2.micro Free tier eligible	1	1	EBS only	-	Low to Moderate	Yes
General purpose	t2.small	1	2	EBS only	-	Low to Moderate	Yes
General purpose	t2.medium	2	4	EBS only	-	Low to Moderate	Yes
General purpose	t2.large	2	8	EBS only	-	Low to Moderate	Yes
General purpose	t2.xlarge	4	16	EBS only	-	Moderate	Yes
General purpose	t2.2xlarge	8	32	EBS only	-	Moderate	Yes
General purpose	t3.nano	2	0.5	EBS only	Yes	Up to 5 Gigabit	Yes
General purpose	t3.micro	2	1	EBS only	Yes	Up to 5 Gigabit	Yes
General purpose	t3.small	2	2	EBS only	Yes	Up to 5 Gigabit	Yes
General purpose	t3.medium	2	4	EBS only	Yes	Up to 5 Gigabit	Yes
General purpose	t3.large	2	8	EBS only	Yes	Up to 5 Gigabit	Yes

Figure 9.25: Choosing the instance type on AMI

7. Clicking on '**Review and Launch**' gets you to step 7 – the **Review Instance Launch** screen:

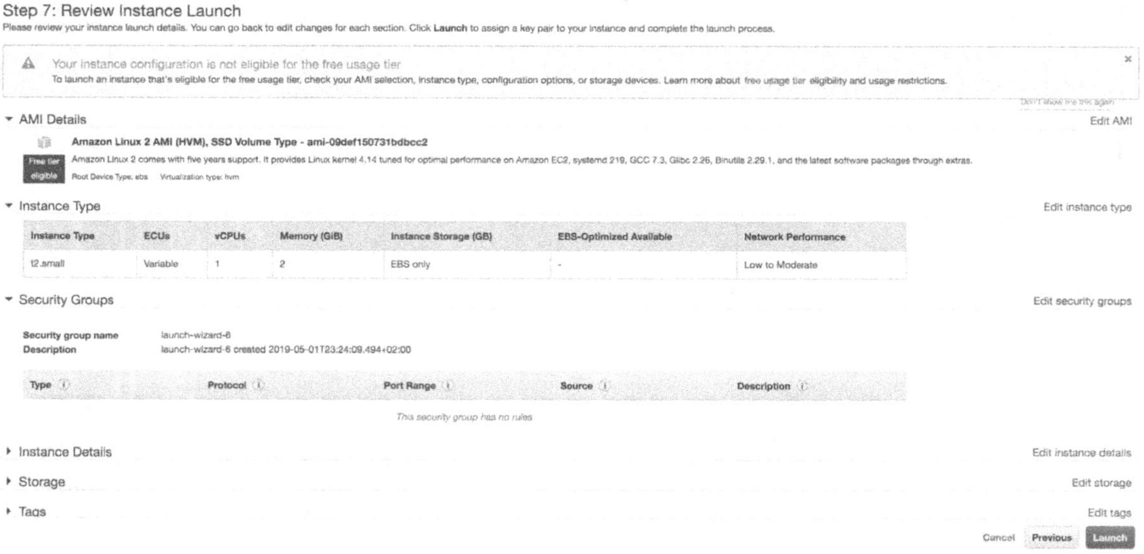

Figure 9.26: The review instance launch screen

8. Now, to make the web service reachable, the security group needs to be modified. To this end, a rule needs to be created. At the end, you should see the following screen:

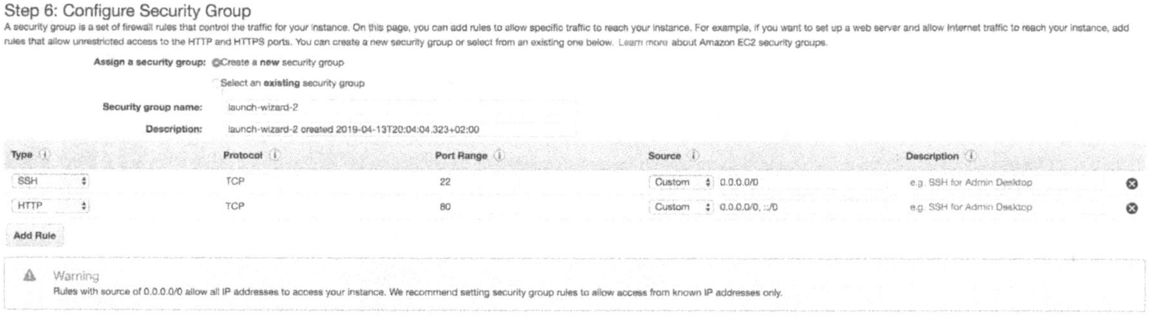

Figure 9.27: Configure the security group

Note

More can be learned about security groups and configuration using the AWS documentation at https://docs.aws.amazon.com/AWSEC2/latest/UserGuide/using-network-security.html.

9. Next, clicking on the 'Launch' icon will trigger a redirection to a **Launch** screen:

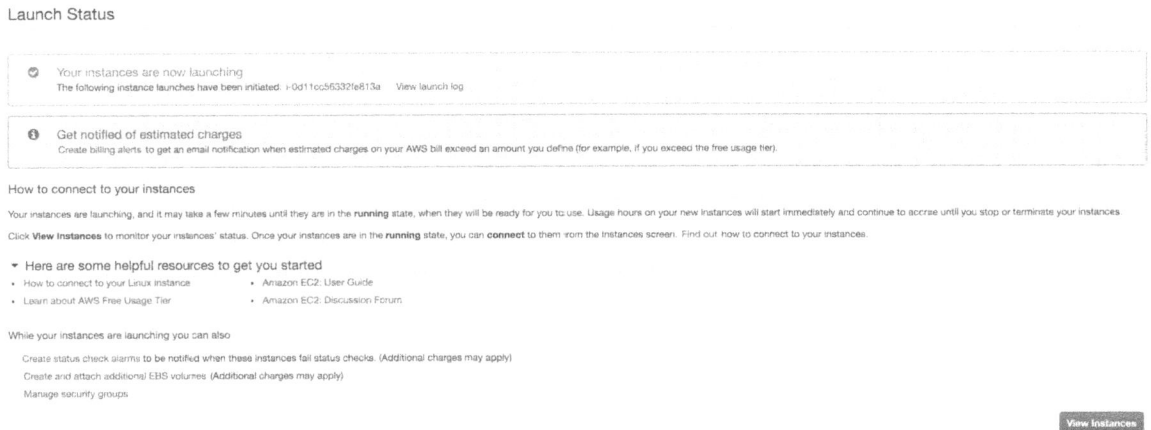

Launch Status

> ✓ Your instances are now launching
> The following instance launches have been initiated: i-0d11cc56332fe813a   View launch log

> ❶ Get notified of estimated charges
> Create billing alerts to get an email notification when estimated charges on your AWS bill exceed an amount you define (for example, if you exceed the free usage tier).

How to connect to your instances

Your instances are launching, and it may take a few minutes until they are in the **running** state, when they will be ready for you to use. Usage hours on your new instances will start immediately and continue to accrue until you stop or terminate your instances.

Click **View Instances** to monitor your instances' status. Once your instances are in the **running** state, you can **connect** to them from the Instances screen. Find out how to connect to your instances.

▾ Here are some helpful resources to get you started
• How to connect to your Linux instance   • Amazon EC2: User Guide
• Learn about AWS Free Usage Tier   • Amazon EC2: Discussion Forum

While your instances are launching you can also

Create status check alarms to be notified when these instances fail status checks. (Additional charges may apply)
Create and attach additional EBS volumes (Additional charges may apply)
Manage security groups

> **View Instances**

Figure 9.28: Launch status on the AWS instance

The '**View Instance**' button is to be used to navigate to a screen that displays the EC2 instance being launched, which is ready to be used when the instance state turns to 'running.'

10. Next, access the EC2 using the following command from the local system terminal with the '**public-dns-name**' field replaced with your EC2 instance name (of the form: ec2-x-x-x-x.compute-1.amazonaws.com) and the path of the key pair **pem** file that was saved earlier:

```
ssh -i /path/my-key-pair.pem ec2-user@public-dns-name
```

This command will take you to the prompt of the EC2 instance where Docker needs to be installed first. Docker installation is required for the workflow since the Docker image will be built within the EC2 instance.

11. For Amazon Linux 2 AMI, the following commands should be used to accomplish this:

```
sudo amazon-linux-extras install docker
sudo yum install docker
sudo service docker start
sudo usermod -a -G docker ec2-user
```

> **Note**
>
> For an explanation of the commands, check out the documentation at https://docs.aws.amazon.com/AmazonECS/latest/developerguide/docker-basics.html.

12. The '**exit**' command should be used to log out of the instance. Next, log back in using the **ssh** command that was used earlier. Verify that Docker is working by issuing the '**docker info**' command. Open another local terminal window for the next steps.

13. Now, copy the files that are needed to build the Docker image within the EC2 instance. Issue the command from the local terminal (not from within EC2!):

```
scp -i /path/my-key-pair.pem file-to-copy ec2-user@public-dns-name:/home/
ec2-user
```

14. The following files should be copied to build the Docker image, as was done earlier: *requirements.txt*, *app.py*, *trained_model.h5*, *trained_tokenizer.pkl*, and *Dockerfile*.

15. Next, log in to the EC2 instance, issue the '**ls**' command to see whether the copied files exist, and build and run the Docker image using the same commands that were used in the local system (ensure that you use port 80 at all locations in the code/commands).

16. Enter the home endpoint from the local browser using the public DNS name to see the '**Hello World!**' message:

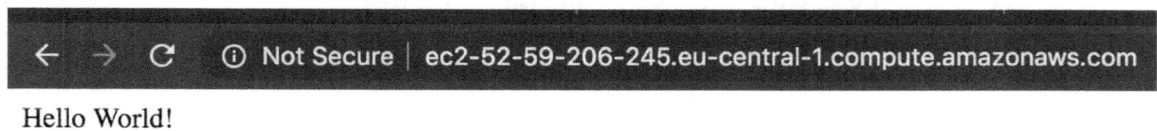

Hello World!

Figure 9.29: Screenshot for the home endpoint

17. Now you can send a curl request to the web service from a local terminal with the test sample data after replacing the **public-dns-name** with yours:

```
curl -X POST \
public-dns-name:80/predict \
-H 'Content-Type: application/json' \
-d '["The book was very poor", "Very nice!", "The author could have done
more", "Amazing product!"]'
```

18. This should return the same review ratings as the ones obtained locally.

This concludes the simple deployment process.

The DS team now shares this **curl** request with the web development team, which can consume the web service with their test samples.

> **Note**
>
> When the web service is not required, stop or terminate the EC2 instance to avoid getting charged.

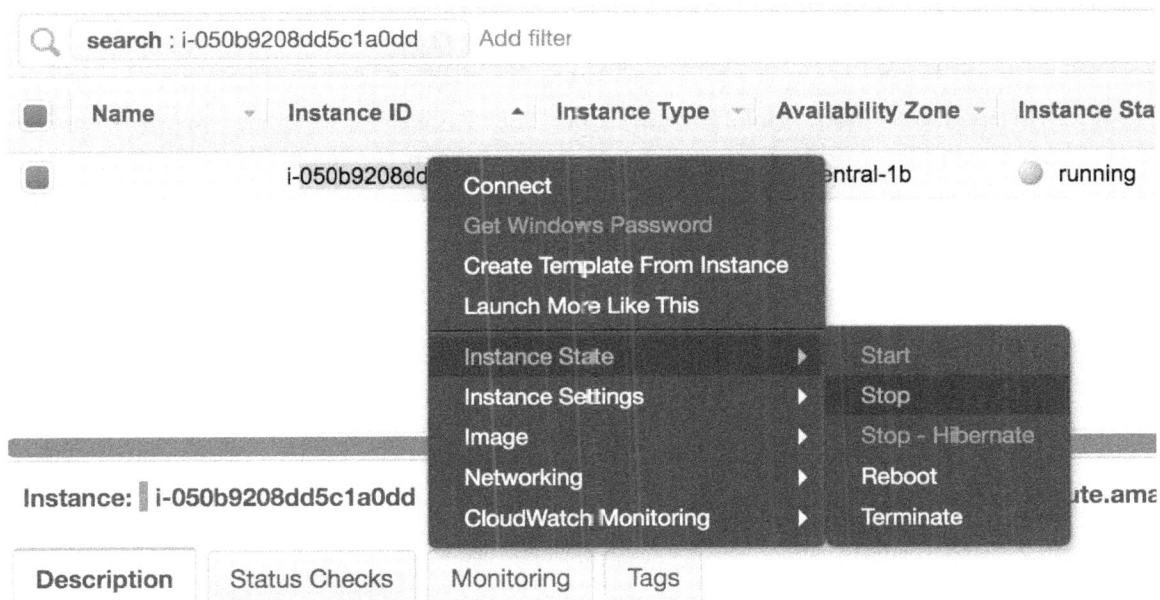

Figure 9.30: Stopping the AWS EC2 instance

From an MVP point of view, the deliverables are now complete!

Improvements

The workflow described in this chapter is only meant to introduce a basic workflow using certain tools (Flask, Colab, Docker, and AWS EC2) and inspire an example plan for a deep learning project in an organization. This is, however, only an MVP, which could be improved in many ways for future iterations.

Summary

In this chapter, we saw the journey of a deep learning project as it flows through an organization. We also learned about Google Colab notebooks to leverage GPUs for faster training. Additionally, we developed a Flask-based web service using Docker and deployed it to a cloud environment, hence enabling the stakeholders to obtain predictions for a given input.

This chapter concludes our efforts toward learning how to leverage deep learning techniques to solve problems in the domain of natural language processing. Almost every aspect discussed in this chapter and the previous ones is a topic of research and is being improved upon continuously. The only way to stay informed is to keep learning about the new and exciting ways to tackle problems. Some common ways to do so are by following discussions on social media, following the work of top researchers/deep learning practitioners, and being on the constant lookout for organizations that are doing cutting-edge work when it comes to this domain.

Appendix

About

This section is included to assist the learners to perform the activities present in the book. It includes detailed steps that are to be performed by the learners to complete and achieve the objectives of the book.

Chapter 1: Introduction to Natural Language Processing

Activity 1: Generating word embeddings from a corpus using Word2Vec.

Solution:

1. Upload the text corpus from the link aforementioned.

2. Import the word2vec from gensim models

```
from gensim.models import word2vec
```

3. Store the corpus in a variable.

```
sentences = word2vec.Text8Corpus('text8')
```

4. Fit the word2vec model on the corpus.

```
model = word2vec.Word2Vec(sentences, size = 200)
```

5. Find the most similar word to 'man'.

```
model.most_similar(['man'])
```

The output is as follows:

```
[('woman', 0.6842043995857239),
 ('girl', 0.5943484306335449),
 ('creature', 0.5780946612358093),
 ('boy', 0.5204570293426514),
 ('person', 0.5135789513587952),
 ('stranger', 0.506704568862915),
 ('beast', 0.504448652267456),
 ('god', 0.50375235080071899),
 ('evil', 0.4990573525428772),
 ('thief', 0.4973783493041992)]
```

Figure 1.29: Output for similar word embeddings

6. 'Father' is to 'girl', 'x' is to boy. Find the top 3 words for x.

```
model.most_similar(['girl', 'father'], ['boy'], topn=3)
```

The output is as follows:

```
[('mother', 0.7770676612854004),
 ('grandmother', 0.7024110555648804),
 ('wife', 0.6916966438293457)]
```

Figure 1.30: Output for top three words for 'x'

Chapter 2: Applications of Natural Language Processing

Activity 2: Building and training your own POS tagger

Solution:

1. The first thing to do is pick a corpus that we want to train our tagger on. Import the necessary Python packages. Here, we use the **nltk treebank** corpus to work on:

```
import nltk
nltk.download('treebank')
tagged_sentences = nltk.corpus.treebank.tagged_sents()
print(tagged_sentences[0])
print("Tagged sentences: ", len(tagged_sentences))
print ("Tagged words:", len(nltk.corpus.treebank.tagged_words()))
```

2. Next, we need to determine what features our tagger will take into consideration when determining what tag to assign to a word. These can include whether the word is all capitalized, is in lowercase, or has one capital letter:

```
def features(sentence, index):
    """ sentence: [w1, w2, ...], index: the index of the word """
    return {
        'word': sentence[index],
        'is_first': index == 0,
        'is_last': index == len(sentence) - 1,
        'is_capitalized': sentence[index][0].upper() == sentence[index]
[0],
        'is_all_caps': sentence[index].upper() == sentence[index],
        'is_all_lower': sentence[index].lower() == sentence[index],
        'prefix-1': sentence[index][0],
        'prefix-2': sentence[index][:2],
        'prefix-3': sentence[index][:3],
        'suffix-1': sentence[index][-1],
        'suffix-2': sentence[index][-2:],
        'suffix-3': sentence[index][-3:],
        'prev_word': '' if index == 0 else sentence[index - 1],
        'next_word': '' if index == len(sentence) - 1 else sentence[index
 + 1],
        'has_hyphen': '-' in sentence[index],
        'is_numeric': sentence[index].isdigit(),
        'capitals_inside': sentence[index][1:].lower() != sentence[index]
[1:]
```

```
            }

      import pprint
      pprint.pprint(features(['This', 'is', 'a', 'sentence'], 2))

      {'capitals_inside': False,
       'has_hyphen': False,
       'is_all_caps': False,
       'is_all_lower': True,
       'is_capitalized': False,
       'is_first': False,
       'is_last': False,
       'is_numeric': False,
       'next_word': 'sentence',
       'prefix-1': 'a',
       'prefix-2': 'a',
       'prefix-3': 'a',
       'prev_word': 'is',
       'suffix-1': 'a',
       'suffix-2': 'a',
       'suffix-3': 'a',
       'word': 'a'}
```

3. Create a function to strip the tagged words of their tags so that we can feed them into our tagger:

```
      def untag(tagged_sentence):
          return [w for w, t in tagged_sentence]
```

4. Now we need to build our training set. Our tagger needs to take features individually for each word, but our corpus is actually in the form of sentences, so we need to do a little transforming. Split the data into training and testing sets. Apply this function on the training set.

```
      # Split the dataset for training and testing
      cutoff = int(.75 * len(tagged_sentences))
      training_sentences = tagged_sentences[:cutoff]
      test_sentences = tagged_sentences[cutoff:]

      print(len(training_sentences))   # 2935
      print(len(test_sentences))       # 979
       and create a function to assign the features to 'X' and append the POS
      tags to 'Y'.
```

```
def transform_to_dataset(tagged_sentences):
    X, y = [], []

    for tagged in tagged_sentences:
        for index in range(len(tagged)):
            X.append(features(untag(tagged), index))
            y.append(tagged[index][1])

    return X, y

X, y = transform_to_dataset(training_sentences)
from sklearn.tree import DecisionTreeClassifier
from sklearn.feature_extraction import DictVectorizer
from sklearn.pipeline import Pipeline
```

5. Apply this function on the training set. Now we can train our tagger. It's basically a classifier since it's categorizing words into classes, so we can use a classification algorithm. You can use any that you like or try out a bunch of them to see which works best. Here, we'll use the decision tree classifier. Import the classifier, initialize it, and fit the model on the training data. Print the accuracy score.

```
clf = Pipeline([
    ('vectorizer', DictVectorizer(sparse=False)),
    ('classifier', DecisionTreeClassifier(criterion='entropy'))
])

clf.fit(X[:10000], y[:10000])   # Use only the first 10K samples if you're
running it multiple times. It takes a fair bit :)

print('Training completed')

X_test, y_test = transform_to_dataset(test_sentences)

print("Accuracy:", clf.score(X_test, y_test))
```

The output is as follows:

```
Training completed
Accuracy: 0.8959505061867267
```

Figure 2.19: Accuracy score

Activity 3: Performing NER on a Tagged Corpus

Solution:

1. Import the necessary Python packages and classes.

```
import nltk
nltk.download('treebank')
nltk.download('maxent_ne_chunker')
nltk.download('words')
```

2. Print the **nltk.corpus.treebank.tagged_sents()** to see the tagged corpus that you need extract named entities from.

```
nltk.corpus.treebank.tagged_sents()
sent = nltk.corpus.treebank.tagged_sents()[0]
print(nltk.ne_chunk(sent, binary=True))
```

3. Store the first sentence of the tagged sentences in a variable.

```
sent = nltk.corpus.treebank.tagged_sents()[1]
```

4. Use **nltk.ne_chunk** to perform NER on the sentence. Set binary to True and print the named entities.

```
print(nltk.ne_chunk(sent, binary=False))
sent = nltk.corpus.treebank.tagged_sents()[2]
rint(nltk.ne_chunk(sent))
```

The output is as follows:

```
(S
  (PERSON Rudolph/NNP)
  (GPE Agnew/NNP)
  ,/,
  55/CD
  years/NNS
  old/JJ
  and/CC
  former/JJ
  chairman/NN
  of/IN
  (ORGANIZATION Consolidated/NNP Gold/NNP Fields/NNP)
  PLC/NNP
  ,/,
  was/VBD
  named/VBN
  *-1/-NONE-
  a/DT
  nonexecutive/JJ
  director/NN
  of/IN
  this/DT
  (GPE British/JJ)
  industrial/JJ
  conglomerate/NN
  ./.)
```

Figure 2.20: NER on tagged corpus

Chapter 3: Introduction to Neural Networks

Activity 4: Sentiment Analysis of Reviews

Solution:

1. Open a new **Jupyter** notebook. Import **numpy**, **pandas** and **matplotlib.pyplot**. Load the dataset into a dataframe.

```
import numpy as np
import matplotlib.pyplot as plt
import pandas as pd
dataset = pd.read_csv('train_comment_small_100.csv', sep=',')
```

2. Next step is to clean and prepare the data. Import **re** and **nltk**. From **nltk.corpus** import **stopwords**. From **nltk.stem.porter**, import **PorterStemmer**. Create an array for your cleaned text to be stored in.

```
import re
import nltk
nltk.download('stopwords')
from nltk.corpus import stopwords
from nltk.stem.porter import PorterStemmer
corpus = []
```

3. Using a for loop, iterate through every instance (every review). Replace all non-alphabets with a ' ' (whitespace). Convert all alphabets into lowercase. Split each review into individual words. Initiate the **PorterStemmer**. If the word is not a stopword, perform stemming on the word. Join all the individual words back together to form a cleaned review. Append this cleaned review to the array you created.

```
for i in range(0, dataset.shape[0]-1):
    review = re.sub('[^a-zA-Z]', ' ', dataset['comment_text'][i])
    review = review.lower()
    review = review.split()
ps = PorterStemmer()
    review = [ps.stem(word) for word in review if not word in
set(stopwords.words('english'))]
    review = ' '.join(review)
    corpus.append(review)
```

4. Import **CountVectorizer**. Convert the reviews into word count vectors using **Count-Vectorizer**.

```
from sklearn.feature_extraction.text import CountVectorizer
cv = CountVectorizer(max_features = 20)
```

5. Create an array to store each unique word as its own column, hence making them independent variables.

```
X = cv.fit_transform(corpus).toarray()
y = dataset.iloc[:,0]
y1 = y[:99]
y1
```

6. Import **LabelEncoder** from **sklearn.preprocessing**. Use the **LabelEncoder** on the target output (**y**).

```
from sklearn import preprocessing
labelencoder_y = preprocessing.LabelEncoder()
y = labelencoder_y.fit_transform(y1)
```

7. Import **train_test_split**. Divide the dataset into a training set and a validation set.

```
from sklearn.model_selection import train_test_split
X_train, X_test, y_train, y_test = train_test_split(X, y, test_size = 0.20, random_state = 0)
```

8. Import **StandardScaler** from **sklearn.preprocessing**. Use the **StandardScaler** on the features of both the training set and the validation set (**X**).

```
from sklearn.preprocessing import StandardScaler
sc = StandardScaler()
X_train = sc.fit_transform(X_train)
X_test = sc.transform(X_test)
```

9. Now the next task is to create the neural network. Import **keras**. Import **Sequential** from **keras.models** and **Dense** from Keras layers.

```
import tensorflow
import keras
from keras.models import Sequential
from keras.layers import Dense
```

10. Initialize the neural network. Add the first hidden layer with **'relu'** as the activation function. Repeat step for the second hidden layer. Add the output layer with **'softmax'** as the activation function. Compile the neural network, using **'adam'** as the optimizer, **'binary_crossentropy'** as the loss function and **'accuracy'** as the performance metric.

```
classifier = Sequential()
classifier.add(Dense(output_dim = 20, init = 'uniform', activation =
'relu', input_dim = 20))
classifier.add(Dense(output_dim =20, init = 'uniform', activation =
'relu'))
classifier.add(Dense(output_dim = 1, init = 'uniform', activation =
'softmax'))
classifier.compile(optimizer = 'adam', loss = 'binary_crossentropy',
metrics = ['accuracy'])
```

11. Now we need to train the model. Fit the neural network on the training dataset with a **batch_size** of 3 and a **nb_epoch** of 5.

```
classifier.fit(X_train, y_train, batch_size = 3, nb_epoch = 5)
X_test
```

12. Validate the model. Evaluate the neural network and print the accuracy scores to see how it's doing.

```
y_pred = classifier.predict(X_test)
scores = classifier.evaluate(X_test, y_pred, verbose=1)
print("Accuracy:", scores[1])
```

13. (Optional) Print the confusion matrix by importing **confusion_matrix** from **sklearn.metrics**.

```
from sklearn.metrics import confusion_matrix
cm = confusion_matrix(y_test, y_pred)
scores
```

Your output should look similar to this:

```
20/20 [==============================] - 0s 160us/step
Accuracy: 1.0
[1.192093321833454e-07, 1.0]
```

Figure 3.21: Accuracy score for sentiment analysis

Chapter 4: Introduction to convolutional networks

Activity 5: Sentiment Analysis on a real-life dataset

Solution:

1. Import the necessary classes

```
from keras.preprocessing.text import Tokenizer
from keras.models import Sequential
from keras import layers
from keras.preprocessing.sequence import pad_sequences
import numpy as np
import pandas as pd
```

2. Define your variables and parameters.

```
epochs = 20
maxlen = 100
embedding_dim = 50
num_filters = 64
kernel_size = 5
batch_size = 32
```

3. Import the data.

```
data = pd.read_csv('data/sentiment labelled sentences/yelp_labelled.
txt',names=['sentence', 'label'], sep='\t')
data.head()
```

Printing this out on a **Jupyter** notebook should display:

	sentence	label
0	Wow... Loved this place.	1
1	Crust is not good.	0
2	Not tasty and the texture was just nasty.	0
3	Stopped by during the late May bank holiday of...	1
4	The selection on the menu was great and so wer...	1

Figure 4.27: Labelled dataset

4. Select the 'sentence' and 'label' columns

```
sentences=data['sentence'].values
labels=data['label'].values
```

5. Split your data into training and test set

```
from sklearn.model_selection import train_test_split
X_train, X_test, y_train, y_test = train_test_split(
    sentences, labels, test_size=0.30, random_state=1000)
```

6. Tokenize

```
tokenizer = Tokenizer(num_words=5000)
tokenizer.fit_on_texts(X_train)
X_train = tokenizer.texts_to_sequences(X_train)
X_test = tokenizer.texts_to_sequences(X_test)
vocab_size = len(tokenizer.word_index) + 1 #The vocabulary size has an
additional 1 due to the 0 reserved index
```

7. Pad in order to ensure that all sequences have the same length

```
X_train = pad_sequences(X_train, padding='post', maxlen=maxlen)
X_test = pad_sequences(X_test, padding='post', maxlen=maxlen)
```

8. Create the model. Note that we use a sigmoid activation function on the last layer and the binary cross entropy for calculating loss. This is because we are doing a binary classification.

```
model = Sequential()
model.add(layers.Embedding(vocab_size, embedding_dim, input_
length=maxlen))
model.add(layers.Conv1D(num_filters, kernel_size, activation='relu'))
model.add(layers.GlobalMaxPooling1D())
model.add(layers.Dense(10, activation='relu'))
model.add(layers.Dense(1, activation='sigmoid'))
model.compile(optimizer='adam',
              loss='binary_crossentropy',
              metrics=['accuracy'])
model.summary()
```

The above code should yield

```
Layer (type)                    Output Shape            Param #
=================================================================
embedding_1 (Embedding)         (None, 100, 50)         87350

conv1d_1 (Conv1D)               (None, 96, 64)          16064

global_max_pooling1d_1 (Glob    (None, 64)              0

dense_1 (Dense)                 (None, 10)              650

dense_2 (Dense)                 (None, 1)               11
=================================================================
Total params: 104,075
Trainable params: 104,075
Non-trainable params: 0
```

Figure 4.28: Model summary

The model can be visualized as follows as well:

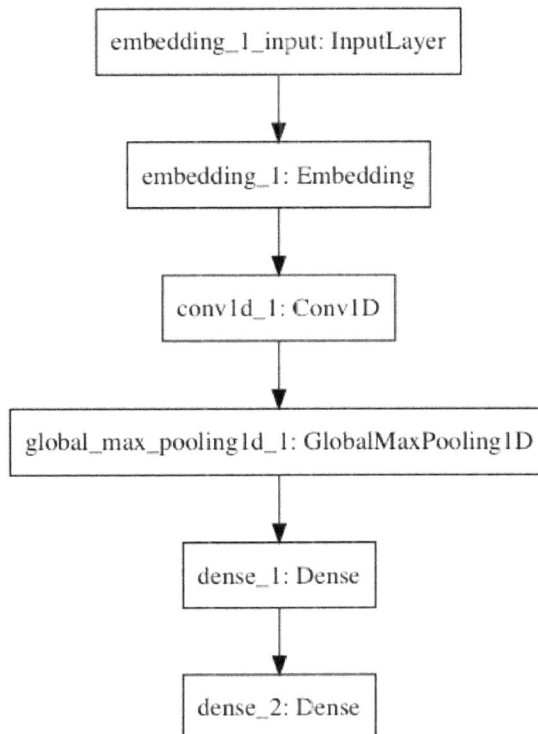

Figure 4.29: Model visualization

9. Train and test the model.

```
model.fit(X_train, y_train,
                    epochs=epochs,
                    verbose=False,
                    validation_data=(X_test, y_test),
                    batch_size=batch_size)
loss, accuracy = model.evaluate(X_train, y_train, verbose=False)
print("Training Accuracy: {:.4f}".format(accuracy))
loss, accuracy = model.evaluate(X_test, y_test, verbose=False)
print("Testing Accuracy:  {:.4f}".format(accuracy))
```

The accuracy output should be as follows:

```
Training Accuracy: 1.0000
Testing Accuracy:  0.8080
```

Figure 4.30: Accuracy score

Chapter 5: Foundations of Recurrent Neural Network

Activity 6: Solve a problem with RNN – Author Attribution

Solution:

Prepare the data

We begin by setting up the data pre-processing pipeline. For each one of the authors, we aggregate all the known papers into a single long text. We assume that style does not change across the various papers, hence a single text is equivalent to multiple small ones yet it is much easier to deal with programmatically.

For each paper of each author we perform the following steps:

1. Convert all text into lower-case (ignoring the fact that capitalization may be a stylistic property)

2. Converting all newlines and multiple whitespaces into single whitespaces

3. Remove any mention of the authors' names, otherwise we risk data leakage (authors names are *hamilton* and *madison*)

4. Do the above steps in a function as it is needed for predicting the unknown papers.

```python
import numpy as np
import os
from sklearn.model_selection import train_test_split


# Classes for A/B/Unknown
A = 0
B = 1
UNKNOWN = -1


def preprocess_text(file_path):

    with open(file_path, 'r') as f:
        lines = f.readlines()
        text = ' '.join(lines[1:]).replace("\n", ' ').replace('  ','
').lower().replace('hamilton','').replace('madison', '')
        text = ' '.join(text.split())
        return text
```

```
# Concatenate all the papers known to be written by A/B into a single long
text
all_authorA, all_authorB = '',''
for x in os.listdir('./papers/A/'):
    all_authorA += preprocess_text('./papers/A/' + x)

for x in os.listdir('./papers/B/'):
    all_authorB += preprocess_text('./papers/B/' + x)

# Print lengths of the large texts
print("AuthorA text length: {}".format(len(all_authorA)))
print("AuthorB text length: {}".format(len(all_authorB)))
```

The output for this should be as follows:

```
AuthorA text length: 216394
AuthorB text length: 230867
```

Figure 5.34: Text length count

The next step is to break the long text for each author into many small sequences. As described above, we empirically choose a length for the sequence and use it throughout the model's lifecycle. We get our full dataset by labeling each sequence with its author.

To break the long texts into smaller sequences we use the **Tokenizer** class from the **keras** framework. In particular, note that we set it up to tokenize according to characters and not words.

5. Choose **SEQ_LEN** hyper parameter, this might have to be changed if the model doesn't fit well to training data.

6. Write a function **make_subsequences** to turn each document into sequences of length SEQ_LEN and give it a correct label.

7. Use Keras **Tokenizer** with **char_level=True**

8. Fit the tokenizer on all the texts

9. Use this tokenizer to convert all texts into sequences using **texts_to_sequences()**

10. Use **make_subsequences()** to turn these sequences into appropriate shape and length

```
from keras.preprocessing.text import Tokenizer
# Hyperparameter - sequence length to use for the model
SEQ_LEN = 30
def make_subsequences(long_sequence, label, sequence_length=SEQ_LEN):

    len_sequences = len(long_sequence)
    X = np.zeros(((len_sequences - sequence_length)+1, sequence_length))
    y = np.zeros((X.shape[0], 1))
    for i in range(X.shape[0]):
        X[i] = long_sequence[i:i+sequence_length]
        y[i] = label
    return X,y


# We use the Tokenizer class from Keras to convert the long texts into a
sequence of characters (not words)

tokenizer = Tokenizer(char_level=True)

# Make sure to fit all characters in texts from both authors
tokenizer.fit_on_texts(all_authorA + all_authorB)

authorA_long_sequence = tokenizer.texts_to_sequences([all_authorA])[0]
authorB_long_sequence = tokenizer.texts_to_sequences([all_authorB])[0]

# Convert the long sequences into sequence and label pairs
X_authorA, y_authorA = make_subsequences(authorA_long_sequence, A)
X_authorB, y_authorB = make_subsequences(authorB_long_sequence, B)

# Print sizes of available data
print("Number of characters: {}".format(len(tokenizer.word_index)))
print('author A sequences: {}'.format(X_authorA.shape))
print('author B sequences: {}'.format(X_authorB.shape))
```

The output should be as follows:

```
Number of characters: 52
author A sequences: (216365, 30)
author B sequences: (230838, 30)
```

Figure 5.35: Character count of sequences

11. Compare the number of raw characters to the number of labeled sequences for each author. Deep Learning requires many examples of each input. The following code calculates the number of total and unique words in the texts.

```
# Calculate the number of unique words in the text

word_tokenizer = Tokenizer()
word_tokenizer.fit_on_texts([all_authorA, all_authorB])

print("Total word count: ", len((all_authorA + ' ' + all_authorB).split('
')))
print("Total number of unique words: ", len(word_tokenizer.word_index))
```

The output should be as follows:

```
Total word count:   74349
Total number of unique words:   6318
```

Figure 5.36: Total word count and unique word count

We now proceed to create our train, validation sets.

12. Stack **x** data together and y data together.

13. Use **train_test_split** to split the dataset into 80% training and 20% validation.

14. Reshape the data to make sure that they are sequences of correct length.

```
# Take equal amounts of sequences from both authors
X = np.vstack((X_authorA, X_authorB))
y = np.vstack((y_authorA, y_authorB))

# Break data into train and test sets
X_train, X_val, y_train, y_val = train_test_split(X,y, train_size=0.8)

# Data is to be fed into RNN - ensure that the actual data is of size
[batch size, sequence length]
X_train = X_train.reshape(-1, SEQ_LEN)
X_val =  X_val.reshape(-1, SEQ_LEN)

# Print the shapes of the train, validation and test sets
print("X_train shape: {}".format(X_train.shape))
```

```
print("y_train shape: {}".format(y_train.shape))

print("X_validate shape: {}".format(X_val.shape))
print("y_validate shape: {}".format(y_val.shape))
```

The output is as follows:

```
X_train shape: (357762, 30)
y_train shape: (357762, 1)
X_validate shape: (89441, 30)
y_validate shape: (89441, 1)
```

Figure 5.37: Testing and training datasets

Finally, we construct the model graph and perform the training procedure.

15. Create a model using **RNN** and **Dense** layers.

16. Since its a binary classification problem, the output layer should be **Dense** with **sigmoid** activation.

17. Compile the model with **optimizer**, appropriate loss function and metrics.

18. Print the summary of the model.

```
from keras.layers import SimpleRNN, Embedding, Dense
from keras.models import Sequential
from keras.optimizers import SGD, Adadelta, Adam
Embedding_size = 100
RNN_size = 256

model = Sequential()
model.add(Embedding(len(tokenizer.word_index)+1, Embedding_size, input_
length=30))
model.add(SimpleRNN(RNN_size, return_sequences=False))
model.add(Dense(1, activation='sigmoid'))

model.compile(optimizer='adam', loss='binary_crossentropy', metrics =
['accuracy'])
model.summary()
```

The output is as follows:

```
Layer (type)                    Output Shape              Param #
=================================================================
embedding_1 (Embedding)         (None, 30, 100)           5300

simple_rnn_1 (SimpleRNN)        (None, 256)               91392

dense_1 (Dense)                 (None, 1)                 257
=================================================================
Total params: 96,949
Trainable params: 96,949
Non-trainable params: 0
```

Figure 5.38: Model summary

19. Decide upon the batch size, epochs and train the model using training data and validate with validation data

20. Based on the results, go back to model above, change it if needed (use more layers, use regularization, dropout, etc., use different optimizer, or a different learning rate, etc.)

21. Change **Batch_size**, **epochs** if needed.

```
Batch_size = 4096
Epochs = 20
model.fit(X_train, y_train, batch_size=Batch_size, epochs=Epochs,
validation_data=(X_val, y_val))
```

The output is as follows:

```
Train on 357762 samples, validate on 89441 samples
Epoch 1/20
357762/357762 [==============================] - 7s 20us/step - loss: 0.6907 - acc: 0.5298 - val_loss: 0.6846 - val_acc: 0.5528
Epoch 2/20
357762/357762 [==============================] - 5s 14us/step - loss: 0.6848 - acc: 0.5521 - val_loss: 0.6864 - val_acc: 0.5457
Epoch 3/20
357762/357762 [==============================] - 5s 14us/step - loss: 0.6832 - acc: 0.5567 - val_loss: 0.6828 - val_acc: 0.5571
Epoch 4/20
357762/357762 [==============================] - 5s 14us/step - loss: 0.6829 - acc: 0.5556 - val_loss: 0.6819 - val_acc: 0.5604
Epoch 5/20
357762/357762 [==============================] - 5s 13us/step - loss: 0.6800 - acc: 0.5621 - val_loss: 0.6760 - val_acc: 0.5718
Epoch 6/20
357762/357762 [==============================] - 5s 14us/step - loss: 0.6713 - acc: 0.5803 - val_loss: 0.6718 - val_acc: 0.5833
Epoch 7/20
357762/357762 [==============================] - 5s 14us/step - loss: 0.6650 - acc: 0.5936 - val_loss: 0.6491 - val_acc: 0.6165
Epoch 8/20
357762/357762 [==============================] - 5s 15us/step - loss: 0.6391 - acc: 0.6309 - val_loss: 0.6230 - val_acc: 0.6488
Epoch 9/20
357762/357762 [==============================] - 6s 17us/step - loss: 0.6113 - acc: 0.6624 - val_loss: 0.6502 - val_acc: 0.6229
Epoch 10/20
357762/357762 [==============================] - 8s 21us/step - loss: 0.5674 - acc: 0.7026 - val_loss: 0.5382 - val_acc: 0.7256
Epoch 11/20
357762/357762 [==============================] - 9s 24us/step - loss: 0.4963 - acc: 0.7568 - val_loss: 0.4697 - val_acc: 0.7745
Epoch 12/20
357762/357762 [==============================] - 13s 36us/step - loss: 0.4178 - acc: 0.8070 - val_loss: 0.4078 - val_acc: 0.8112
Epoch 13/20
357762/357762 [==============================] - 16s 46us/step - loss: 0.3448 - acc: 0.8483 - val_loss: 0.3798 - val_acc: 0.8328
Epoch 14/20
357762/357762 [==============================] - 24s 67us/step - loss: 0.2898 - acc: 0.8759 - val_loss: 0.2925 - val_acc: 0.8746
Epoch 15/20
357762/357762 [==============================] - 24s 68us/step - loss: 0.2364 - acc: 0.9021 - val_loss: 0.2538 - val_acc: 0.8920
Epoch 16/20
357762/357762 [==============================] - 24s 66us/step - loss: 0.1934 - acc: 0.9225 - val_loss: 0.2153 - val_acc: 0.9104
Epoch 17/20
357762/357762 [==============================] - 24s 67us/step - loss: 0.1662 - acc: 0.9345 - val_loss: 0.1931 - val_acc: 0.9206
Epoch 18/20
357762/357762 [==============================] - 24s 67us/step - loss: 0.1400 - acc: 0.9455 - val_loss: 0.1325 - val_acc: 0.9254
Epoch 19/20
357762/357762 [==============================] - 27s 76us/step - loss: 0.1249 - acc: 0.9520 - val_loss: 0.1666 - val_acc: 0.9329
Epoch 20/20
357762/357762 [==============================] - 33s 91us/step - loss: 0.1079 - acc: 0.9591 - val_loss: 0.1503 - val_acc: 0.9400
<keras.callbacks.History at 0x20f3a8d9ef0>
```

Figure 5.39: Epoch training

Applying the Model to the Unknown Papers

Do this all the papers in the Unknown folder

1. Preprocess them same way as training set (lower case, removing white lines, etc.)

2. Use **tokenizer** and **make_subsequences** function above to turn them into sequences of required size.

3. Use the model to predict on these sequences.

4. Count the number of sequences assigned to author **A** and the ones assigned to author **B**

5. Based on the count, pick the author with highest votes/count

```
for x in os.listdir('./papers/Unknown/'):
    unknown = preprocess_text('./papers/Unknown/' + x)
    unknown_long_sequences = tokenizer.texts_to_sequences([unknown])[0]
    X_sequences, _ = make_subsequences(unknown_long_sequences, UNKNOWN)
    X_sequences = X_sequences.reshape((-1,SEQ_LEN))

    votes_for_authorA = 0
    votes_for_authorB = 0

    y = model.predict(X_sequences)
    y = y>0.5
    votes_for_authorA = np.sum(y==0)
    votes_for_authorB = np.sum(y==1)


    print("Paper {} is predicted to have been written by {}, {} to {}".
format(
            x.replace('paper_','').replace('.txt',''),
            ("Author A" if votes_for_authorA > votes_for_authorB else
"Author B"),
            max(votes_for_authorA, votes_for_authorB), min(votes_for_
authorA, votes_for_authorB)))
```

The output is as follows:

```
Paper 1 is predicted to have been written by Author B, 11946 to 8828
Paper 2 is predicted to have been written by Author B, 11267 to 8379
Paper 3 is predicted to have been written by Author B, 6738 to 6646
Paper 4 is predicted to have been written by Author A, 5254 to 4519
Paper 5 is predicted to have been written by Author A, 6570 to 5184
```

Figure 5.40: Output for author attribution

Chapter 6: Foundations of GRUs

Activity 7: Develop a sentiment classification model using Simple RNN

Solution:

1. Load the dataset.

```
from keras.datasets import imdb
max_features = 10000
maxlen = 500

(train_data, y_train), (test_data, y_test) = imdb.load_data(num_words=max_
features)
print('Number of train sequences: ', len(train_data))
print('Number of test sequences: ', len(test_data))
```

2. Pad sequences so that each sequence has the same number characters.

```
from keras.preprocessing import sequence
train_data = sequence.pad_sequences(train_data, maxlen=maxlen)
test_data = sequence.pad_sequences(test_data, maxlen=maxlen)
```

3. Define and compile model using **SimpleRNN** with 32 hidden units.

```
from keras.models import Sequential
from keras.layers import Embedding
from keras.layers import Dense
from keras.layers import GRU
from keras.layers import SimpleRNN

model = Sequential()
model.add(Embedding(max_features, 32))
model.add(SimpleRNN(32))
model.add(Dense(1, activation='sigmoid'))

model.compile(optimizer='rmsprop',
              loss='binary_crossentropy',
              metrics=['acc'])

history = model.fit(train_data, y_train,
                    epochs=10,
                    batch_size=128,
                    validation_split=0.2)
```

4. Plot the validation and training accuracy and losses.

```
import matplotlib.pyplot as plt

def plot_results(history):
    acc = history.history['acc']
    val_acc = history.history['val_acc']
    loss = history.history['loss']
    val_loss = history.history['val_loss']

    epochs = range(1, len(acc) + 1)
    plt.plot(epochs, acc, 'bo', label='Training Accuracy')
    plt.plot(epochs, val_acc, 'b', label='Validation Accuracy')

    plt.title('Training and validation Accuracy')
    plt.legend()
    plt.figure()
    plt.plot(epochs, loss, 'bo', label='Training Loss')
    plt.plot(epochs, val_loss, 'b', label='Validation Loss')
    plt.title('Training and validation Loss')
    plt.legend()
    plt.show()
```

5. Plot the model

```
plot_results(history)
```

The output is as follows:

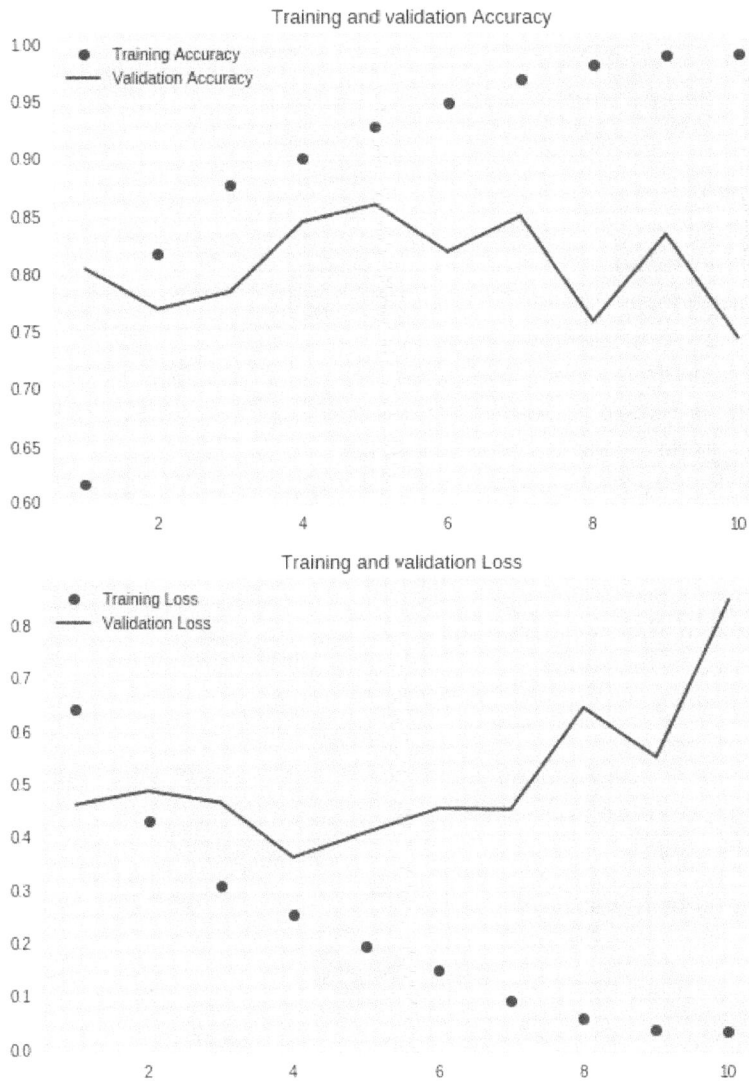

Figure 6.29: Training and validation accuracy loss

Activity 8: Train your own character generation model with a dataset of your choice

Solution:

1. Load the text file and import the necessary Python packages and classes.

```python
import sys
import random
import string
import numpy as np
from keras.models import Sequential
from keras.layers import Dense
from keras.layers import LSTM, GRU
from keras.optimizers import RMSprop
from keras.models import load_model

# load text

def load_text(filename):
    with open(filename, 'r') as f:
        text = f.read()
    return text

in_filename = 'drive/shakespeare_poems.txt' # Add your own text file here
text = load_text(in_filename)
print(text[:200])
```

The output is as follows:

```
THE SONNETS

by William Shakespeare

From fairest creatures we desire increase,
That thereby beauty's rose might never die,
But as the riper should by time decease,
His tender heir might bear his mem
```

Figure 6.30: Sonnets from Shakespeare

2. Create dictionaries mapping characters to indices and vice-versa.

```
chars = sorted(list(set(text)))
print('Number of distinct characters:', len(chars))
char_indices = dict((c, i) for i, c in enumerate(chars))
indices_char = dict((i, c) for i, c in enumerate(chars))
```

The output is as follows:

Number of distinct characters: 61

Figure 6.31: Distinct character count

3. Create sequences from the text.

```
max_len_chars = 40
step = 3
sentences = []
next_chars = []
for i in range(0, len(text) - max_len_chars, step):
    sentences.append(text[i: i + max_len_chars])
    next_chars.append(text[i + max_len_chars])
print('nb sequences:', len(sentences))
```

The output is as follows:

nb sequences: 31327

Figure 6.32: nb sequence count

4. Make input and output arrays to feed the model.

```
x = np.zeros((len(sentences), max_len_chars, len(chars)), dtype=np.bool)
y = np.zeros((len(sentences), len(chars)), dtype=np.bool)
for i, sentence in enumerate(sentences):
    for t, char in enumerate(sentence):
        x[i, t, char_indices[char]] = 1
    y[i, char_indices[next_chars[i]]] = 1
```

5. Build and train the model using GRU and save the model.

```
print('Build model...')
model = Sequential()
model.add(GRU(128, input_shape=(max_len_chars, len(chars))))
model.add(Dense(len(chars), activation='softmax'))

optimizer = RMSprop(lr=0.01)
model.compile(loss='categorical_crossentropy', optimizer=optimizer)
model.fit(x, y,batch_size=128,epochs=10)
model.save("poem_gen_model.h5")
```

6. Define sampling and generation functions.

```
def sample(preds, temperature=1.0):
    # helper function to sample an index from a probability array
    preds = np.asarray(preds).astype('float64')
    preds = np.log(preds) / temperature
    exp_preds = np.exp(preds)
    preds = exp_preds / np.sum(exp_preds)
    probas = np.random.multinomial(1, preds, 1)
    return np.argmax(probas)
```

7. Generate text.

```
from keras.models import load_model
model_loaded = load_model('poem_gen_model.h5')
def generate_poem(model, num_chars_to_generate=400):
    start_index = random.randint(0, len(text) - max_len_chars - 1)
    generated = ''
    sentence = text[start_index: start_index + max_len_chars]
    generated += sentence
    print("Seed sentence: {}".format(generated))
    for i in range(num_chars_to_generate):
        x_pred = np.zeros((1, max_len_chars, len(chars)))
        for t, char in enumerate(sentence):
            x_pred[0, t, char_indices[char]] = 1.

        preds = model.predict(x_pred, verbose=0)[0]
```

```
            next_index = sample(preds, 1)
            next_char = indices_char[next_index]

            generated += next_char
            sentence = sentence[1:] + next_char
        return generated
    generate_poem(model_loaded, 100)
```

The output is as follows:

```
Seed sentence: pretty looks have been mine enemies,
And
'pretty looks have been mine enemies,\nAnd summmmmite it Time swill hold love and ust.\nAnd thou heart whereferayed me henule,\nThat which have,'
```

Figure 6.33: Generated text output

Chapter 7: Foundations of LSTM

Activity 9: Build a Spam or Ham classifier using a Simple RNN

Solution:

1. Import required Python packages

```
import pandas as pd
import numpy as np
from keras.models import Model, Sequential
from keras.layers import SimpleRNN, Dense,Embedding
from keras.preprocessing.text import Tokenizer
from keras.preprocessing import sequence
```

2. Read the input file containing a column that contains text and another column that contains the label for the text depicting whether the text is spam or not.

```
df = pd.read_csv("drive/spam.csv", encoding="latin")
df.head()
```

The output is as follows:

	v1	v2	Unnamed: 2	Unnamed: 3	Unnamed: 4
0	ham	Go until jurong point, crazy.. Available only ...	NaN	NaN	NaN
1	ham	Ok lar... Joking wif u oni...	NaN	NaN	NaN
2	spam	Free entry in 2 a wkly comp to win FA Cup fina...	NaN	NaN	NaN
3	ham	U dun say so early hor... U c already then say...	NaN	NaN	NaN
4	ham	Nah I don't think he goes to usf, he lives aro...	NaN	NaN	NaN

Figure 7.35: Input data file

3. Label the columns in the input data.

```
df = df[["v1","v2"]]
df.head()
```

The output is as follows:

	v1	v2
0	ham	Go until jurong point, crazy.. Available only ...
1	ham	Ok lar... Joking wif u oni...
2	spam	Free entry in 2 a wkly comp to win FA Cup fina...
3	ham	U dun say so early hor... U c already then say...
4	ham	Nah I don't think he goes to usf, he lives aro...

Figure 7.36: Labelled input data

4. Count spam, ham characters in the **v1** column.

```
df["v1"].value_counts()
```

The output is as follows:

```
ham      4825
spam      747
Name: v1, dtype: int64
```

Figure 7.37: Value counts for spam or ham

5. Get **X** as feature and **Y** as target.

```
lab_map = {"ham":0, "spam":1}
X = df["v2"].values
Y = df["v1"].map(lab_map).values
```

6. Convert to sequences and pad the sequences.

```
max_words = 100
mytokenizer = Tokenizer(nb_words=max_words,lower=True, split=" ")
mytokenizer.fit_on_texts(X)
text_tokenized = mytokenizer.texts_to_sequences(X)
text_tokenized
```

The output is as follows:

```
[[50, 64, 8, 89, 67, 58],
 [46, 6],
 [47, 8, 19, 4, 2, 71, 2, 2, 73],
 [6, 23, 6, 57],
 [1, 98, 69, 2, 69],
 [67, 21, 7, 38, 87, 55, 3, 44, 12, 14, 85, 46, 2, 68, 2],
 [11, 9, 25, 55, 2, 36, 10, 10, 55],
 [72, 13, 72, 13, 12, 51, 2, 13],
 [72, 4, 3, 17, 2, 2, 16, 64],
 [13, 96, 26, 6, 81, 2, 2, 5, 36, 12, 47, 16, 5, 96, 47, 18],
 [30, 32, 77, 7, 1, 98, 70, 2, 80, 40, 93, 88],
 [2, 48, 2, 73, 7, 68, 2, 65, 92, 42],
 [3, 17, 4, 47, 8, 91, 73, 5, 2, 38],
 [12, 5, 2, 3, 12, 40, 1, 1, 97, 13, 12, 7, 33, 11, 3, 17, 7, 4, 29, 51],
 [1, 17, 4, 18, 36, 33],
 [2, 13, 5, 8, 5, 73, 26, 89],
 [93, 30],
 [6, 49, 19, 1, 69, 1],
 [34, 5, 6, 5, 61],
 [94, 5, 73, 35, 2, 2],
 [9, 20, 49, 3],
 [75, 2, 12, 19, 64],
 [23, 57, 45, 9, 90],
```

Figure 7.38: Tokenized data

7. Train the sequences

```
max_len = 50
sequences = sequence.pad_sequences(text_tokenized,maxlen=max_len)
sequences
```

8. Build the model

```
model = Sequential()
model.add(Embedding(max_words, 20, input_length=max_len))
model.add(SimpleRNN(64))
model.add(Dense(1, activation="sigmoid"))
model.compile(loss='binary_crossentropy',
              optimizer='adam',
              metrics=['accuracy'])
model.fit(sequences,Y,batch_size=128,epochs=10,
          validation_split=0.2)
```

9. Predict the mail category on new test data.

```
inp_test_seq = "WINNER! U win a 500 prize reward & free entry to FA cup
final tickets! Text FA to 34212 to receive award"
test_sequences = mytokenizer.texts_to_sequences(np.array([inp_test_seq]))
test_sequences_matrix = sequence.pad_sequences(test_sequences,maxlen=max_
len)
model.predict(test_sequences_matrix)
```

The output is as follows:

```
array([[0.979119]], dtype=float32)
```

Figure 7.39: Output for new test data

Activity 10: Create a French to English translation model

Solution:

1. Import the necessary Python packages and classes.

```
import os
import re
import numpy as np
```

2. Read the file in sentence pairs.

```
with open("fra.txt", 'r', encoding='utf-8') as f:
    lines = f.read().split('\n')

num_samples = 20000 # Using only 20000 pairs for this example
lines_to_use = lines[: min(num_samples, len(lines) - 1)]
```

3. Remove **\u202f** character

```
for l in range(len(lines_to_use)):
    lines_to_use[l] = re.sub("\u202f", "", lines_to_use[l])


for l in range(len(lines_to_use)):
    lines_to_use[l] = re.sub("\d", " NUMBER_PRESENT ", lines_to_use[l])
```

4. Append '**BEGIN_** ' and ' **_END**' words to target sequences. Map words to integers.

```python
input_texts = []
target_texts = []
input_words = set()
target_words = set()

for line in lines_to_use:
    target_text, input_text = line.split('\t')
    target_text = 'BEGIN_ ' + target_text + ' _END'
    input_texts.append(input_text)
    target_texts.append(target_text)
    for word in input_text.split():
        if word not in input_words:
            input_words.add(word)
    for word in target_text.split():
        if word not in target_words:
            target_words.add(word)


max_input_seq_length = max([len(i.split()) for i in input_texts])
max_target_seq_length = max([len(i.split()) for i in target_texts])

input_words = sorted(list(input_words))
target_words = sorted(list(target_words))
num_encoder_tokens = len(input_words)
num_decoder_tokens = len(target_words)
```

5. Define encoder-decoder inputs.

```python
input_token_index = dict(
    [(word, i) for i, word in enumerate(input_words)])
target_token_index = dict(
    [(word, i) for i, word in enumerate(target_words)])

encoder_input_data = np.zeros(
    (len(input_texts), max_input_seq_length),
    dtype='float32')
decoder_input_data = np.zeros(
    (len(target_texts), max_target_seq_length),
    dtype='float32')
decoder_target_data = np.zeros(
    (len(target_texts), max_target_seq_length, num_decoder_tokens),
```

```
    dtype='float32')

for i, (input_text, target_text) in enumerate(zip(input_texts, target_
texts)):
    for t, word in enumerate(input_text.split()):
        encoder_input_data[i, t] = input_token_index[word]
    for t, word in enumerate(target_text.split()):
        decoder_input_data[i, t] = target_token_index[word]
        if t > 0:
            # decoder_target_data is ahead of decoder_input_data #by one
timestep
            decoder_target_data[:, t - 1, target_token_index[word]] = 1.
```

6. Build the model.

```
from keras.layers import Input, LSTM, Embedding, Dense
from keras.models import Model

embedding_size = 50
```

7. Initiate encoder training.

```
encoder_inputs = Input(shape=(None,))
encoder_after_embedding = Embedding(num_encoder_tokens, embedding_size)
(encoder_inputs)

encoder_lstm = LSTM(50, return_state=True)_,
state_h, state_c = encoder_lstm(encoder_after_embedding)
encoder_states = [state_h, state_c]
```

8. Initiate decoder training.

```
decoder_inputs = Input(shape=(None,))
decoder_after_embedding = Embedding(num_decoder_tokens, embedding_size)
(decoder_inputs)
decoder_lstm = LSTM(50, return_sequences=True, return_state=True)
decoder_outputs, _, _ = decoder_lstm(decoder_after_embedding,
                                    initial_state=encoder_states)
decoder_dense = Dense(num_decoder_tokens, activation='softmax')
decoder_outputs = decoder_dense(decoder_outputs)
```

9. Define the final model.

```
model = Model([encoder_inputs, decoder_inputs], decoder_outputs)
model.compile(optimizer='rmsprop', loss='categorical_crossentropy',
metrics=['acc'])
model.fit([encoder_input_data, decoder_input_data],
            decoder_target_data,
            batch_size=128,
            epochs=20,
            validation_split=0.05)
```

10. Provide inferences to encoder and decoder

```
# encoder part
encoder_model = Model(encoder_inputs, encoder_states)

# decoder part
decoder_state_input_h = Input(shape=(50,))
decoder_state_input_c = Input(shape=(50,))
decoder_states_inputs = [decoder_state_input_h, decoder_state_input_c]

decoder_outputs_inf, state_h_inf, state_c_inf = decoder_lstm(decoder_
after_embedding, initial_state=decoder_states_inputs)

decoder_states_inf = [state_h_inf, state_c_inf]
decoder_outputs_inf = decoder_dense(decoder_outputs_inf)
decoder_model = Model(
    [decoder_inputs] + decoder_states_inputs,
    [decoder_outputs_inf] + decoder_states_inf)
```

11. Reverse-lookup token index to decode sequences

```
reverse_input_word_index = dict(
    (i, word) for word, i in input_token_index.items())
reverse_target_word_index = dict(
    (i, word) for word, i in target_token_index.items())


def decode_sequence(input_seq):
```

12. Encode input as a state vector

```
states_value = encoder_model.predict(input_seq)
```

13. Generate empty target sequence of length 1.

```
target_seq = np.zeros((1,1))
```

14. Populate the first character of target sequence with the start character.

```
target_seq[0, 0] = target_token_index['BEGIN_']
```

15. Sampling loop for a batch of sequences

```
stop_condition = False
    decoded_sentence = ''

    while not stop_condition:
        output_tokens, h, c = decoder_model.predict(
            [target_seq] + states_value)
```

16. Sample a token.

```
sampled_token_index = np.argmax(output_tokens)
sampled_word = reverse_target_word_index[sampled_token_index]
decoded_sentence += ' ' + sampled_word
```

17. Exit condition: either hit max length or find stop character.

```
if (sampled_word == '_END' or
    len(decoded_sentence) > 60):
        stop_condition = True
```

18. Update the target sequence (of length 1).

```
target_seq = np.zeros((1,1))
target_seq[0, 0] = sampled_token_index
```

19. Update states

```
states_value = [h, c]

    return decoded_sentence
```

20. Inference for user input: take in a word sequence, convert the sequence word by word into encoded.

```
text_to_translate = "Où est ma voiture??"

encoder_input_to_translate = np.zeros(
    (1, max_input_seq_length),
    dtype='float32')

for t, word in enumerate(text_to_translate.split()):
    encoder_input_to_translate[0, t] = input_token_index[word]

decode_sequence(encoder_input_to_translate)
```

The output is as follows:

```
' Get a lot. _END'
```

Figure 7.47: French to English translator

Chapter 8: State of the art in Natural Language Processing

Activity 11: Build a Text Summarization Model

Solution:

1. Import the necessary Python packages and classes.

```
import os
import re
import pdb
import string
import numpy as np
import pandas as pd
from keras.utils import to_categorical
import matplotlib.pyplot as plt
%matplotlib inline
```

2. Load the dataset and read the file.

```
path_data = "news_summary_small.csv"
df_text_file = pd.read_csv(path_data)
df_text_file.headlines = df_text_file.headlines.str.lower()
df_text_file.text = df_text_file.text.str.lower()

lengths_text = df_text_file.text.apply(len)
dataset = list(zip(df_text_file.text.values, df_text_file.headlines.values))
```

3. Make vocab dictionary.

```
input_texts = []
target_texts = []
input_chars = set()
target_chars = set()

for line in dataset:
    input_text, target_text = list(line[0]), list(line[1])
    target_text = ['BEGIN_'] + target_text + ['_END']
    input_texts.append(input_text)
    target_texts.append(target_text)


    for character in input_text:
        if character not in input_chars:
            input_chars.add(character)
```

```
    for character in target_text:
        if character not in target_chars:
            target_chars.add(character)

input_chars.add("<unk>")
input_chars.add("<pad>")
target_chars.add("<pad>")

input_chars = sorted(input_chars)
target_chars = sorted(target_chars)

human_vocab = dict(zip(input_chars, range(len(input_chars))))
machine_vocab = dict(zip(target_chars, range(len(target_chars))))
inv_machine_vocab = dict(enumerate(sorted(machine_vocab)))

def string_to_int(string_in, length, vocab):
    """
    Converts all strings in the vocabulary into a list of integers
representing the positions of the
    input string's characters in the "vocab"

    Arguments:
    string -- input string
    length -- the number of time steps you'd like, determines if the
output will be padded or cut
    vocab -- vocabulary, dictionary used to index every character of your
"string"

    Returns:
    rep -- list of integers (or '<unk>') (size = length) representing the
position of the string's character in the vocabulary
    """
```

4.   Convert lowercase to standardize.

```
    string_in = string_in.lower()
    string_in = string_in.replace(',','')

    if len(string_in) > length:
        string_in = string_in[:length]

    rep = list(map(lambda x: vocab.get(x, '<unk>'), string_in))
```

```python
    if len(string_in) < length:
        rep += [vocab['<pad>']] * (length - len(string_in))

    return rep

def preprocess_data(dataset, human_vocab, machine_vocab, Tx, Ty):

    X, Y = zip(*dataset)
    X = np.array([string_to_int(i, Tx, human_vocab) for i in X])
    Y = [string_to_int(t, Ty, machine_vocab) for t in Y]
    print("X shape from preprocess: {}".format(X.shape))

    Xoh = np.array(list(map(lambda x: to_categorical(x, num_
classes=len(human_vocab)), X)))
    Yoh = np.array(list(map(lambda x: to_categorical(x, num_
classes=len(machine_vocab)), Y)))

    return X, np.array(Y), Xoh, Yoh

def softmax(x, axis=1):
    """Softmax activation function.
    # Arguments
        x : Tensor.
        axis: Integer, axis along which the softmax normalization is
applied.
    # Returns
        Tensor, output of softmax transformation.
    # Raises
        ValueError: In case 'dim(x) == 1'.
    """
    ndim = K.ndim(x)
    if ndim == 2:
        return K.softmax(x)
    elif ndim > 2:
        e = K.exp(x - K.max(x, axis=axis, keepdims=True))
        s = K.sum(e, axis=axis, keepdims=True)
        return e / s
    else:
        raise ValueError('Cannot apply softmax to a tensor that is 1D')
```

5. Run the previous code snippet to load data, get vocab dictionaries and define some utility functions to be used later. Define length of input characters and output characters.

```
Tx = 460
Ty = 75
X, Y, Xoh, Yoh = preprocess_data(dataset, human_vocab, machine_vocab, Tx,
Ty)
Define the model functions (Repeator, Concatenate, Densors, Dotor)
# Defined shared layers as global variables

repeator = RepeatVector(Tx)
concatenator = Concatenate(axis=-1)
densor1 = Dense(10, activation = "tanh")
densor2 = Dense(1, activation = "relu")
activator = Activation(softmax, name='attention_weights')
dotor = Dot(axes = 1)
Define one-step-attention function:
def one_step_attention(h, s_prev):
    """

    Performs one step of attention: Outputs a context vector computed as a
dot product of the attention weights
    "alphas" and the hidden states "h" of the Bi-LSTM.

    Arguments:
    h -- hidden state output of the Bi-LSTM, numpy-array of shape (m, Tx,
2*n_h)
    s_prev -- previous hidden state of the (post-attention) LSTM, numpy-
array of shape (m, n_s)

    Returns:
    context -- context vector, input of the next (post-attetion) LSTM cell
    """
```

6. Use **repeator** to repeat **s_prev** to be of shape (**m**, **Tx**, **n_s**) so that you can concatenate it with all hidden states "**a**"

```
s_prev = repeator(s_prev)
```

7. Use concatenator to concatenate a and s_prev on the last axis ($\approx$ 1 line)

```
concat = concatenator([h, s_prev])
```

8. Use **densor1** to propagate **concat** through a small fully-connected neural network to compute the "intermediate energies" variable e.

```
e = densor1(concat)
```

9. Use **densor2** to propagate e through a small fully-connected neural network to compute the "**energies**" variable energies.

```
energies = densor2(e)
```

10. Use "**activator**" on "**energies**" to compute the attention weights "**alphas**"

```
alphas = activator(energies)
```

11. Use **dotor** together with "**alphas**" and 'a' to compute the context vector to be given to the next (post-attention) LSTM-cell

```
context = dotor([alphas, h])

    return context
Define the number of hidden states for decoder and encoder.
n_h = 32
n_s = 64
post_activation_LSTM_cell = LSTM(n_s, return_state = True)
output_layer = Dense(len(machine_vocab), activation=softmax)
Define the model architecture and run it to obtain a model.
def model(Tx, Ty, n_h, n_s, human_vocab_size, machine_vocab_size):
    """

    Arguments:
    Tx -- length of the input sequence
    Ty -- length of the output sequence
    n_h -- hidden state size of the Bi-LSTM
    n_s -- hidden state size of the post-attention LSTM
    human_vocab_size -- size of the python dictionary "human_vocab"
    machine_vocab_size -- size of the python dictionary "machine_vocab"

    Returns:
    model -- Keras model instance
    """
```

12. Define the inputs of your model with a shape (**Tx**,)

13. Define **s0** and **c0**, initial hidden state for the decoder LSTM of shape (**n_s,**)

```
X = Input(shape=(Tx, human_vocab_size), name="input_first")
s0 = Input(shape=(n_s,), name='s0')
c0 = Input(shape=(n_s,), name='c0')
s = s0
c = c0
```

14. Initialize empty list of outputs

```
outputs = []
```

15. Define your pre-attention Bi-LSTM. Remember to use return_sequences=True.

```
a = Bidirectional(LSTM(n_h, return_sequences=True))(X)

# Iterate for Ty steps
for t in range(Ty):

    # Perform one step of the attention mechanism to get back the
context vector at step t
    context = one_step_attention(h, s)
```

16. Apply the post-attention LSTM cell to the "**context**" vector.

```
    # Pass: initial_state = [hidden state, cell state]
    s, _, c = post_activation_LSTM_cell(context, initial_state =
[s,c])
```

17. Apply **Dense** layer to the hidden state output of the post-attention LSTM

```
out = output_layer(s)
```

18. Append "out" to the "outputs" list

```
outputs.append(out)
```

19. Create model instance taking three inputs and returning the list of outputs.

```
model = Model(inputs=[X, s0, c0], outputs=outputs)

return model
```

```
model = model(Tx, Ty, n_h, n_s, len(human_vocab), len(machine_vocab))
#Define model loss functions and other hyperparameters. Also #initialize
decoder state vectors.
```

```
opt = Adam(lr = 0.005, beta_1=0.9, beta_2=0.999, decay = 0.01)
```

```
model.compile(loss='categorical_crossentropy', optimizer=opt,
metrics=['accuracy'])

s0 = np.zeros((10000, n_s))
c0 = np.zeros((10000, n_s))
outputs = list(Yoh.swapaxes(0,1))
Fit the model to our data:
model.fit([Xoh, s0, c0], outputs, epochs=1, batch_size=100)
#Run inference step for the new text.
EXAMPLES = ["Last night a meteorite was seen flying near the earth's
moon."]
for example in EXAMPLES:

    source = string_to_int(example, Tx, human_vocab)
    source = np.array(list(map(lambda x: to_categorical(x, num_
classes=len(human_vocab)), source)))
    source = source[np.newaxis, :]
    prediction = model.predict([source, s0, c0])
    prediction = np.argmax(prediction, axis = -1)
    output = [inv_machine_vocab[int(i)] for i in prediction]

    print("source:", example)
    print("output:", ''.join(output))
```

The output is as follows:

```
source: Last night a meteorite was seen flying near the earth's moon.
output: aaaaa          <pad><pad><pad><pad><pad><pad><pad><pad><pad><pad><pad><pad><pad><pad><pad><pad>
```

Figure 8.18: Text summarization model output

Chapter 9: A practical NLP project workflow in an organisation

Code for LSTM model

1. Check if GPU is detected

```
import tensorflow as tf
tf.test.gpu_device_name()
```

2. Setting up collar notebook

```
from google.colab import drive
drive.mount('/content/gdrive')


# Run the below command in a new cell


cd /content/gdrive/My Drive/Lesson-9/


# Run the below command in a new cell
!unzip data.csv.zip
```

3. Import necessary Python packages and classes.

```
import os
import re
import pickle
import pandas as pd

from keras.preprocessing.text import Tokenizer
from keras.preprocessing.sequence import pad_sequences

from keras.models import Sequential
from keras.layers import Dense, Embedding, LSTM
```

4. Load the data file.

```
def preprocess_data(data_file_path):
    data = pd.read_csv(data_file_path, header=None) # read the csv
    data.columns = ['rating', 'title', 'review'] # add column names
    data['review'] = data['review'].apply(lambda x: x.lower()) # change
all text to lower
```

```
    data['review'] = data['review'].apply((lambda x: re.sub('[^a-zA-z0-
9\s]','',x))) # remove all numbers
    return data
```

```
df = preprocess_data('data.csv')
```

5. Initialize tokenization.

```
max_features = 2000
maxlength = 250

tokenizer = Tokenizer(num_words=max_features, split=' ')
```

6. Fit tokenizer.

```
tokenizer.fit_on_texts(df['review'].values)
X = tokenizer.texts_to_sequences(df['review'].values)
```

7. Pad sequences.

```
X = pad_sequences(X, maxlen=maxlength)
```

8. Get target variable

```
y_train = pd.get_dummies(df.rating).values
```

```
embed_dim = 128
hidden_units = 100
n_classes = 5

model = Sequential()
model.add(Embedding(max_features, embed_dim, input_length = X.shape[1]))
model.add(LSTM(hidden_units))
model.add(Dense(n_classes, activation='softmax'))
model.compile(loss = 'categorical_crossentropy', optimizer='adam',metrics
= ['accuracy'])
print(model.summary())
```

9. Fit the model.

```
model.fit(X[:100000, :], y_train[:100000, :], batch_size = 128, epochs=15,
validation_split=0.2)
```

10. Save model and tokenizer.

```
model.save('trained_model.h5')  # creates a HDF5 file 'trained_model.h5'

with open('trained_tokenizer.pkl', 'wb') as f: # creates a pickle file
'trained_tokenizer.pkl'
    pickle.dump(tokenizer, f)

from google.colab import files
files.download('trained_model.h5')
files.download('trained_tokenizer.pkl')
```

Code for Flask

1. Import the necessary Python packages and classes.

```
import re
import pickle
import numpy as np

from flask import Flask, request, jsonify
from keras.models import load_model
from keras.preprocessing.sequence import pad_sequences
```

2. Define the input files and load in dataframe

```
def load_variables():
    global model, tokenizer
    model = load_model('trained_model.h5')
    model._make_predict_function()  # https://github.com/keras-team/keras/
issues/6462
    with open('trained_tokenizer.pkl',  'rb') as f:
        tokenizer = pickle.load(f)
```

3. Define preprocessing functions similar to the training code:

```python
def do_preprocessing(reviews):
    processed_reviews = []
    for review in reviews:
        review = review.lower()
        processed_reviews.append(re.sub('[^a-zA-z0-9\s]', '', review))
    processed_reviews = tokenizer.texts_to_sequences(np.array(processed_
reviews))
    processed_reviews = pad_sequences(processed_reviews, maxlen=250)
    return processed_reviews
```

4. Define a Flask app instance:

```python
app = Flask(__name__)
```

5. Define an endpoint that displays a fixed message:

```python
@app.route('/')
def home_routine():
    return 'Hello World!'
```

6. We'll have a prediction endpoint, to which we can send our review strings. The kind of HTTP request we will use is a '**POST**' request:

```python
@app.route('/prediction', methods=['POST'])
def get_prediction():
  # get incoming text
  # run the model
    if request.method == 'POST':
        data = request.get_json()
    data = do_preprocessing(data)
    predicted_sentiment_prob = model.predict(data)
    predicted_sentiment = np.argmax(predicted_sentiment_prob, axis=-1)
    return str(predicted_sentiment)
```

7. Start the web server.

```python
if __name__ == '__main__':
  # load model
  load_variables()
  app.run(debug=True)
```

8. Save this file as **app.py** (any name could be used). Run this code from the terminal using **app.py**:

```
python app.py
```

The output is as follows:

```
Using TensorFlow backend.
2019-03-24 23:08:25.948604: I tensorflow/core/platform/cpu_feature_guard.cc:141] Your CPU supports instructions
that this TensorFlow binary was not compiled to use: AVX2 FMA
 * Serving Flask app "app" (lazy loading)
 * Environment: production
   WARNING: Do not use the development server in a production environment.
   Use a production WSGI server instead.
 * Debug mode: on
 * Running on http://127.0.0.1:5000/ (Press CTRL+C to quit)
 * Restarting with stat
Using TensorFlow backend.
2019-03-24 23:08:31.730337: I tensorflow/core/platform/cpu_feature_guard.cc:141] Your CPU supports instructions
that this TensorFlow binary was not compiled to use: AVX2 FMA
 * Debugger is active!
 * Debugger PIN: 150-665-765
```

Figure 9.31: Output for flask

Index

About

All major keywords used in this book are captured alphabetically in this section. Each one is accompanied by the page number of where they appear.

A

absolute:82
abstract: 102, 143
access: 92, 232, 234, 266, 286, 289
accuracy: 22, 28, 47, 55, 69-72, 91-92, 94, 112-113, 116, 121, 150, 172, 175-177, 208-209, 253, 275-276
activate: 98, 185
activated:75
activation: 73-78, 83, 86, 90, 102-103, 106-107, 115-116, 121, 143-144, 146-148, 150, 158, 160, 162-166, 168, 170-171, 174, 181, 190-191, 193, 196-197, 201-203, 208, 212-213, 220, 242, 249-252, 275
algorithm: 14, 22-25, 28-29, 36, 38-39, 46, 49, 54, 57-58, 60-61, 79-84, 86-87, 90-91, 94, 110, 112, 178
alphas: 238, 250-251
amazon: 124, 267, 280, 284-285, 287-289
amazonaws:289
amazonecs:289
analytics:92
app-packt: 283-284
arbitrary: 100, 238
argmax: 183, 225, 254, 278
arrays: 173, 185, 218
asarray:183
astype:183
asymmetry:159

B

backend: 143, 242
biases: 73, 76, 78, 83
bi-lstm: 250-252
binary: 60, 63, 80, 90-91, 115, 120-121, 172, 174, 189, 203, 208-209, 211, 228

C

calculus:110
categories: 7, 21, 36, 56-57, 59-61, 63, 87, 94
chatbot:7
chunked: 51-52
chunking: 35, 49-53, 57
chunks: 50-53
classes: 87, 93, 99, 106-107, 109, 115-116, 247, 254, 275
cluster: 22, 39, 88
cnn-based:117
coding:272
command: 3, 5, 10, 25, 31, 44, 89, 111, 271-272, 281, 283-284, 286, 289-290
composite:86
configure: 286, 288
console: 285-286
constant: 72, 127, 192, 292
corpora: 1, 5-8, 11, 33, 39, 42, 49, 56-57, 61, 65
corpus: 5, 8-9, 11, 13-15, 17-20, 22-24, 26, 29-32, 36, 39-40, 43, 47, 50-51, 53-55, 57, 59, 63-64, 90, 171, 178, 206, 216, 218, 220, 257

cortana: 7, 124
cortex:98
crosstropy:150

D

daemon:282
darrell:119
dashboard: 285-286
database: 15, 236, 241, 266
dataframe: 15-16, 89, 93, 273
dataset: 54, 69, 73-74, 78, 80-81, 87-88, 93, 99, 111, 114-116, 120, 172-173, 175, 177, 184-185, 210, 243-244, 247-248, 264
debugging:281
decode: 223, 225-226
deploy: 92, 261, 276, 282-284
docker: 280, 282-284, 289-292
dockerfile: 282-283, 290
dockerhub:283
domain: 231-232, 262, 292
dominant:233
dummies:274

E

e-commerce: 265-266
embedding: 21-22, 26, 29, 115, 156, 173-174, 203, 208-209, 219-220, 222-223, 272, 275
employ:116
entity: 7, 33, 35-36, 42, 50, 55-63, 65, 234
entropy:59
entrypoint:282
enumerate: 179, 181, 183,

217-218, 226, 244

epochs: 30, 91, 111-113, 115-116, 150-151, 175-176, 182, 208-209, 222, 227, 254, 275

F

feature: 22, 38, 79-80, 90, 101-102, 109, 265, 274
fields: 68, 94, 102, 266, 273
filename:178
fine-tuned: 105, 256
flatten: 106-107
flattened: 105-106
flattening: 105, 108
framework: 71, 92, 143, 152, 277
free-tier:285
function: 10, 12, 16-17, 19, 50-51, 54, 73, 75-77, 80-84, 86-87, 89-91, 94, 102-103, 106-107, 109-112, 120-121, 128, 134, 146, 151, 157-158, 160, 162-166, 168-171, 173-176, 178, 182-184, 193, 196-197, 201, 203, 209, 235-236, 239-243, 246-247, 249-250, 253, 258, 272-274, 277, 281

G

gdrive:271
generic:256
genres:58
glorot:143
google: 6-7, 114, 124, 255-256, 261, 267-269, 271, 277, 292
googleblog:256

googling:29
gradient: 80, 82-87, 91, 94, 110, 112, 134-136, 142, 151, 157-160, 186, 190, 228, 232-233, 255

H

header:272
hierarchy:98

I

import: 12, 14, 16-19, 25, 30, 32, 44, 48, 54-55, 63, 89-90, 93, 99, 103, 106, 111-112, 114-115, 120, 145, 149, 152, 164, 173-175, 178, 183, 194, 203, 211, 213, 219, 242, 258, 270-272, 277
initialize: 55, 174, 195, 197-198, 200, 202, 206, 212, 218, 224, 233, 252, 254, 258, 273
install: 19, 25, 30, 48, 114, 233, 277, 282, 289
instance: 9, 14, 16, 45-46, 51, 54, 56, 73-74, 80, 93, 124, 172, 226, 252-253, 265, 278, 280, 284-291
integer: 179, 206-207, 217, 247, 249
iterate: 93, 252

J

jupyter: 9-10, 12, 14, 16-19, 25, 30, 43-44, 89, 93, 99, 120, 172, 185

K

keepdims:249
keras-team:277
kernel: 102, 106, 115, 143

L

lambda: 242, 247, 254, 272
lemmatize:16
library: 8, 12, 19, 24, 30, 50, 68, 89
lstm-based: 203, 210
lstm-cell:251

M

macosx:272
matmul: 165, 167, 169, 195, 198, 202
matplotlib: 51, 99, 103, 175
maxpooling:106
multiclass:182
multi-head:255

N

networking:116
neural: 2, 22, 28, 65, 67-68, 71-79, 83-84, 86-88, 90-94, 97-99, 101-102, 105, 109, 111, 118, 121, 123-125, 128, 155-157, 189-190, 211-212, 222, 228, 231-233, 236-237, 239, 251, 257-258
newaxis:254

O

one-coded:246
onehot: 90-91
one-hot: 111, 114, 248
openai:257
overfit:98

P

package: 89, 178, 244, 256
pickle: 114, 276-277, 283
primary:69
private:286
pyplot: 99, 103-104,
    150, 175
python: 3, 8-9, 12, 18,
    29, 40, 51, 68, 92-93,
    99, 103, 145, 149, 152,
    164, 167, 172, 178, 194,
    197, 203, 211, 241, 244,
    252, 256, 258, 268,
    277, 279, 282-283
pytorch:143

R

randint:183
random: 149, 164-165,
    167, 169, 178, 183,
    194-195, 197-198,
    200, 202, 242-243
regression: 71, 76, 78-81,
    83, 86-87, 134, 274
repository: 99, 120,
    204, 227, 283
reshape:111
return: 12, 15, 89, 103,
    143-147, 149-150, 164,
    178, 183, 194, 220,
    223, 226, 243-244,

247-249, 251-253,
    271-272, 278, 290
rmsprop: 174, 178, 181, 220

S

scikit:120
session: 175, 209,
    227, 267, 276
setosa:74
sigmoid: 77, 90, 121,
    142, 158, 162, 164-167,
    174, 193-195, 197-198,
    201, 208-209
softmax: 107, 109, 116,
    146-148, 150, 181,
    212-213, 220, 223,
    239, 249-251, 275
stemmer: 14-15
stride:103
string: 10, 44-45, 178, 180,
    243, 246-247, 254, 265
supervised: 38-40,
    42-43, 57, 65, 70,
    79-80, 87-88, 171

T

tensor: 145, 240,
    249-250, 256
tensorflow: 143, 172,
    241, 256, 270, 282
threshold: 75, 142
torque:257
trigger: 175, 289

U

untagged: 39, 42-43
update: 81, 83-84, 86,
    110, 133-136, 158-159,
    162-165, 167,

169-170, 196-199, 201,
    225-226, 244

V

validate:93
valueerror:249
v-class:257
vector: 21-22, 26-29,
    33, 105, 111, 129, 132,
    148, 164, 170-171, 181,
    193, 197, 201, 203, 212,
    223, 225, 233-240,
    246, 250-252, 254
verbose: 30, 91,
    113, 116, 183

W

weblink:271
website: 58, 124, 265
wordnet: 15-16
workdir: 282-283
workflow: 88, 184,
    261-265, 289, 291

Y

yyyy-mm-dd: 236,
    238, 241

Z

zipped: 271-272

www.ingramcontent.com/pod-product-compliance
Lightning Source LLC
Chambersburg PA
CBHW061756210326
41599CB00034B/6803